D0974695

Ten
Talks

Parents Must Have
With Their Children

About Drugs
& Choices

Robe-T Eby
604-807-6132

Ten Talks

Parents Must Have
With Their Children

About Drugs
& Choices

**Dominic Cappello and
Xenia G. Becher, M.S.W., C.S.W.**

HYPERION

New York

Copyright © 2001 Dominic Cappello

All rights reserved. No part of this book may be used or reproduced in
any manner whatsoever without the written permission of the Publisher.
Printed in the United States of America. For information address
Hyperion, 77 W. 66th Street, New York, New York 10023-6298.

ISBN 0-7868-8664-1

FIRST EDITION
10 9 8 7 6 5 4 3 2 1

To April Roseman—
whose expression of compassion and commitment
taught me volumes about making healthy choices.
D.C.

To my children, Chelsea, Timothy, and Gabriel,
my husband, Patrick, and my parents, Ksenia and Andrij Guzelak,
all of whom show me love, patience, and strength
to light my way.
X.G.B.

Contents

Contents

Acknowledgments

The Ten Talks Team

The development of any *Ten Talks* book is always a team effort. This book on drugs and choices is the result of thousands of conversations with parents, educators, children, young people, and representatives from religious organizations, law enforcement, and public health departments from across the country. Packaging their insight into book form involved the invaluable contributions of some very committed colleagues and thoughtful editorial consultants: Susan Durón, Ph.D., an education specialist and evaluator in Denver, Colorado; Bonnie Faddis, Ph.D., a researcher and education specialist in Portland, Oregon; Susan Burgess, M.S., M.A., an organizational development consultant and director of the Ten Talks Center in New York; Susan Coots, a sexuality educator and program development consultant in Syracuse, New York; Lynn Delevan at the Center for Social and Emotional Learning in New York; Cassie Barber at the School Improvement Counsel Assistance in Columbia, South Carolina; Christopher Yu in New York City; and Skylar Fein in Philadelphia. Special thanks to Paula Brooks for her editorial review of the entire manuscript in addition to coordinating the sample talks with parents and children. Much gratitude is expressed to our medical reviewer, Ted Eytan, M.D., M.P.H., in Seattle, Washington, who gave us the benefit of his invaluable insight.

We are indebted to our national reviewers and advisors: Lauri Halderman; Tom Shea, Psy.D.; Sheriff Joe Gerace; Deputy Sheriff James Quattrone; Joy Guarino; Dr. Matthew Goulet; Barbara Sullivan; Linda Goldstein; Michael Day; Lisa Frank; Paul Didonato; Lisa Perry; Ellen Leach; Norma Straw; Mary Jo McHaney; Diana Rivera; Dennis Worsham; Srdjan Stakic; Faith Mary Gault; Robin Weeks; Kate Thomsen; Emily Sharp; Courtney Ramirez; Diane Toscano; Paul Riker, M.S., C.A.S.A.C.; Linda Vincent, R.N., M.S.W., C.S.W.; Rita Creighton of the Washington State PTA; Richard Pargament; Judy Walruff, Ph.D., of the Flinn Foundation; Tina Hoff and Julia Davis, of the Henry Kaiser Family Foundation; and the staff at Ten Thousand Waves. We also want to thank our family reviewers: Aubyn, Sara, and Taylor Gwinn; Chelsea, Timothy, and Gabriel Becher; Gabriel, Gabriela, and Anastasia Romero; Sharon and Cherice Ledbetter; Paula, Joseph, Lee, and Robert Brooks; Pam and Betsy Parr; Megen, Kevin, and Matt Opsahl; Grace, Sarah, Laura, David, and Jared Richards; Ken, Patti, Alex, and Anne Goodling; Divina, William, and Natalie Vernigor; Norman, Caitlin, and Justin Vinner; Bruce, Debbie, Max, and Marley Kabin; Lorna Glubb; Ross Emerick; and Penny, Laura, Ellen, and Alex Jansen, as well as the families who wish to be anonymous.

Special thanks to Jerald Newberry, Paul Sathrum, and Vicki Harrison at the National Education Association Health Information

Network, for their strong support of the "Can We Talk?" and "¿Conversamos?" parent-child communication programs and their commitment to health promotion for parents, youth, and educators. Thanks to Jerry Painter and Frieda Takamura at the Washington Education Association, and Debra Delgado at the Annie E. Casey Foundation. We offer our gratitude to Pepper Schwartz, Ph.D., at the University of Washington, for her ongoing inspiration and support, Fred Morris for supporting the *Ten Talks* series throughout its continuing growth, and our ever-vigilant editor at Hyperion, Mary Ellen O'Neill.

Of course, this book would not have been possible without the thousands of parents across the country who attended our presentations and workshops and helped us refine the Ten Talks approach. Those moms and dads proved that parents are the experts, and with the right resources can nurture family talks about alcohol, tobacco, and other drugs, and other controversial social issues. A big thank-you to the families in Dayton, Georgia; New York City, Syracuse, Buffalo, and Jamestown, New York; Seattle, Yakima, Olympia, Vancouver, and Everett, Washington; Portland, Bend, and Salem, Oregon; Memphis, Tennessee; Kansas City, Missouri; Dallas, Austin, and San Antonio, Texas; Great Falls, Montana; Des Moines, Iowa; Pine Ridge Indian Reservation in South Dakota; Flint, Michigan; Idaho Falls and Boise, Idaho; Orlando and Miami, Florida; Sels, Arizona; Oklahoma City, Oklahoma; Asheville, Greenville, Lafayette, and Charlotte, North Carolina; Virginia Beach and Fairfax, Virginia; Santa Fe, Las Cruces, and Albuquerque, New Mexico; San Diego, San Francisco, and Los Angeles, California; and Columbia and Charleston, South Carolina.

Ten
Talks

Parents Must Have
With Their Children

About Drugs
& Choices

Welcome to Ten Talks

How to Use This Book

When I was growing up, my parents never discussed drugs. I just grew up watching the adults partying, smoking, and getting drunk.
—Ed, father of three, Sels, Arizona

I was about ten years old and visiting an older cousin of mine and her friend. We were putting on makeup and listening to music when all of a sudden they lit up what I thought was a cigarette. Then the room started to smell funny. When my cousin offered me a toke, I was so scared I ran home. When I told my mom what happened she said that I'd done the right thing. That was the entire extent of the talking I did with my mom on the subject of drugs. —Lisa, mother of two, Orlando, Florida

A clear "window of opportunity" exists for parents of younger children. Between the ages of ten and twelve, most children name their parents as their primary source of guidance, advice and information about issues like sex, violence, and drugs and alcohol.
—Kaiser Family Foundation and Children Now, "Talking With Kids About Tough Issues: A National Survey of Parents and Kids"

If you're like most people, then alcohol, tobacco, and other drugs were part of your childhood. How often did you and your parents sit down and really talk about drugs? If you're like most people, the answer is easy: never.

Perhaps your parents thought you'd get all the information you needed at school, or that the public service announcements on TV would scare you away from pot, ecstasy, and triple scotches. The data on drug use suggest otherwise.

Why aren't parents having these conversations about drugs and healthy decision making with their children? If you're a parent yourself, you can probably come up with plenty of reasons. First of all, just because you're a parent doesn't mean you're an expert on drugs—many parents don't feel prepared to have the conversation. Even parents who know a thing or two about drugs will tell you that it's different discussing them with their own children. Lots of parents trust their kids and hope for the best. Compounding the problem, most of us don't have role models for this work. Since our parents didn't have open and frank talks on alcohol and other drug use with us, we didn't learn how to start sensitive and potentially controversial talks with our own kids.

Many parents breathe a sigh of relief when they hear drug prevention education is being taught in their kids' schools. They assume students will get the essential information from teachers and that parents may be off the hook. Parents who look more closely see that just isn't the case.

School-based programs usually focus on the dangers of illegal drugs, an important topic. But they rarely ask why young people and adults are turning to alcohol and drugs in the first place. They probably don't look at drugs as an escape route from difficult feelings, explore how kids feel about peer influences, or help young people interpret the media's depictions of legal drugs, like the appearance of alcohol, nicotine, or prescription drugs in just about every movie they see. Only parents can help their children put drug use and misuse within a larger context. Only parents can listen to kids' concerns and help them think through the difficult choices that are already arising in their everyday lives.

> "I'm trying to instill my values in my child so that when he faces decisions about using drugs he will have some guidance. My hope is that the values can serve as a reference point."
>
> —Sally, mother of three, Syracuse, New York

Kids can't miss the references to alcohol, tobacco, and prescription drugs—they're everywhere. Magazines feature ads for antidepressants, radio ads hawk diet pills, their favorite sitcom characters joke about "getting blasted," beer ads promote alcohol as a quick road to fun and excitement, and TV shows include no-holds-barred depictions of all kinds of drug use. Meanwhile, a few well meaning public service announcements are bombarding kids with messages about the horrors of drugs, some of which the kids may have already tried without ill effect.

Now that's what we call mixed messages. Which ones do you think are hitting home?

> "To be honest, I have found the talks with my teenager about drug use to be both confusing and scary. But I know that I need to keep having them." —Elsa, mother of two, Sels, Arizona

> "My mother had several brothers—they were all heavy drinkers, and four of them were heroin addicts. It was just understood, sort of unspoken, that they were the junkies in the family. By the time I was eleven, all four of them were living not far from us, and I was

very impressionable. Long story short: The four of them have passed away, all due to drunk driving accidents or drug overdoses. None of them were out of their thirties."

—Maria, mother of three, Seattle, Washington

"My twelve-year-old has bought the campaign that all drugs are bad. She even takes my cigarettes and throws them away! But alcohol is different—she thinks it's sophisticated."

—Lynn, mother of one, New York City

Why Ten Talks?

This book was written as a collaborative effort between a social worker specializing in community health and a communication specialist with years of experience working with parents and educators. Both of us have spoken to young people and their parents all over the country and feel it's time we faced the facts: Few families are talking about drug use.

But there is hope. We continue to hear from parents all around the country who speak candidly about having gotten little guidance about dealing with peer pressure from their own parents. Now they are breaking the cycle of silence with their own children. With their conversations as models, we can help you do the same.

Parents want to keep their children safe and help them make healthy choices. *Ten Talks* is designed to do just that. Our mutual concerns as well as our different professional perspectives have been brought together in this book. The result is a process that parents can use to help their kids understand the complexities of life, develop strategies for dealing with the stresses and anxieties of everyday living, avoid the temptation to misuse substances that are readily available, and learn about their families' own values, rules, and the law.

How to Use This Book

Each chapter focuses on a different aspect of drug use and is divided into four sections. In the first section, Preparing for the Talk, you'll find ways to clarify your values and family rules about each aspect of drug use that we discuss.

The second section, The Talk, is centered around situations for you and your child to read and includes illustrations to help set the scene in your child's mind. These stories illustrate challenging situations that your child might face in everyday life. Each story is followed by questions for you to ask. Your child's answers will give you insight into how she thinks and would act in particular situations. The questions encourage kids to share their views, and gives you an opportunity to articulate your personal values and the importance of following family rules and guidelines.

The third section, After the Talk, gives you an opportunity to reflect on your child's responses and to identify any potential problems. It also gives you a chance to hear your child's beliefs and attitudes. You might be pleasantly surprised by what you hear.

The fourth section contains sample talks with excerpts of actual conversations between parents and their children. Some talks are very animated and show what can happen when a child is fully engaged. Others illustrate what happens when a child starts squirming from the moment the parent starts the conversation. Some talks will engage a particular child more than others. Even conversations with resistant children show that they learn something about the topic—and that parents learn more about the child. Each of the ten talks may range in time from two minutes to an unhurried hour. Even a two-minute talk can be considered worthwhile.

> "I realize that the time I spend talking with my children shows my interest in their feelings and gives the unspoken message of love and respect." —Marlene, mother of three, Buffalo, New York

> "I spent about eighty hours of scheduled course work and another thirty hours going over materials to learn how to talk with school kids about drugs. I also spent about another eighty hours learning about drug recognition. Learning how to talk to kids about drugs, whether as a parent or a police officer, takes time and commitment." —Deputy Sheriff James Quattrone, Chautauqua County, New York

Families ARE Talking: More about Sample Talks

In many ways, the sample talks form the centerpiece of this book. As we tested each activity with real families, we found that most children will open up and talk about drug use, but only if they're asked, by someone they love and trust. Many children were grateful for the talks—some reported that they felt that unspoken rules about drug use needed to be spoken aloud. The sample talks in this book almost prompted us to change the title of our book from *Ten Talks Parents Must Have* . . . to *Ten Talks Parents and Children ARE Having* . . . When you read the sample talks, you may notice that some conversations meander and seem to go nowhere for some time; that can be a reality of talking with children, as you already know! But keep reading the sample talks and you'll see that with patience, important issues arise with even the most noncommunicative young person.

Every Talk Is a Success

We have learned from our other books in the Ten Talks series that it's not always clear during discussions whether your child is getting the message. It's particularly hard when you feel you are barely being tolerated, or when your child feels that he is doing you a big favor to sit through two questions. But the real impact of the talks may be hard to see at first. You might find at some future date that you really did make a lasting impression.

And even if your child didn't get everything out of the talk that you would have wanted, remember this: Your child got the knowledge that you care. Your child will know that you are approachable when tough choices arise. Our goal is to help you build pathways of communication between you and your child. That doesn't happen in an instant, but conversation by conversation.

We actually believe there is no wasted time or effort in sitting down with your kids to talk about drugs. Yes, there may be long pauses in your talk. Allow your child to fill in the silences. The effort will always pay off. Not convinced? Read a few sample talks and see for yourself.

One, Two, or Ten Talks

The Ten Talks philosophy is that when it comes to your child, you are the expert. You know which chapters of this book will be most important and appropriate to your child's level of development. Of course, not every chapter pertains to your child's life and your family's situation, so choose the chapters that make the most sense to you. Also, each chapter contains more than one story— you do not need to read each one with your child for the talk to be effective. Feel free to innovate. For example, you might want to change the sequence of the talks depending on your child's interests. We've repeated certain themes in the stories to reinforce particular concepts. If those stories don't inspire a dialogue, feel free to skip them.

There are three chapters, however, that we suggest you do not skip—Chapter One: What Are Drugs?, Chapter Two: How Do You Feel?, and Chapter Seven: Different Drugs/Different Dangers, which illustrates the laws regarding drug use and the consequences for breaking them. These chapters will help you establish the larger framework of values, concerns, and beliefs within which your family works.

What Can You Expect from Ten Talks*?*

The Ten Talks process, first published in *Ten Talks Parents Must Have With Their Children About Violence,* and further developed in *Ten Talks Parents Must Have With Their Children About Sex and Character,* has shown that following the guidelines in this book can bring huge rewards for both parent and child. Stick with the ten conversations and you may

- increase the amount of time you spend in meaningful discussions with your child.
- increase your understanding of your child's views about drug use and healthy decision making.
- feel more confident that your child can keep himself safe and healthy.
- be able to describe the local laws and family rules about alcohol, tobacco, and other drug use, and the consequences for breaking them.

Do these objectives seem daunting? If so, you're not alone. In Ten Talks workshops around the country we hear parents ask, "Can I really do this?" The answer is: Yes, you can! Thousands of parents in cities across the country have proved it. We think that if you're reading this book you're already on the right track.

The Role of School

"I've already learned this in school!" That's a common response from teens when parents approach them to talk about drugs. What's a good response? First, you can reassure your child that these talks are not meant to accuse them of anything or to pry into their lives; you simply want to hear their opinions on different topics. Second, you can tell them that health class is *not* a substitute for your own concerns, values, and house rules. Remember, the ultimate responsibility for kids' alcohol, tobacco, and other drug use doesn't rest with health teachers, but with parents—in other words, you.

Talking with the Noncommunicative Child

When parents sit down to have the first talk, they often find their child trying to make a quick exit! If that happens to you, don't worry. You're not alone in trying to engage a less-than–enthusiastic child. Here are five common ways that young people try to derail the discussion.

Child's rejection #1: "I've already heard this at school."
Child's rejection #2: "I'll talk about this, but I don't want to talk about it with you."

Child's rejection #3: "I'm not doing drugs."
Child's rejection #4: "I'm not gonna do it."
Child's rejection #5: "It's none of your business."

Here are some ways that parents have steered their conversations back on track.

- "I care about you, and having these talks means a lot to me."
- "School doesn't cover our family values or all of the concerns that I have."
- "Okay, if you still don't want to discuss it with me, I'll let you pick someone else from our family or friends to discuss it with."
- "This is an important issue that affects everyone in our family. It's about our family rules and the law. It's my job to make sure you know the rules and what happens if you break them."
- "You know you are my business. My job is making sure that you've considered how you might behave before you are presented with an important choice. All I am doing is helping you prepare for that moment. I wouldn't be doing my job as a parent if I didn't help you think about drugs and choices."

The Setting

Where and when you have the talk will affect how well it goes. You may find that talking with your child one-on-one, rather than with other people present, will give you the best results. Remember that some places are better than others to initiate a talk. Some parents have had their best luck in the car, on walks, or while doing chores. One mom in Seattle came up with her own approach:

"When I have an important talk to initiate, I get my son in the car and start the discussion. He doesn't have to maintain eye contact with me and he also can't escape!"

Family Rules: Your Duty as a Parent

Cigarettes, alcohol, and other drugs are everywhere, and you can't keep your child from being exposed to the topic or to the temptations. We can't pretend that all young people will abstain from drinking or smoking until they are of legal age, or that they'll never experiment with an illegal substance. (Did you or your peers?)

But you can come up with some family rules about following the law, keeping healthy, and staying away from illegal drugs. You can communicate your rules and the laws to your child and make sure your child understands them. Enforcing these rules isn't easy, especially with teens. That's why it's vital to establish them early on.

To avoid confusion, the rules need to be spoken, rather than unspoken, as many parents said their family rules about drinking and drugs were. Each chapter ends with a section called The Bare Minimum, which comprises a quick review of terms, sample family rules, and a checkup on your child's understanding of the law.

"I didn't know what my teenage daughter would say when I started the talk about drugs and dating, but she opened up and told me things I was almost unprepared to hear. She talked about her peers using pot, cocaine, and ecstasy at parties that she attended—and in a very matter-of-fact way, as though it was no big deal."

—Barbara, mother of two, Columbia, South Carolina

"My parents never talked about a single rule that had to do with drugs. Looking back, it seems as though I grew up in a world of unspoken rules which I found confusing."

—Tim, father of two, Vancouver, British Columbia, Canada

The Support of Aunts, Uncles, and Grandparents

If you feel overwhelmed at the thought of having these talks with your child, or have been rebuffed too many times by a noncommunicative teenager, consider calling in the reserves: grandparents, aunts, uncles, stepparents, trusted friends, or people from your religious community.

Some parents admit that when they were teens the last people they wanted to talk to about social issues were parents. Some say they actually turned to their favorite aunt, uncle, or grandparent. One mom found that she simply couldn't talk with her son about anything important. She called her brother and asked if he would do some "uncle duty" and take her son out for some meals and a few good conversations. The uncle reported to his sister that he and his nephew were actually able to have good talks. Single moms might ask a trusted adult male to talk to a son, as many young boys report the desire for healthy male role models whom they can trust and depend on.

Just make sure that if you ask another adult to talk with your child, his or her values are compatible with your own. And you don't have to hand off responsibility for the whole set of conversations. There will be several of these talks you can do yourself.

When Is a Child Old Enough for Ten Talks*?*

Ten Talks is designed for children in grades three through twelve. However, most substance abuse educators believe that even very young children can talk about alcohol and nicotine as an introduction to drug use and misuse. What's important is that you use simple words and don't introduce issues that are not easily understood by your child. You need to tailor the talks to your child's age and maturity level; obviously, the talk you would have with a fourth grader would not be the same as the one you'd have with a high-school senior.

Many of the discussion topics in *Ten Talks* will be familiar to your kids from TV or school. The main ingredient of the *Ten Talks* process—storytelling—is an activity that young children are very familiar with. We have found that parents talking with their fourth, fifth, and sixth graders were the most successful. But even younger kids can usually understand the importance of at least one or two of the topics.

For example, in the chapter on tobacco, young children know what chain-smoking looks like, since they see it everywhere, including on TV, and they easily grasp the concept of peer pressure from older kids to have a puff. The nice part about talking to the younger children is that they usually are more willing to seek guidance from a parent. Some middle- and many high-school students may see this book as something for "children," but the family rules and laws outlined in each chapter are relevant to any child or adult in your extended family. If your child watches TV, uses the Internet, or goes to school, then the ten topics in this book need to be discussed. Above all, remember that you know best how you can frame the talks in a way your child will understand.

You will find that your child's reaction to the talks will change as she moves from elementary school to middle school to high school. Just as any good schoolteacher does, you can revisit the topics in this book yearly to reinforce the lessons learned, review the family rules and the law, and make adjustments if needed.

About Quotes and Pronouns

Most of the quotes from parents and youths come from feedback we received during presentations and workshops on parent-child communication that were conducted across the country. Quite a few have been added from parents who tested the *Ten Talks* book for us. Their names have been changed to protect their privacy. Also, in the interest of succinctness, *Ten Talks* alternates pronouns throughout the text: In one paragraph we may refer to your child as "she" and in the next we might say "he."

Special Note

Ten Talks has been developed to help parents and children talk about alcohol, tobacco, and other drug use. *Ten Talks* is not intended to replace professional evaluation and treatment by a licensed mental health professional, if needed. If any concerns arise about potential alcohol or other drug abuse, please contact a licensed child psychologist, psychiatrist, physician, or social worker. Also, laws regarding alcohol, tobacco, and other drug use change from state to state and year to year. Consult your local police department to clarify any questions or concerns you have about illegal substance use or possession.

1

What Are Drugs?

Talking about *Your* Definitions

My mom mixed scotch with antidepressants all the time, and no one ever talked about it. —Tad, father of two, Chicago, Illinois

I remember years ago sitting in a PTA presentation on drugs, when they warned us that kids might try getting high on the gas shooting out of cans of whipped cream.
—Lee, mother of three, Columbia, South Carolina

My husband and I have different opinions about drug use—and this creates a lot of conflict between us and with the kids.
—Dana, mother of two, Seattle, Washington

My second grader just learned the term "weed"—on the school bus. —Jan, mother of one, New York City

When you hear the word "drugs," which drugs come to mind? And when you think about your child, which ones concern you the most? Most parents' concerns center on illegal drugs like pot, ecstasy, heroin, and crack cocaine. Some parents see danger in alcohol, some parents worry most about tobacco, and other parents are concerned about the abuse of prescription drugs.

Clearly, drugs are a common part of our lives. Where would we be without aspirin, caffeine, antihistamines, and a cabinet full of prescription drugs? Many of us use a cup of coffee to give us a boost in the morning. Some look forward to a glass of wine or a beer after a day at work. Antidepressants have become accepted by many as a normal way to deal with anxiety or depression. Using drugs—including alcohol, tobacco, and medical prescriptions—which chemically alter our feelings is commonplace for most of us.

But it's not easy to talk about all drugs at once. Legal drugs can save lives and can also ruin them if used improperly. There's a thin line between therapeutic use and abuse. Talking about that line can be complicated. Talking about illegal drug use can be more complicated still, and can bring up memories of childhood, youthful experimentation, and family patterns of drug use. These are tough topics, but as parents we cannot avoid them. What's more, we have to start these conversations early in our children's lives. This chapter is designed to help you clarify your definition of "drugs" and to help you compare your definitions with those of your children.

Preparing for the Talk

This talk will give you the chance to introduce the topic of alcohol and other drugs with your children. It also will help you explain why it's important to discuss drug use. This first chapter will help you and your child discuss your values and feelings about drugs.

In this talk you will help your child understand that

- alcohol and other drugs are a part of everyday life.
- there is a difference between drug use and drug abuse.
- alcohol and other drugs alter our feelings and it's important to know how they are altered.

- the use and abuse of alcohol and other drugs does not excuse harmful behavior.
- there are family rules about alcohol and drug use.

What You Can Expect from This Talk

After the talk your child will be able to

- define the term "drug."
- describe alcohol and drug use and abuse.
- express the family rules about alcohol and other drug use.

Is Your Child at Risk?

Why do some children misuse alcohol and drugs, while others do not? There is no simple answer to this complex question. But one key element can help us understand children's behaviors when it comes to drugs: risk factors. Risk factors are the conditions in a child's life that increase the likelihood that a boy or girl will develop one or more health behavior problems during their teens. Researchers have noted risk factors that can lead to a variety of serious situations, including alcohol and drug misuse, teen pregnancy, and violence.

But risk factors are not the end of the story. Today many health educators are focusing on "protective factors," things that can strengthen a young person and promote a safer and healthier adolescence. In order to help your child develop healthy behaviors, there are some protective factors that need to be set in place and reinforced:

- Ongoing family and community dialogue about values that promote health, safety, and respect
- Continued nurturing of the child's relationship to the family
- Continued support of the relationship between the child and the school
- A long-term relationship with a trusted adult who models support, respect, and caring
- Active involvement in extracurricular activities to build self-esteem and confidence
- Trusted friends

According to the U.S. Department of Health and Human Services' "Prevention Primer," if the high-risk environment is the family itself—for instance if children are growing up in an alcoholic or drug-abusing family, studies suggest that they have a better chance of growing into healthy adulthood if they

- can learn to do one thing well that is valued by themselves, their friends, and their community.
- are required to be helpful as they grow up.
- are able to ask for help for themselves.
- are able to distance themselves from the dysfunctional family member(s).
- are able to bond with a socially valued, positive entity, such as the family, school, community group, or religious organization.

Though this list may seem like common sense, some children lack the most basic items on it. As a result, they end up making uninformed and unhealthy decisions. Your kids are making choices every day, choices that will be smarter and healthier with the support of a vigilant parent, a supportive teacher, and a nurturing community. Look at the list again. How many protective factors are in place for your child?

Let's Start by Defining Our Terms

Before we can talk about drugs and choices, we need to clarify our use of the word "drugs." "Drugs" is a provocative word. When most parents of a young child hear "drugs," they think pot, crack, heroin, or other street drugs. But what does the child think of? We suggest starting your first talk by defining the term "drug" and comparing your definition with your child's. Do both of you view wine, beer, cigarettes, coffee, and marijuana the same way? If not, how does your definition of "drug" differ from your child's?

There are other terms to define as well. Consider the difference between drug "use," drug "misuse," and drug "abuse." "Misuse" may refer to a situation in which alcohol was inappropriately used, while abuse may refer to something more serious, including addiction. Many parents using the Ten Talks activities have found that defining these terms with their children is eye-opening.

"When I started getting ready to talk with my daughter about drugs I realized that I had never really sat down and thought about my values and feelings about drinking and smoking and everything else. I had not given much thought to my own childhood and I could not remember a thing my parents told me about drugs. Getting ready to have the talk has been an interesting time of reflection." —Sandra, mother of two, Providence, Rhode Island

What Kinds of Choices Does Your Child Make?

Like adults, young people make hundreds of decisions every day. Many of these choices have to do with whether or not to use alcohol, nicotine, or other drugs—some very adult choices indeed. Learning how to make healthy choices will be a lifelong process for them. Your early involvement is key. You need to clarify what you believe in and what you expect from your child's decision making.

Quotes to Consider

"Parent-child communication about drugs and alcohol should begin early—before children are exposed to drugs. According to a survey from Columbia University's National Center on Addiction and Abuse, 'Few twelve-year-olds know how to buy marijuana or know someone who has used hard drugs, but about three times as many do by the time they are thirteen.'" — *K.I.D.S. Link,* fall, 1998, Vol. 1, Issue 1

"In the United States, from 5 to 10 million young people between the ages of twelve and seventeen are using alcohol, tobacco or illicit drugs. This represents as many as half of all the kids this age." —U.S. Department of Health and Human Services, "Keeping Youth Drug Free: A Guide for Parents, Grandparents, Elders, Mentors and Other Caregivers," 1996

"Unfortunately, there are many drugs teenagers abuse in addition to tobacco, alcohol, and marijuana. Common illegal drugs abused by adolescents include cocaine, crack, speed, LSD, PCP, heroin, and ecstasy. Other drugs parents need to be aware of are legal drugs, which can be just as deadly and addicting as illegal drugs. These include prescribed medications, inhalants (fumes from glues, aerosols and solvents), over-the-counter cough, cold, sleep, and diet medications as well as illegal drugs."

—American Academy of Child and Adolescent Psychiatry,
"Tobacco and Kids," www.aacap.org

"A well-established law of recreational drug use: Once users find a substance they like, they will snort or shoot or drop whatever version is available, at any cost. Which is why you must look to the market to understand the future of drugs used for anything other than doctor-approved healing. That market can be divided into three groups: the partiers, who just want to have fun (and who sometimes become addicts), the shrinks and shamans, who believe drugs can expand your consciousness, and the scientists, who suspect that illegal drugs—or their chemical cousins—may have marketable legal uses."

—John Cloud, "Recreational Pharmaceuticals,"
Time magazine, Jan. 15, 2001

"If you want to save taxpayer dollars and you want to reduce violence in your communities, if you want to accomplish all of these larger social goals, you have to draw users into effective drug treatment."

—General Barry R. McCaffrey, former White House director of
national drug policy, quoted in "A Drug Warrior Who Would
Rather Treat than Fight," *New York Times*, Jan. 8, 2001

"Most of us have something in our lives that's important enough to stand between us and drugs. As these pages show, we are making good choices—great choices—for ourselves."

—Special supplement to *USA Today* sponsored by the
White House Office of National Drug Control Policy's
National Youth Anti-Drug Media Campaign, 2000

Different Families: Different Values

Everyone interprets behavior in his or her own way. Here are some behaviors that may be experienced differently depending on a person's background:

A grandfather is visiting the family. As he does most nights, he drinks almost an entire bottle of wine at dinner. He is getting loud and slurring his words.

Some parents might say that it's not a big deal if an adult gets drunk—they might excuse the behavior as "Gramps getting silly." Others would see the behavior as a problem and not want their child to be around someone acting like that, even a family member. Other parents would explain how some adults can enjoy wine in moderation and that problems begin when drinking is in excess. What would you do?

■

An aunt is visiting the family and chain-smokes in the kitchen.

Some parents would see nothing to worry about, since the aunt is an adult and can make up her own mind about whether or not to smoke. Others would ask her to smoke outside, away from the children, and would want to explain to the kids that the aunt may suffer serious health consequences as a result of smoking. What would you do?

■

A daughter is home from college on vacation when her mother discovers a bottle of prescription painkillers in the bathroom. When she asks her daughter what they are for, the daughter says she had an athletic injury six months ago and "sometimes needs them."

Some parents would ask why the daughter is using painkillers. Others would want to talk with their daughter about whether she's become dependent on the painkillers and the feelings that the pills give. What would you do?

■

A teenage girl is at a dance club when she is offered a pill by a friend. All her friends are taking them. She swallows it, and a few minutes later feels nauseous, then relaxed and happy, totally uninhibited.

Many parents would be very upset to hear that their daughter was taking drugs. Some would try to get her to change her friends, while others would not let her go to those types of clubs or parties at her age. What would you do?

■

A mom's brother is visiting from out of town. The mom knows her brother has a history of smoking marijuana. Later that night, her son smells something funny coming from his uncle's bedroom.

Some parents would make a point to tell their visiting relatives or other friends about their values regarding drug use in the home and what they do and don't want their kids exposed to. What would you do?

Different Perspectives

"My son likes stories from my life the best. I told him about how my two best friends locked me in a bathroom once to try to force me to smoke dope. I refused. My son said why didn't I just do it, who cares? I told him that I had simply made a decision that drugs were not something I wanted for myself, no matter what everyone else was doing. I have other stories, too. Both of my parents were chain-smokers and alcoholics. I saw how they behaved. My mother was angry and abusive, and my father got way too loose with other women and made a fool of himself. I told my son about my college friends who did 'ludes and speed. They threw up on my shoes, took their clothes off in public, and ended up in bed with people they didn't even know. I told my son that I didn't want to lose control of myself and do any of those things. When I painted the picture in this way, I think he got it!"

—Cassie, mother of two, Columbia, South Carolina

"I tried to keep my definitions really simple. So I told my daughter, any chemical you put into you that changes your ability to think clearly would be considered a drug. Kids are smart, because she asked me if my morning coffee fit into that category."

—Karen, mother of three, Columbia, South Carolina

"I see these ads for not doing drugs and I know they cost a lot of money to run them on TV and billboards. And I see my kid's school crumbling, and no after-school programs for our children. And it doesn't make sense. You've got to invest in kids to make real change." —Patricia, mother of two, Atlanta, Georgia

"All my parents ever said to me about drugs was, 'We did our dirt and I hope you learned from our mistakes.'"

—Tracy, mother of three, Orlando, Florida

What the Media Is Telling Your Child

What messages is your child getting about alcohol from TV shows? Many scenes are set in bars, parties always include alcohol, some characters smoke, and jokes are made about whatever illegal drug is sweeping the country at the time. Beer ads are all over TV: The ads' themes are partying, sexuality, macho sports, recreation, and youthful, healthy lifestyles. Beer commercials also use talking animals that children find amusing and engaging. If you read a magazine, you'll see slick ads for alcohol indicating that if you want to enjoy life, a drink will help. If you want to be sexy, you'll drink one brand; to be masculine, you'll drink another. Since alcohol and nicotine are technically drugs, you can see that drug use is heavily promoted everywhere.

Illegal or "street drugs" are portrayed differently. Stories about cocaine or heroin usually have unhappy endings, and typically the drug use isn't glorified. Still, there are scenes of people using marijuana that suggest that hip people use it recreationally and without problems. If your kids watch MTV, a few of the rockers they idolize talk and act like they are on drugs and your kids may assume they are. Parents can get discouraged when they see how drugs, sex, and youth music are deeply intertwined. Fortunately, you can talk with your kids about the difference between fantasy and reality!

Last-minute Checkups before the Talk

Before you talk with your child, try to remember what, if anything, your parents taught you about alcohol and other drugs when you were growing up.

- Did a parent ever talk to you about alcohol use?
- Did they ever talk to you about the difference between drug use and abuse?
- Did they model healthy coping skills to deal with stress without using alcohol or other drugs?

As a parent, what are you teaching your child about alcohol and other drugs?

- Do you encourage her to talk about the drug use she sees?
- How do you let your child know that you welcome any concerns she has about alcohol or other drugs?
- Do you talk to your child about her friends and what they do?
- Do you talk with your child about having fun without alcohol and other drugs?
- Do you model the ability to deal with stress without alcohol or other drugs?
- If people in your family drink, do they designate a driver?

Do you have any stories you can share with your child about alcohol or other drug use, or how you confronted someone who was abusing alcohol or other drugs? For example:

- The time a friend tried to get you drunk
- The time you were the designated driver

- The time you used alcohol to deal with sadness or anger and what happened
- The time you called your mom when you were drunk and she came and picked you up
- The time you felt scared by a family member's or your own alcohol or other drug use

Sharing your stories lets your child know how you feel about alcohol and drug use and what impact it had on you when you were growing up.

What Are Your Family Rules?

Do you have family rules about alcohol and other drug use, along with clear consequences for breaking the rules? If not, this is a good time to think about them.

The illustrated scenarios in the next section are meant to give you a chance to discuss your definition of "drug use," how alcohol and other drugs are used and abused, and how there is pressure to use drugs of all kinds. The stories and questions are open-ended, allowing your child to reflect on a range of topics, including the things friends do to protect one another, peer influence, and any other problems or concerns. Depending on your child, the talk could even include issues of mixed messages in the media, and mixed messages about drug use from adult family members. Discussing these situations will give you an opportunity to share your family rules about alcohol and other drug use as well as your views on acceptable behavior.

The Talk

Introduce the Talk

To start this talk you could say, "I've got some questions for you about drugs."

Your child may offer the following: "We've already gone over that in school." Or he may say, "You're always getting into my business." As we will mention throughout this book, this talk is much easier with a fourth grader than with a high-school student well along on the road to independence. Our advice is to persevere even if you are able to talk for only two or three minutes each time. For older children, it is vital to address your family rules and the reasons you want to put them in place.

You can ask, "Which drugs can alter a person's feelings?" Your child might respond with, "Your coffee gets you up in the morning" or "Your wine calms you down at night." A child who's older and more candid might try to challenge you with, "I hear that Uncle Ray smokes pot." A favorite conversation stopper used by kids is, "What did you do when you were young?" (And yes, this book offers helpful quotes from parents who share how they responded to that very question.)

Review These Words

Please review the terms in this section. You know which are appropriate for your child's age and maturity level. More than likely, even the youngest children have heard these words on TV or at school.

addiction: losing control over the use of a substance, like alcohol, or an activity, like gambling.

alcohol: wine, beer, liquor, and other beverages that impact the body by causing loss of motor control. They impact a person's feelings by promoting relaxation, loss of inhibitions, and emotional changes including happy, angry, or sad feelings, depending on the person.

alcoholism: the continued and compulsive use of alcohol, despite negative consequences.

antidepressant: a drug that is most often prescribed to treat depression. It may impact a person's feelings by reducing feelings of hopelessness and sadness, and increase confidence and ability to engage in enjoyable activities.

caffeine: a drug that stimulates the brain and heart, elevates alertness and concentration, and sometimes causes nervousness and agitation. Caffeine is found in coffee, tea, some sodas, over-the-counter medicines, and prescription drugs. Caffeine can be addictive.

choice: an ability people have to use free will to make a decision for themselves. This ability can be affected by the use of alcohol and other drugs.

cocaine: a substance that is found in the leaves of several types of plants. It is a stimulant that can induce a variety of reactions, including feelings of euphoria, extreme happiness, aggression, anxiety, sleeplessness, loss of appetite, and complacency. Cocaine is a white powder that is snorted.

crack: cocaine that's in a rocklike form. When heated, the vapors are inhaled and delivered quickly to the bloodstream through the lungs. Crack is typically smoked.

Definitions

coping mechanisms: ways people deal with stress or painful feelings without drugs. Examples include sports, exercise, meditation, and talking with a friend.

designer drugs: a slang term for synthetic drugs, often used in clubs, that alter a person's consciousness and perceptions, stimulate euphoria, and increase energy.

drug: any substance, legal or illegal, that is used to alter a person's consciousness, perceptions, or feelings. Drugs are thought of by doctors as compounds used to combat disease and improve health. Drugs are defined by courts and police officers as illegal substances whose sale or use has legal consequences.

ecstasy (also called MDMA, "e," or "x"): a compound manufactured illegally and used to create feelings of joy and happiness for three to six hours. It impacts a person's feelings by causing lack of stress and loss of inhibitions, and is often used in combination with other drugs. Taken in the form of a pill, it elevates the body temperature and can cause dehydration, muscle cramping, and nausea. Studies indicate MDMA causes destruction in the brain.

enabling: protecting a drug user from the consequences of his or her actions (for example: not mentioning a person's rude behavior when he was drunk, ignoring clear signs that one's child is using alcohol or other drugs).

feelings: sensations that help us regulate our choices and behaviors. Stress, anger, sadness, depression, lack of self-esteem, and fear are some feelings that may be difficult to experience and may serve as catalysts for alcohol, tobacco, or drug use.

hallucinogens (examples include LSD, or "acid"; mushrooms; peyote): synthetic or natural substances that impact a person's feelings by creating visual and auditory hallucinations and a feeling of "mind expansion" or altered reality.

heroin: an opiate, a drug similar to morphine but many times more powerful. It impacts a person's feelings by reducing pain, creating euphoria, reducing stress, and removing inhibitions. It can be injected, smoked, or snorted.

inhalants: chemical vapors (found in many household products like hair spray and paint thinner) that can be inhaled to produce a mind-altering effect. Inhalants can be deadly.

marijuana (called "pot," "herb," "weed"): A plant which is smoked or eaten. It can produce a sense of euphoria, stimulate hunger, and can sometimes cause anxiety and paranoia. Forms of marijuana can be used for medicinal purposes. For example, patients recovering from chemotherapy might receive marijuana to reduce nausea and stimulate appetite.

nicotine: The addictive ingredient in tobacco is highly habit-forming and impacts a person's body by increasing heart rate and constricting blood vessels. Nicotine users continuously experience, to varying degrees, a state of withdrawal. Tobacco can be smoked or absorbed through the mouth.

opiates: group of drugs derived from the opium poppy, including morphine, heroin, and several other medications used to treat pain by doctors. They impact a person's feelings by reducing pain awareness, promoting sleep, and for some, inducing a feeling of complacency or euphoria.

recovery: the process of becoming sober and learning to live without addictive drugs.

recreational drug use: using a drug for the purpose of enjoying its effects rather than because of a chemical addiction.

This term is often misused by those who are in fact addicted but who may be in denial about it.

sedative: also referred to as a depressant or tranquilizer, a drug that is often prescribed to treat anxiety or insomnia. It impacts a person's feelings by promoting sleep and feelings of relaxation.

self-medicating: using alcohol or other drugs to alter one's feelings. People often report drinking alcohol or taking another mind-altering substance because of boredom, sadness, anger, fear, or depression.

set and setting: the environment a drug is taken in, which affects your reaction to how a drug feels. Taking a drug with a group of people who are all using the same drug feels different psychologically and physically from taking it when one is alone or among people who are not using the same drug.

speed: a synthetic stimulant. Speed affects a person's central nervous system in the same way adrenaline (the body's natural stimulant) works. It speeds up the body's functioning by increasing heart rate, which in turn intensifies concentration and thought processes.

stimulants (other terms: amphetamines, speed): substances that impact a person's feelings by creating increased alertness and feelings of euphoria, which people find pleasurable. However, they also experience central nervous system stimulation, which increases heart rate and blood pressure.

withdrawal syndrome (also "Jones-ing"): a physical and psychological reaction to not having a drug that one has developed a dependence on. Examples include withdrawal from caffeine (severe headaches); marijuana, or cocaine (psychological symptoms); or opiates (shaking, altered sensations, runny nose, feelings of pain and nausea). Withdrawal from alcohol is considered one of the most severe.

"My sixteen-year-old son informed me that 'cheese' means pot and 'jelly pills' means ecstasy."

—Carrie, mother of two, Columbia, South Carolina

"I was trying to explain to my ten-year-old son that some people take drugs to numb their feelings, and he looked at me bewildered and asked, 'Why would anybody want to do that?'"

—Pam, mother of two, Gaithersburg, Maryland

Why Is Talking about Alcohol and Other Drugs Important?

Ask your child whether talking about alcohol and other drug use seems important. Here are some reasons you might want to offer. Talking about alcohol and other drugs means

- learning to identify drug misuse in others or oneself.
- seeing how drug use can change our relationships.
- clarifying family rules about legal and illegal drug use, both healthy and unhealthy.
- clarifying the school rules and laws about drug use.

The Stories

In the next part of the talk, you'll be reading short stories to your child and discussing them together. You don't have to read all of the stories. Pick the ones that you think are appropriate for your child. The stories are very simple. Feel free to embellish them, adding details that you think might make the story more believable to your child.

A Story about Mom and Dad's Drinks

This story provides an opportunity to talk about alcohol and its moderate use by adults.

"Both mom and dad had a long day at work. At dinner, the brother and sister are drinking juice, while their parents each drink a beer."

Ask these questions of your child:

- What is the mom thinking?
- What is the dad thinking?
- What is the daughter thinking?
- What is the son thinking?

Now that your child has completed this scenario, ask the following questions:

- Do the kids want to drink alcohol? Why or why not?
- When people drink alcohol, how does it change their personalities?
- Is alcohol a drug?
- What should the parents say to the kids about responsible, adult use of alcohol?

- If you were in a situation like this, how would you feel? What would you do?

A Story about Being Offered "a Smoke"

This story provides an opportunity to talk about tobacco and how friends can influence our behavior.

"A high-school senior and a high-school freshman are talking at a party. The senior offers the freshman a cigarette."

Ask these questions of your child:

- What is the senior thinking?
- What is the freshman thinking?
- What is the senior saying?
- What is the freshman saying?

Now that your child has completed this scenario, ask the following questions:

- Would the freshman accept the cigarette? Why or why not?
- What addictive drug does tobacco contain? (Tobacco contains nicotine.)
- How can the freshman refuse a cigarette?
- What do people usually do in a situation like this?
- What's the difference between being offered "a smoke" and being offered a "cancer-causing drug"?

- If you were in a situation like this, how would you feel? What would you do?

A Story about a Girl and Her Aunt

This story provides an opportunity to talk about the misuse of drugs and how family members model behavior.

"An aunt is visiting her sister and her niece. The niece walks in on the aunt in the bathroom by accident while the aunt is taking some painkillers, pills that the aunt just found in the medicine cabinet."

Ask these questions of your child:

- What is the girl thinking?
- What is the aunt thinking?
- What is the girl saying?
- What is the aunt saying?

Now that your child has completed this scenario, ask the following questions:

- Should the aunt explain why she is using the mom's painkillers?
- Are painkillers a drug?
- Would the daughter be curious and want to take a painkiller even though it was not prescribed to her? Why or why not?

- Why might the girl be curious as to why her aunt is using her mom's painkillers?
- How would you feel if you were in a situation like this? What would you do?

A Story about a Girl at a Party

This story gives you a chance to talk about illegal drugs, commitments to parents, and feeling the influence of peers.

"A girl is at a party with some friends. The girl is offered a pill by a popular kid at school. The kid says that the pill will make her feel totally relaxed and happy."

Ask these questions of your child:

- What is the girl thinking?
- What is the girl saying?
- What is the popular kid thinking?

Now that your child has completed this scenario, ask the following questions:

- Might the girl want to take the pill? Why or why not?
- What kinds of reasons might the girl offer?
- Is the pill a drug?

- What are the kinds of consequences the girl might face if she takes the pill?
- If she takes the pill, will the girl have betrayed her parents' trust? What if this is the first time the daughter has taken an illegal drug?
- How would you feel if you were in a situation like this? What would you do?

Clarify Your Family's Values

Discuss these questions with your child as a way of sharing your values about alcohol and drug use. We have included a number of potential responses from children to help you formulate your own responses.

Ask your child: "When people have painful feelings and want to stop feeling sad, angry, or afraid, what can they do to feel better besides drinking alcohol or taking other drugs?"

Child response #1: "Talk to a friend."
Parent: Right. Sometimes talking about problems with a trusted friend or even an acquaintance can help someone feel better. Talking to a parent or grandparents or aunt or uncle might be helpful, too.

Child response #2: "See a school counselor to help with the problem."
Parent: Asking for help is definitely a good idea. There are all kinds of people who can help, including relatives [name some

that you trust], people from our religious community, and people at school.

Child response #3: "Well, one beer couldn't hurt."

Parent: That may be true sometimes. A beer or a glass of wine might not hurt an adult at all. In some families and cultures it might be fine. It all depends on the situation and the age and emotional maturity of the person who wants to drink. If an adult uses alcohol moderately that might be fine. But some people—both young and old—become addicted to alcohol, or sedate themselves in order to mask difficult feelings. For these people, even one glass of alcohol can hurt.

Child response #4: "I don't know."

Parent: Well, when you feel really bad—or when you feel good and want to change your feelings, a common motivation for recreational drug use—what do you do to feel better? Take a long walk, talk on the phone with a friend, write in a journal, play a game, go for a run, watch TV, or just sleep?

The Bare Minimum: A Quick Quiz for Kids

Ask your child the following questions to assess her knowledge and perceptions of alcohol and other drug use.

1. Can you give me an example of three drugs that are legal for adults?
   Sample answers:
* alcohol

- tobacco
- drugs prescribed for you by a doctor

2. Can you give me an example of three illegal drugs?
   Sample answers:
- pot
- ecstasy
- crack

3. What is a substance that is legal only for adults but can be deadly?
   Sample answer:
- tobacco (which contains nicotine)

Talk about Your Family Rules

This is an opportunity to review your family rules. Ask your child the following question:

1. What are our family rules about using alcohol and other drugs?
   Sample answers:
- Adults may use alcohol responsibly, in moderation.
- We never drink alcohol and drive.
- No one in this family breaks the law regarding alcohol or other drug use.
- We don't drink alcohol or use drugs.
- We talk about our alcohol, tobacco, and drug use openly and honestly to learn about how it can be healthy or unhealthy.

After the Talk

How did your first talk go? Were you surprised by anything you heard? The results of this talk vary widely. Some parents are surprised by how much their kids know about drug use, or by how open their children are to the topic. Parents of teenagers usually report more resistance than parents of younger children. If that's what you experienced, don't let it get you down. Talking about the consequences of drug abuse takes time, energy, and patience. When it comes to letting your kids know that you love them and that you care, there is no wasted effort.

A Moment to Reflect

Take a moment to reflect on the talk you just had with your child. How do you feel about it?

- What surprised you about your child's view of alcohol and other drug use?
- Do you think your child has the confidence and critical thinking skills to deal with life's pressures without relying on alcohol or other drugs? Does your child seem susceptible to peer influence?
- Think about whether your child has the ability to deal with everyday stresses that accompany childhood and adolescence.
- What did you learn about how to listen and talk to your child?

Warning Signs

Did your talk give you any cause for concern? In some cases, this talk reveals potential problems that the child might be facing. Review the following warning signs to see if your child might be using alcohol or other drugs:

- She doesn't see anything wrong with kids drinking alcohol or using other drugs.
- He makes up serious problems for the characters in the illustrated stories.
- She expresses ideas about drug use that are dangerous or illegal.
- He hints at having problems with alcohol, cigarettes, or other drugs.
- She reports feeling isolated or alienated from peers.
- He says people who go into rehab to deal with drug use are weak or stupid.
- He says he doesn't care about school and his grades drop.
- She shares some problems in the course of the talk that sound like they could be serious.

You observe your child all the time. Trust your instincts. When you meet your child's friends, observe whether they appear alert, sober, and attentive. If grades take a quick downturn, ask about the cause, and note whether there is a corresponding change in behavior. You don't need a special degree to know when your child needs support. You are the expert. Don't be afraid to express your concerns and ask how you can help.

Finding Help

This talk or your child's recent behaviors may indicate problems that require outside support. Help for your child—and you—is available. Most teachers, school counselors, principals, religious leaders, and employee assistance programs can refer parents to caring professionals with expertise in working with young people and family members. Finding a counselor requires time, energy, and persistence, but their help may be invaluable. You may need to interview a few professionals before you find one you and your child are comfortable with.

Success Stories

You have made it through an important talk. Congratulations! What did you learn? One mom in Sels, Arizona, reported that her sixteen-year-old son revealed in the course of a talk that he had indeed gotten drunk at a party. This led to a series of talks about drinking, trust, and respect for the family rules and the law.

This talk is only the beginning. One talk can't cover all your concerns about drug use. That will take many conversations, over time. With this talk, no matter how brief, you have started to create an environment of awareness and openness. You have let your child know that you can talk about drugs together and that help is available for people who need it. Not bad for a first try.

Sample Talks

Between Parents and Children

If you are wondering how a talk based on this chapter might really sound, take a look at the following excerpts from real family talks. Notice how moms and dads embellish the stories, changing details to make them work better for their kids. Some parents skip certain questions and focus on other issues that they think are important. Some of the kids in these stories talk easily about drug use, while others are more resistant—that's the reality of talking with young people about drugs.

Discussing the Story about Mom and Dad's Drinks

Participants: a mother and her twelve-year-old daughter

Mom: Okay, here's our first story. "Both mom and dad had a long day at work. At dinner, the brother and sister are drinking juice while their parents each drink a beer." What is the mom thinking?

Daughter: That the beer's good but maybe she shouldn't be drinking it in front of her children.

Mom: Great. What is the dad thinking?

Daughter: The dad's thinking the same thing as the mom.

Mom: What is the daughter thinking?

Daughter: That her parents shouldn't be drinking because there could be serious consequences, such as them getting drunk. She's thinking that she'd never do that when she grew up. And it's the same thing the boy's thinking.

Mom: Why would the kids want to drink alcohol?

Daughter: They wouldn't.

Mom: When someone drinks alcohol, how does it change their personality?

Daughter: It could make them violent.

Mom: Is alcohol a drug?

Daughter: Yes.

Mom: What should the parents say to the kids about responsible, adult use of the drug, alcohol?

Daughter: They should say . . . well there's nothing to say because it's not responsible for adults, either.

Mom: Um, okay. If you were in a situation like this, how would you feel?

Daughter: Worried about the parents.

Mom: What would you do?

Daughter: I'd get them involved in a program about, against drugs, but find one for adults.

Mom: All right, great job! Thank you so much for having this talk.

Lessons Learned from This Sample Talk

In this talk, the mom learned something important about her daughter: She thinks alcohol is a drug like any other. That makes her daughter a rare twelve-year-old indeed! It's important to note, however, that no one in this family drinks alcohol. Could that be the reason the daughter finds alcohol an issue of great concern? Why does she say that alcohol might make people violent? Is that opinion based on watching TV or real people? In her next talk, the mom could probe more on that question. She might also want to point out that responsible adults who drink socially don't necessarily need a treatment program.

Discussing the Story about Being Offered "a Smoke"

Participants: a mother and her twelve-year-old daughter

Mom: Okay, here's a story for us. "A high-school senior and a high-school freshman are talking at a party. The senior offers the freshman a cigarette." What is the senior thinking?

Daughter: That she's going to take it.

Mom: What is the senior saying?

Daughter: "You should take this to be cool. Everyone's doing it."

Mom: What is the freshman saying?

Daughter: "No."

Mom: Why would the freshman accept the cigarette?

Daughter: She wouldn't.

Mom: Does tobacco contain a drug?

Daughter: Yeah.

Mom: What drug is it?

Daughter: Nicotine.

Mom: Nicotine, very good. How can the freshman refuse a cigarette?

Daughter: By saying no aggressively—assertively.

Mom: What do people usually do in a situation like this?

Daughter: Take it.

Mom If you were in a situation like this, how would you feel?

Daughter: That I should say no.

Mom: What would you do?

Daughter: Say no.

Lessons Learned from This Sample Talk

What did this mom learn about her daughter? That the daughter has clearly seen peer pressure to smoke—but that she feels confident in her ability to say no. It's obvious that the daughter views nicotine as a drug. In a later talk, the mom might want to underline the long-term health consequences of smoking and the risks associated with secondhand smoke.

Discussing the Story about a Girl and Her Aunt

Participants: a dad and his twelve-year-old son

Dad: Let's read the next story. "An aunt is visiting her sister and the sister's children. A girl walks in on the aunt in the bathroom by accident while the aunt is taking some of her sister's painkillers. (These are pills that the girl's mother got from the dentist a few weeks ago after some work on her teeth.)" So, in other words, the aunt is in the bathroom taking pills that aren't hers. What is the girl thinking?

Son: She's like, "Yo, what are you doing? That's not yours."

Dad: You think she'd say that?

Son: Or she'd just walk away.

Dad: What would the aunt be thinking about when the girl walks in and sees her?

Son: "Um, er, uh . . . I thought these were aspirin!"

Dad: Should the aunt explain why she is using the mom's painkillers?

Son: Yeah.

Dad: Are painkillers a drug? Like aspirin?

Son: Yeah.

Dad: Would the daughter be curious and want to take a painkiller? Why or why not?

Son: Probably not, because she doesn't want to get sick.

Dad: Why might the girl be curious as to why her aunt is using her mom's painkillers?

Son: Well, they're not hers.

Dad: That question seems somewhat—

Son: Obvious!

Dad: How would you feel if you were in a situation like this? What would you do?

Son: I would say, "What are you doing?"

Dad: You'd say that to an adult?

Son: Yeah.

Dad: Anything else?

Son: No.

Lessons Learned from This Sample Talk

This talk is a great springboard to further conversations and questions. The dad may want to ask the son why he thinks it "obvious" that the girl would be curious about the aunt's taking some of Mom's painkillers. Are all kids curious in the same way, or as concerned? The son also said that he would ask an adult relative about how pills should be used. How realistic is this? Would he really tell on a favorite aunt or uncle? Or could he be encouraged to tell a parent without confronting an adult?

Discussing the Story about a Girl at a Party

Participants: a mother and her twelve-year-old daughter

Mom: Here's another story for us. "A girl is at a party with some friends. The girl is offered a pill by a popular kid at school whom she likes. The kid says that this pill will make her feel totally relaxed and happy." What is the girl thinking?

Daughter: The girl's thinking that she shouldn't take the pill.

Mom: What's the girl saying?

Daughter: Nothing.

Mom: Why might the girl want to take the pill?

Daughter: She doesn't.

Mom: What kinds of reasons might the girl offer?

Daughter: Because there could be some stuff in it that she's allergic to.

Mom: Is a pill a drug?

Daughter: I don't know. Is it?

Mom: Well, they are at the party and they're offering pills. Are they offering drugs?

Daughter: Maybe.

Mom: Yes, they are offering drugs. If you are at a party and someone offers you a pill, it's drugs. What are the kinds of consequences the daughter might face if she takes the pill?

Daughter: If it's a drug, she could get, uh, drunk?

Mom: If she took the pill, has the daughter betrayed her parents' trust? If they let her go to the party in the first place?

Daughter: Yeah.

Mom: What if this is the first time the daughter has taken an illegal drug?

Daughter: I don't get the question.

Mom: Well, if this is the first time she's had to make a choice like this, maybe we should cut her some slack. How would you feel if you were in this situation?

Daughter: Uncomfortable?

Mom: What would you do?

Daughter: Say no.

Mom: Would you call your mother and ask her to come get you?

Daughter: Yeah.

Mom: Okay.

Lessons Learned from This Sample Talk

As you can see, the daughter in this talk was a little reluctant to have the conversation, but Mom bravely soldiered on and got right to the points that were most important to her: She emphasized what to do in such a situation and she made it clear that any pill offered at a party should be considered a drug. The mom got some good information about her daughter's knowledge of drug use at parties.

2

How Do You Feel?

Talking about How Drugs Alter Your Feelings

Talking to my son about feelings is not something that comes naturally to me—or to him. If I ever said something like, "It's important to feel your feelings," my son would just laugh.
—Anthony, father of three, Seattle, Washington

Why do kids turn to drugs? A lot of it has to do with their emotional state. As parents, educators, and community members, it is time to come to terms with the fact that we have to teach our children how to cope with and experience unpleasant feelings. The good news in all of this is that it can be taught. Simple conversations between adults and children are the beginning.
—Lynn Delevan, Center for Social and Emotional Learning, New York

I grew up on cowboy movies where the hero would get mad, down a whiskey, and then shoot the bad guy. I guess that taught me that strong emotions equals booze. —Ed, father of two, Los Angeles

You can't talk about recreational drug use without discussing feelings. In writing this book we interviewed hundreds of parents, educators, and young people about drug use, and everyone's story included a part about the "tough times" the drug user was going through. Adults talked about their own parents' dealing with stress and turning to alcohol. Teens spoke of feeling lonely and desperate to fit into a peer group, even at the cost of using street drugs. Educators remembered times when they felt disillusioned with work and found themselves smoking marijuana every day—to deal with the feelings.

Many of us can identify with Anthony, the father above, who'd rather not talk about feelings with his son. We think we might feel silly or embarrassed. But that's a small price to pay for safeguarding our children's lives and futures.

And the truth is that parents across the country are successfully teaching their kids to deal with difficult feelings—first by identifying them, and then by experiencing them. We know that it's not always easy in a culture that says, "Happiness is only a beer away!" But that shouldn't stop us from doing all we can.

We chose to focus on feelings up front, because we didn't want to write another book about drugs that didn't look at why people turn to drugs and incorporate their use into their daily lives. We think understanding how drugs work in the body is important. But we think that what parents really need is a book that helps them talk to their children about how to deal with difficult feelings and the stresses of living in a very complex society—the very things that turn us toward drugs in the first place.

Parents also need to talk with their children about guidelines for behavior and about appropriate ways to act on our feelings. Parents need a way to communicate with their children about family rules and values, and how we can express our feelings fully within those limits.

This chapter will help you think about how you model expressing feelings, especially ones that are not always easy to deal with. You'll also help your child develop the ability to deal with stress and other uncomfortable feelings. We believe that's a crucial step in preparing your kids for an emotionally healthy life as an adult.

How are feelings affected by alcohol, tobacco, and drugs?

Why do some people use a drug only occasionally, while others feel they need to use it daily? Why do some teens experiment briefly with drugs and grow up to lead lives free from drug dependence, while others quickly become addicted?

Our genes probably play a role, a connection scientists are just beginning to unravel. But we can't change our genes. We can change how we deal with feelings.

We believe one of the keys to preventing addiction is in our capacity to manage our feelings of stress and pain. A young person needs to find some way to cope with difficult feelings, from day-to-day loneliness to the pain of abuse. Some cope by doing sports, making art, or talking to friends, while others use a drug instead.

We've found that children can be taught to express pain, fear, or anger in a healthy, productive, and nonviolent manner. We've seen parents helping their kids to identify their feelings and to express them in ways that are useful and healthy.

Talking about Feelings

"My son knows how to express anger. He hits and fights. I'm trying to show him other ways that are healthy."

—Mona, mother of two, Syracuse, New York

"I'm trying to teach my kids that we make choices every day—either to express or suppress feelings." —Ann, mother of three, New York City

What does one mean when saying "feel your feelings"? Would your child understand what you are talking about? Children have all the feelings adults do, although learning to express them takes time. That's something they'll learn from their environment—from neighbors and friends, teachers and coaches, movies and TV, and of course, from you.

Messages about how to cope with difficult feelings are everywhere. Television shows include many different kinds of people using alcohol or other drugs as a way of dealing with stress. Perhaps as a result, words to describe alcohol or other drug use are an ordinary part of kids' vocabulary. The terms "drunk," "stoned," "wasted," and "high" can be heard in any schoolyard in the country.

Ads on TV, on the radio, and in magazines hawk alcohol, cigarettes, and prescription drugs as a route to happiness and a way to avoid pain. Internet pharmacies bombard everyone—adults and kids alike—with e-mails promoting Viagra and hair-loss cures. The message? If something is wrong, a drug can fix it.

Thankfully, there are thoughtful messages about drugs, too. Your kids' school may offer lessons on drugs and drug abuse. But talk to your kids, and you'll find that their classes probably don't ask why people turn to drugs in the first place. You'll find that they haven't thought through their own values or how they'd handle specific situations. That's where you come in.

The talk in this chapter will give you a chance to discuss how your child feels about life and its everyday stresses. You and your child will discuss personal qualities and skills for coping with feelings that each person needs to have in order to be happy, healthy, and safe.

"When Heather first started acting rude and rebellious, I should have suspected that she was using drugs—her personality changed so drastically. But it was months before I was able to get her to talk about what she was going through. In the meantime, she got into a lot of trouble and I nearly lost her."

—Maria, mother of two, New York City

Talking about Identifying and Coping with Your Feelings

"In counseling, we work with people to help them identify feelings and behaviors. We work on ways to separate the two—so that a feeling like anger does not have to lead to behavior like hitting."

—Susan Burgess, therapist, New York

What do we mean when we say someone is good at expressing feelings? Here are some difficult feelings most people would agree are experienced by most people at one time or another.

- Worry
- Fear
- Loneliness
- Loss
- Anger
- Sadness

Perhaps you can think of other difficult feelings that people often face. Has your child felt or expressed any of these feelings? The answer is almost certainly yes. As your child gets older and the life situations presented become more complex, the temptation to avoid difficult feelings is normal. Who wants to be stressed or angry? But life never stops presenting us with challenges. By the time kids are in late elementary school and beginning puberty, they need to have the ability to manage those feelings.

Parents need to help their child develop skills to process difficult feelings associated with adolescence, including feelings of insecurity and confusion. The person who has the ability to deal with unpleasant feelings and get through a school day without alcohol or drugs is doing pretty well. Asking kids to fully experience their feelings during adolescence is not always an easy request. If you think back on your teenage years, you may recall that this was a time of mood swings and unpredictable feelings. Filled with some of the highest emotional highs and lowest lows, the years from ten to eighteen are an important time to learn and practice strategies for coping with and communicating feelings.

Developmental psychologists agree that we pass through a number of critical periods during which specific events must occur if development is to happen normally. Likewise, emotional development and expression are key to children and adults making healthy decisions with respect to the use and abuse of drugs.

Your goal is to raise a child who can deal with tough feelings without dependence on alcohol or other drugs. And you can.

Feelings Are a Part of Life

"My daughter was surprised when I told her that I still grapple with difficult feelings. I think she would be surprised to know about the grab bag of feelings that I have. I don't think she understands that learning to deal with tough feelings is a lifelong process."   —Cindy, mother of two, Denver, Colorado

Even though this talk is about dealing with tough situations and feelings, your conversation with your child should not be about frightening, shaming, or intimidating her to the point that she doesn't ever want to leave her bedroom. Parents understand that life is complex and filled with wonderful experiences as well as challenging ones. We also know that decisions about drinking or using legal drugs come with big responsibilities and serious consequences.

This talk is about empowering your child with communication skills and critical-thinking skills. These skills can help her navigate through life and make informed decisions about whom she spends time with and how to deal with situations she might find herself in. At the end of this talk, your child should understand that there are many ways to cope with stress, painful feelings, or infatuations. She'll also understand that using alcohol and other drugs to mute or mask feelings has a variety of negative consequences. She'll see that there are many choices she can make based on her own and her family's values. Most important, she'll understand that coping with stress and complex feelings are things families can and should discuss.

Preparing for the Talk

This talk opens the door to ongoing conversations that will deepen your child's understanding of feelings and how to deal with them. In this talk you will let your child know that

- it's okay to talk about feelings.
- he can depend on you for support when facing difficult feelings.
- you have expectations about her behavior as it relates to coping with difficult feelings.

- there are family guidelines and rules about healthy, respectful ways to express and cope with difficult feelings.

What You Can Expect from This Talk

After the talk your child will

- be able to identify healthy ways to deal with difficult feelings.
- understand that there are many kinds of stressful situations people face and that learning to cope with them is a natural and important part of growing up.
- understand your family guidelines and rules about coping with stress and expressing difficult feelings.
- understand that we can share our feelings with our families and find support.

"Growing up I knew that my parents would have grounded me for life if they knew I'd tried any kind of drugs. But that didn't stop me from experimenting. I'm really worried about my twelve-year-old son, who's facing the same decisions. He is already bottling up his feelings."   —Lisa, mother of one, Seattle, Washington

"Who are we kidding? I know my kids have tried drugs. Most kids in college do. That doesn't make them addicts. And it doesn't mean they can't cope."   —Bill, father of one, Orlando, Florida

"In our family, all feelings were expressed. When my mom and dad yelled, we knew they were mad. But they were very loving and supportive."   —Mario, father of two, New York City

What Does "Coping with Feelings" Mean?

First, you need to find out what your child thinks "coping with feelings" means. Does she think of coping as saying what's on her mind or keeping her feelings a secret? Does he think that being a man means suffering in silence? If you talk to your child about "coping" you may be surprised by what your child thinks.

Your child learns about coping with feelings in all kinds of ways. You are the primary role model. Your child hears your comments about TV shows or ads and sees how you and your friends relate to one another. Those are the primary models that your child will use in finding ways to cope. Any time you communicate your thoughts or feelings, you're helping to define coping.

As you read this chapter, there will be opportunities to discuss your strategies for coping with stressful feelings and the situations that may cause them.

Making Healthy Choices

Jen and her mom have been fighting about the phone bill. Her mom thinks Jen is spending too much money on long distance calls. The mother is overwhelmed with bills she can't pay and is feeling very stressed. She considers having a few glasses of wine and putting off the bills till later. Instead, she firmly tells her daughter that she is worried—and sits down to start paying the bills.

The daughter saw her mom feeling stress, then making a healthy choice. Do you think seeing something like that can affect a young child? How would you act in this situation if you were the mom? What else could the mom have done to deal with her feelings of stress? Do you think that drinking a glass of wine might have been a good idea?

Your Parents' Family Rules and Yours

When you were growing up, did your family have spoken or unspoken rules about how you or other family members could express feelings? Was expressing feelings something that was nurtured in your home? If not, why not? Who set the rules? Some families come from cultures where discussing feelings is normal, while in other cultures that's far from the case. *Ten Talks* refers to family rules throughout. We don't think that most families have stated rules about expressing feelings, but many do have unspoken rules regarding stress or difficult feelings—especially anger.

If you were to ask your child, "What are the family rules about expressing anger in this house?" what would she say? A goal of *Ten Talks* is to help you identify and set the rules that you feel comfortable with and to make sure that your child knows what the rules are. These rules also help your child understand how feelings—even difficult ones like anger—can be communicated in appropriate ways.

"In our house, when our mom got mad, she screamed at us. We knew that Mom had a temper and we got out of her way when she was upset."　　　　　—Tracy, mother of two, Gaithersburg, Maryland

"I grew up with a mother who was always angry about something, and it made me very reluctant to express anger as an adult."
　　　　　　　　　　　　　　　—Lisa, mother of three, New York City

"My dad seemed stressed from work every night. He used to drink too much on the weekends. We learned he was different during those times than the rest of the week. My brother and I always hung out at friends' houses just to keep out of trouble. Dad was never there for us." —J.B., father of one, Yakima, Washington

"To be honest, it wasn't until I got into counseling that I understood that I could make choices. Up until then my feelings and my behavior were one and the same. When I felt fear, I drank."

—Ed, father of two, Portland, Oregon

Influence of the Media

TV and movies are full of images of people getting drunk or using other drugs as a way to cope with difficult feelings. These images are not designed to offer insight into the complex issues around drugs and feelings. That's your job.

The media plays a big role in shaping our ideas about expressing feelings—especially when it comes to how males show feelings, as opposed to females. Stereotypes about how men and women are supposed to feel and how they should express those feelings are as strong as ever. This may be the twenty-first century, but the strong, silent male and the emotional, expressive female can be found on just about every movie screen in the country.

What do you think are appropriate ways for men to express their feelings? For women to express theirs? Don't leave that task to TV. Talk to your kids about it.

Influence of Peers

How can parents help kids learn to deal with stress and anxiety? Many parents find it helpful to think back to their own childhood and what helped them deal with difficult situations and confusing feelings. Adults say that having friends who successfully coped with stress without alcohol or drugs was an important factor in learning to cope with their own daily stresses in healthy ways.

Think back to your childhood. Did you have friends who were able to communicate their feelings in healthy ways? Did stress increase as you moved from elementary to middle to high school?

"When I started high school, I was constantly threatened by older guys. I lived in fear for two years, but never told anyone."

—Rich, father of two, Jamestown, New York

"My best friend and I didn't drink or do drugs in high school. Then her dad died and she changed. She started hanging out with the drug crowd." —Pat, mother of two, Boise, Idaho

"In junior high school, the bottom fell out for me. I left my secure little grade school with teachers and friends I had known for years and entered a big, new school that was impersonal and frightening." —Jeffrey, New York City

"I had a clique that I hung around with. We did everything together. We were a five-girl social club. As I think back, we served as a therapy and support group for each other. That's what got me through some excruciatingly painful teenage years!"

—Gretchen, mother of one, Denver, Colorado

Quotes to Consider

"Adolescents who are at risk for developing alcohol and drug problems include teens with a family history of substance abuse, who are depressed, who have low self-esteem, and who feel they don't fit in." —American Academy of Child and Adolescent Psychiatry, "Tobacco and Kids," www.aacap.org

"The emotional system is immature in early adolescence. Emotions are extreme and changeable. Small events can trigger enormous reactions. A negative comment about appearance or a bad mark on a test can hurl a teenager into despair." —Mary Pipher, *Reviving Ophelia,* 1994

"There are hundreds of studies showing that how parents treat their children, whether with harsh discipline, emphatic understanding, indifference or warmth, has deep and long-lasting consequences for the child's emotional health." —Daniel Goleman, *Emotional Intelligence,* 1994

"Parents say that open communication best prepares children to make wise decisions. And kids who have had conversations with their parents say they were glad to have talked and got good ideas about how to handle the issues."
—Kaiser Family Foundation and Children Now, "Talking With Kids About Tough Issues: A National Survey of Parents and Kids," 1999

A New World for Children

Is life more stressful now than it was fifty years ago? Are more of us turning to drugs to cope with stress? Do we have more choices to make? Fifty years ago, more families had a working dad and a mom who stayed home to raise the kids. This "traditional family" no longer represents the majority of U.S. households.

Most Americans are in blended families. Over half of the country's moms work outside the home. Many households are headed by only one parent. Many parents have been married numerous times and see kids from each union at different times during the week, while still other households have two moms or two dads. Some experts think that a lack of family stability is a major added stress for today's kids.

Young people today also have access to more information, much of it violent or confusing. Hyper-violent video games compete for their attention, along with 500 channels of cable TV and a nearly infinite number of websites with dubious content.

The good news is that you have considerable control over the development of your child's attitudes and feelings. You are the most important influence on your child. You are your child's role model for developing sound relationships, communicating feelings, and making healthy choices.

"Even though I didn't try hard drugs when I was a teenager, I recognize it's a different time and my kids are under different pressures than I was. The Internet chat rooms are enough to confuse anyone."
—Nina, mother of three, Denver, Colorado

"I don't so much as take an aspirin in front of my children without talking about how drugs should be used prudently. Pretty soon they'll be too old to influence, so I'm trying to get my point across while I still can." —Rachel, mother of two, Everett, Washington

Different Families: Different Values

Your child is presented with many values about expressing feelings. You have your own values and attitudes, but your child's friends, teachers, or coaches may have different ones. The following scenarios illustrate how your child may get different messages from different people.

Your child is playing at a neighbor's home with a group of boys. One boy punches your child and the other boys laugh. Your child is upset and cries.

One father might hear about the punching and write it off as boys being boys. Another parent might take the boy who was struck aside, comfort him, and give him time to express his feelings. Still another parent would encourage the boy to fight back next time. How would you react? What if it was a girl being hit? How comfortable would your child be communicating this situation and his feelings to you?

■

In class, some sixth graders are working on a math problem. The teacher calls on your son and he gives the correct answer. The kid who sits behind your son whispers, "You think you're so smart—I'm gonna pound you after school." Your son feels scared.

What would you like your child to do in a situation like this? If he tells the teacher he could get in more trouble with the bully. Then again, the teacher might be able to resolve it. How would you want to see this situation addressed? How comfortable would your child be communicating this situation and his feelings to you?

∎

Your daughter is going out with a guy. They are kissing at a party when he lets her know that he wants to have sex. Your daughter does not want to have sex, but she thinks she loves him. She is very stressed and unsure what to do. He is pressuring her to relax, have a beer, and have fun.

What kinds of feelings do you think the daughter is experiencing? How might the beer impact her feelings? How would you want your daughter to respond? How comfortable would your child be communicating this situation and her feelings to you?

The father of the boy who was hit, the bully, and the boyfriend all have their own ways of creating situations that cause stress. Your child may face situations similar to these at some point in his or her life. Many situations require both critical thinking and the ability to communicate one's feelings. What do you tell your kids about standing up for themselves if it might mean getting hurt? Other people, like the dad mentioned in the first scenario, are communicating their values to your child in subtle or not-so-subtle ways. Your values need to be communicated in a way that's equally loud and clear.

Different Perspectives

"I tell my son, 'I don't know how you feel, but I do know the feeling.' I try to teach him words to be able to talk about his feelings, but I know that sometimes it's hard even for me to put my finger on what's going on with me. It's really complicated and scary, because

I won't always be right there to ask him what's going on. Even when there's no easy answer, we still talk about how it feels to go through hard times, and I hope the feeling of being loved is what he'll remember most when he's out there."

—Patti, mother of one, Buffalo, New York

Last-minute Checkups before the Talk

This is a good time to think back to when you were a child and wanted to talk about feelings and situations that were causing you stress. When you were a child:

- Did a parent ever talk to you about feelings?
- Did you ever tell your parents about difficult feelings you experienced? What did they say?
- Did your parents ever discuss ways to communicate feelings like anger?

How do you think your childhood experiences have affected the way you're raising your child?

- What have you told your child about feelings?
- Have you told her to expect some pressures and stresses from schoolmates? Is she supposed to avoid situations that cause worry and stress?
- Has your family discussed appropriate ways to express anger and how people might respond to it?

Do you have any stories that you could share with your child? For example:

- A story about a neighbor or schoolmate who was very angry and expressed it in a manner that scared you
- An experience confronting a person's anger or fear
- A time when you felt afraid or insecure

Keep these stories in mind as you talk with your child. She needs to hear that you have faced these situations yourself and made tough decisions.

What Are Your Family Rules?

Do you have family rules about how, when, and where to express feelings—especially feelings of anger, frustration, sadness, or fear? We are not suggesting that these rules control how your child can feel. The truth is quite the opposite—we hope that your child feels she can safely express her feelings. The point is to help create respect for people's boundaries so that expressions of anger, fear, insecurity, and frustration are not used as attacks. Have you talked about ways to deal with stress? If not, this is a good time to think about them. You'll also want to discuss family rules and school rules about dealing with violence or threats of violence.

Discussing the illustrated scenarios in the next section will give you a chance to discuss your family rules. What would you want your child to do in each situation? What are your expectations? Before the talk, think about what rules you want to communicate to your child. At the end of the talk, you will have the chance to review the rules together.

The Talk

Introduce the Talk

All right—you are almost ready to have the talk about feelings with your child. To fully understand the *Ten Talks* process, make sure to read the entire chapter before starting the talk. You may find the sample talks at the end of this chapter particularly helpful.

Find a time for an uninterrupted ten minutes or so. With this book in hand, tell your child: "I'd like to talk with you about this chapter I'm reading about feelings and drugs. I don't think we've ever talked about this. I think it's really important."

Some younger children may be happy to talk with you, while others may be completely uninterested. Many children assume that they actually know more about real life than you do. Some common responses from a resistant child: "I already know all this!" or "I learned that in school."

If your child doesn't want to talk, be patient. Many parents report that timing is everything. Some kids do better during a walk (boys especially seem to do better when they can move and talk at the same time). And remember, you can use the following statement as many times as necessary: "It's part of my job as a parent to have this talk, to listen to you and answer your questions. It's part of your job as my child to listen and ask me questions."

Remember how you liked to be spoken to when you were young—kids still don't want to be talked down to or treated like babies. At the first sign of a patronizing speech, they'll shut down.

Next, you could say, "I've got some questions to discuss. First, what have you learned about why people get stressed?" Or you could ask, "What stresses you?" Next, ask if she's had any lessons or talks at school about how people deal with stress or difficult feelings. School lessons on drug abuse may not talk about feelings; instead, they may be general talks about how to stay away from strangers offering drugs. Ask what your child has learned.

You could say something like, "There are many reasons people misuse alcohol and drugs. One reason is to escape from difficult feelings like stress, anger, and sadness. I'd like to start by talking about the stresses you feel."

Review These Words

Please review the terms in this section. Discussing all the terms with your child is optional. You know what's appropriate for your child's age and maturity level.

coping: how a person decides how to manage a situation.

coping behaviors: These could be either positive or negative ways to respond to a situation. For example, a person feeling a lot of anxiety could choose to talk with a friend (a positive coping behavior) or get drunk (a negative one).

counseling: advice and help in dealing with a problem, provided by a trained individual.

critical thinking: a process of questioning, information gathering, looking at different perspectives, and problem solving.

risk factors: parts of a person's life that can potentially lead to problems with alcohol and other drugs. For example, living with someone who abuses drugs is a high risk factor.

protective factors: parts of a person's life that can provide stability and security to the individual. For example, having a strong family bond, clear rules, and supportive parents are protective factors that can help keep a person from turning to drugs.

sex role stereotypes: This refers to the notion that there are traditional, specific roles for males and females. According to traditional sex roles in the United States, males do not communicate feelings openly, while females can and should. Today we know that sex roles are learned behaviors and that males and females have a wide choice in how to behave, rather than a limited set of behaviors.

Why Is Talking about Feelings Important?

Ask your child whether he thinks talking about feelings is important. Here are some reasons you might want to offer. Talking about feelings helps us:

- identify situations that are bothering us.
- understand that the ability to communicate feelings is important for healthy self-esteem.
- learn how to talk about problems and solve them.
- learn how to ask for what we need from others.
- clarify our family rules on healthy, respectful ways to communicate feelings.

The Stories

In the next part of the talk, you'll be reading short stories to your child and discussing them together. You don't have to read all of the stories. Pick the ones that you think are appropriate. The stories are very simple. Feel free to embellish them, adding details that you think might make the stories more believable. For example, some parents change the gender of the characters to make the story mirror their own families. These stories focus on feelings and choices rather than specific drug use.

Some children will express their concerns in a candid way. Others may say, "Well, I know this boy who has some problems," but they really may be talking about themselves. Remember that sometimes you may have to read between the lines to get to your child's true feelings and concerns.

A Story about a Boy on the Run

This story provides an opportunity to talk about what a boy might feel if he was threatened.

"A boy is running home from school after being threatened by some bigger boys."

Ask this question of your child:

• What is the boy feeling and thinking?

Now that your child has completed this scenario, ask the following questions:

• What might make the boy feel better?
• Would the boy tell his mom or dad about this situation? Why or why not?

- What would the boy's parents say about this situation?
- What could the boy's parents do to help the boy resolve this situation?
- What if the boy doesn't want to tell a parent? Who else could he tell?
- Have you seen or been in a situation like this? If so, how did you feel? What did you do?

Clarify Your Family's Values

Discuss these questions with your child as a way of sharing your values about communicating feelings.

Ask your child: "How would you feel if you were threatened by someone at school?"

Child: I don't know.

Parent: Would you feel scared or angry, or would you try to laugh it off?

Child: Angry.

Parent: I would want to know if something like that ever happened to you. Would you feel comfortable telling me about that?

A Story about a Girl Being Teased

This story gives you a chance to talk about what a girl might feel if she was being teased.

"A girl is walking by a table where a

group of girls are sitting. The other girls snicker and look over at her and start whispering and laughing."

Ask this question of your child:

• What is the girl feeling and thinking?

Now that your child has completed this scenario, ask the following questions:

• What might make the girl feel better?
• Would the girl tell her mom or dad about this situation? Why or why not?
• What would the girl's parents say about this situation?
• What could the girl's parents do to help her resolve this situation?
• What if the girl does not tell a parent? Who else could she tell?
• Have you seen or been in a situation like this? If so, how did you feel? What did you do?

Clarify Your Family's Values

Discuss these questions with your child as a way of sharing your values about communicating feelings.

Ask your child: "How would you feel if you were laughed at or made fun of by someone at school?"

Child: I would tell them to leave me alone.
Parent: Would you feel scared or angry, or would you try to laugh it off?

Child: Sad.

Parent: I would want to know about such a situation if it occurred. Would you feel comfortable telling me about it?

Stories for Older Children

The following stories deal with more mature behaviors. While some younger children may not be able to relate to them, you may find that to your child, these stories make perfect sense.

A Story about Homework

This story provides an opportunity to discuss how your child deals with stress, manages his time, and makes choices.

"A boy spent Saturday playing rather than doing his big homework assignment. Now he's staying up late to do his homework. He knows he can't finish it in time for class tomorrow."

Ask this question of your child:

• What is the boy feeling and thinking?

Now that your child has completed this scenario, ask the following questions:

- How might the boy deal with the situation in the morning?
- Why is the boy behind?
- How does the boy feel about his choice to play rather than do homework?
- Will he tell his parents about his situation? Why or why not?
- If you were in a situation like this, how would you feel? What would you do? Would your choice be different from the boy's?

A Story about an Argument

This story provides an opportunity to discuss how your child feels about witnessing conflict.

"A girl is staying up late and hears her parents fighting about bills, money, and divorce."

Ask this question of your child:

- What is the girl feeling and thinking?

Now that your child has completed this scenario, ask the following questions:

- How do you think the girl might feel when she wakes up in the morning?

- What kinds of questions might she have for her parents? Would she feel comfortable discussing her concerns with her parents? Why or why not?
- What is the girl thinking about her parents' relationship?
- If you were in a situation like this, how would you feel? What would you do?

The Bare Minimum: A Quick Quiz for Kids

Ask your child the following questions to assess his knowledge of how to express feelings.

1. Why is it important to talk about our feelings?
   Sample answers:
- It can relieve stress.
- It helps others to understand you better.
- It's not good to bottle up feelings, because that can lead to emotional problems.
- It can let people know how their behavior affects you.
- It can let people know that you need help solving a problem.

2. Which feelings might be the most difficult to talk about?
   Sample answers:
- It depends on the person, but sadness, fear, and anger can be really hard to talk about.
- Sometimes it's not easy to talk about being left out, lonely, or scared.
- It's not always easy to talk about not feeling "normal."

3. Why is it important to talk about the stresses we feel?
- Stress is a part of life, and often grows as one gets older. Learning how to discuss things that are stressful can help make life easier.

4. Can you give me one example of how a person learns to talk about feelings?
   Sample answers:
- By listening to a dad, uncle, or grandfather talk about his feelings (especially true for boys)
- By listening to a mom, aunt, or grandmother talk about her feelings (especially true for girls)
- By spending time with friends who talk about their feelings
- By watching people who talk out their problems on TV

5. Why might a person drink alcohol or take other drugs if they were feeling lonely or overwhelmed?
   Sample answer:
- Sometimes people feel that they cannot deal with their feelings of discomfort and want a way to escape from them for a while.

6. What are some ways to deal with difficult feelings that don't involve drinking alcohol or taking other drugs?
   Sample answers:
- Talking with a friend
- Talking with parents or another relative
- Playing sports
- Taking a walk
- Seeing a movie
- Writing in a diary or journal
- Taking a long, hot bath
- Working on a hobby
- Crying

Talk about Your Family Rules

These must be *your* rules. Be prepared for your child to ask about the reasons behind the rules. You may find it helpful to talk with relatives or friends about developing your family rules. Sample answers from other parents follow.

Ask your child the following questions:

1. What is our family rule about expressing anger?
Sample answers:
- Talking about what makes you angry is a very healthy way to sort out your feelings and figure out what's upsetting you. Yelling or screaming at someone is not the way to do it.
- There is no such thing as a strange or stupid question about your feelings. We can talk about anything with one another.
- Sometimes talking about feelings can lead to disagreements. Talking about different points of view is okay in this family as long as the talking is done respectfully.

2. What is our family rule about using insults, threats, or name-calling—or being insulted or threatened by anyone?
Sample answers:
- When you are called names or threatened, you should tell a responsible adult. We want to hear about it. We need to know if any member of this family feels unsafe.
- We do not call other people names or threaten others at home, at school, or in the neighborhood.
- We treat people the same way we want others to treat us.

After the Talk

Take a moment to reflect on the talk you just had with your child. How do you feel about it? What surprised you about your child's attitudes about expressing feelings? How do you feel about your ability to talk with your child about feelings? How do you think your child felt about the talk? What will you do differently in the next talk?

After the talk with their child, many parents report a variety of feelings: accomplishment at sustaining even a three-minute talk, frustration at not being able to get more information from their child, or even a sense of fear that their child may be involved in situations he can't handle.

Warning Signs

This talk can reveal problems that a child may be facing. Was your child reluctant to talk about any situations? Did he appear anxious or did he get angry? Did the way he responded to your questions seem like normal behavior, or did you get the feeling that something may be wrong? There may be cause for concern if you hear from the school, from other parents, or from child-care providers that your child

- is treating other children inappropriately.
- does not seem to have any friends.
- is using inappropriate language in jokes or insults.
- is hurting or threatening others.
- is being hurt or threatened by others.
- is distant and withdrawn.

In any of these situations, you need to find out what is happening by talking with your child. If, after your discussion, you feel your child needs more help than you alone can offer, visit the school counselor or social worker to find out about other resources available in your community.

Finding Help

Support and help for your child is available. Most schoolteachers, principals, religious center staff, or employee assistance programs can refer parents to professionals with expertise in working with young people. Often a short-term intervention can do a world of good. If you have a good relationship with your child's grandparents, aunts, uncles, or other extended family members, tell them what's going on with your child and seek out the support you and your child need.

Success Stories

You have made it through talk number two. Congratulations! Many parents say that getting their kids (especially boys) to talk about feelings wasn't easy at first. Some parents were pleasantly surprised by some of what they heard, while other things were hard to hear. In the course of the talks, some children told stories of being called names or insults at school, or of having fights with siblings or neighbors. Other children shared great news—about how they learned to solve problems, talk problems over with older siblings, or deal with negative emotions in a positive way.

No matter what you've heard from your child, you've continued an important process that will have a powerful ripple effect. You're the thoughtful parent who's taken the time to listen attentively and get a clearer picture of your child's real world. That's a huge accomplishment.

Remember, this is only your second talk. Future talks will be a little easier. Even with the noncommunicative child, you're planting a seed that may not bear fruit for years to come. We hope you feel a sense of accomplishment, because you've earned it.

Sample Talks

Between Parents and Children

Before you begin your first talk, you might want to read this sample conversation. The following are excerpts of actual talks between parents and children.

Discussing the Story about the Boy on the Run

Participants: a mother and her fourteen-year-old son

Mom: Here's the story. "A boy is running home from school after being threatened by some bigger boys." What is the boy feeling and thinking?

Son: He's feeling like he needs to get away from the older boys so he doesn't get beat up. And he's feeling, "What if they find me again?" as he's running, and "What are they going to do?"

Mom: What might make the boy feel better?

Son: He'd feel better if the boys didn't tease him and they didn't bully him, because they make people feel pretty bad.

Mom: What if he ran into someone he knew? Would that help?

Son: Yes, it would help because he could tell them the kids were after him and then if the kids found him, that person could just tell them to stop and go home.

Mom: Would the boy tell his mom or dad about this situation?

Son: Well, he might try and deal with it on his own, at first, but then he'd probably tell his parents about the situation so it doesn't happen again.

Mom: What if the boy doesn't tell a parent?

Son: He'll probably continue to get bullied around and he'll continue to feel bad—maybe even worse.

Mom: What would the boy's parents say about this situation?

Son: That he needs to try and stay away from those boys and stand up for himself. Whenever he sees those boys he just needs to run somewhere so they don't see him and he needs to go directly home.

Mom: What if there were an adult nearby?

Son: They would probably tell them to stop, or they'd help the boy.

Mom: And the boy could—well, nobody really likes to tattle, but he could use the adults to help.

Son: Yeah.

Mom: If he needed to. Or he could go into an area where adults are and that might discourage the kids from bothering him anymore. Okay, what could the boy's parents do to help the boy resolve this situation?

Son: They could talk to him about peer pressure and tell him some things about how to deal with this situation. Or they could go to his counselor and they could talk about it.

Mom: Yeah, good ideas! Have you seen or been in a situation like this?

Son: Yes, but not necessarily someone threatening to beat me up.

Mom: Something similar? How did you feel?

Son: I felt pretty bad. I felt I wasn't wanted anywhere and stuff.

Mom: So what did you do?

Son: I tried to talk with the kid and I asked you and Dad for help.

Mom: Okay. Anything else you want to say about this?

Son: No.

Lessons Learned from This Sample Talk

As you can see from the talk, something like this situation has already happened in this boy's life. In fact, the boy has a physical disability, which, although very minor, makes a teenager's life even more challenging. As he notes, his response to the bullying was to ask his parents for help. That gave them a great opportunity to reinforce the family rules about what responses to bullies were acceptable. His parents also reminded him that they were ready to give him support and that "tattling" is nothing to be ashamed of when it can save someone's life. The son seems to be aware of his feelings and has the ability to talk about them, a skill that should be nurtured throughout high school.

Discussing the Story about a Girl Being Teased

Participants: a mother and her twelve-year-old daughter

Mom: Okay, ready for our first story? "A girl is walking by a table where a group of girls are sitting. The girls snicker and look over at her and start whispering and laughing." What is the girl feeling and thinking?

Daughter: That the girls are snickering and laughing at her.

Mom: So how does she feel?

Daughter: Anxious to know what they're saying.

Mom: What might make the girl feel better?

Daughter: Telling the girls she doesn't like it when they snicker at her?

Mom: Do you think that would make them stop?

Daughter: It might make her feel better.

Mom: Would the girl tell her mom or dad about this situation?

Daughter: No.

Mom: What if the girl does not tell a parent? Then what is she going to do?

Daughter: Tell the counselor.

Mom: What would the girl's parents say about this situation?

Daughter: I don't know.

Mom: What could the girl's parents do to help her resolve this situation?

Daughter: Talk to the principal.

Mom: Have you seen or been in a situation like this?

Daughter: Maybe I've seen one.

Mom: How did you feel?

Daughter: Like I shouldn't get into it.

Mom: What did you do?

Daughter: Nothing.

Mom: Why did you feel you shouldn't get into it?

Daughter: Because it's better to stay out of things like that.

Lessons Learned from This Sample Talk

The daughter in this talk didn't think the girl in the story should tell her parents about a distressing situation at school. That could be a cause for concern, and the mom might want to ask in further talks about what happens when people keep problems to themselves. The daughter also revealed that she had seen harassment at school but hadn't wanted to interfere. The mom could go over her values about being a witness to harassing or violent behaviors, and could under-line how she'd like her daughter to respond. The daughter revealed attitudes and values that the mom can address more in future talks.

Discussing the Story about Homework

Participants: a mother and her fourteen-year-old son

Mom: "A boy spent Saturday playing rather than doing his big homework assignment."

Son: Not a very good idea.

Mom: "He is now staying up late to do his homework. He knows he cannot finish it in time for class tomorrow." What is the boy feeling and thinking?

Son: He's feeling pressured about what his parents will say and he feels pressure that he's going to get a bad grade from the teacher.

Mom: Right. How might the boy deal with the situation in the morning?

Son: He might get up a little early and try to finish it or stay after school to finish it and turn it in late.

Mom: Why is the boy behind?

Son: He's behind because he stayed up late and he played all day.

Mom: How do you think he feels now about his choice to play rather than do his homework?

Son: He feels he should get his homework done first and then he should play.

Mom: Do you think he will tell his parents about his situation? Why or why not?

Son: No. Because he doesn't like the feeling of his parents getting angry at him for not doing his homework.

Mom: If you were in a situation like this, how would you feel?

Son: I'd feel pretty bad. But I would get my homework done first.

Mom: You would most of the time, but not always. What if you hadn't gotten your homework done? Then how would you feel?

Son: Like I hadn't done my job right. I'd feel like I'd have to work really fast to get it done. Or I'd have to turn it in late.

Mom: So what would you do if you couldn't finish it that night?

Son: I'd try and finish it after that class.

Mom: And turn it in late? Okay. How would your choice be different from the boy's?

Son: I'd organize myself. I'm going to get my homework done first before I go out and do whatever I want. Then I don't have anything to worry about the whole day.

Mom: Okay. Good job.

Lessons Learned from This Sample Talk

Here's a productive talk that doesn't address issues of drug use at all. The mom laid the foundation for later talks about feelings and the kinds of stresses that can lead people to turn to alcohol and other drugs. Mom and son appear to share similar values about getting homework done on time and being responsible. The mom might want to explore the son's statement that letting parents know about late homework might make them angry.

Discussing the Story about an Argument

Participants: a mother and her fourteen-year-old son

Mom: "A girl is staying up late and hears her parents fighting about bills, money, and divorce." What is the girl feeling and thinking?

Son: Her parents aren't getting along, so her parents might get a divorce, and she doesn't want that.

Mom: Why do you think she wouldn't want that?

Son: Because they're her parents. She wouldn't want them to separate. That'd be hard on her.

Mom: Okay. How would that be hard?

Son: Because . . . um . . .

Mom: Well, what happens to kids when their parents get a divorce?

Son: Well . . .

Mom: Are they given away?

Son: No! [laughs]

Mom: What happens?

Son: No, they, like, have to go back and forth between parents and, I don't know, it'd be hard on the kid because . . .

Mom: You just know it would be hard?

Son: Yeah.

Mom: Okay. How do you think the girl might feel when she wakes up in the morning? That's after listening to this arguing all night long.

Son: Well, she'd probably still be worried that her parents might get a divorce. She might not say anything, but she might.

Mom: What kinds of questions might she have for her parents? Would she feel comfortable discussing her concerns with her parents?

Son: Well . . .

Mom: You said she might not say anything?

Son: She's worried about what the parents might say. She just doesn't feel comfortable talking about it.

Mom: What questions might she have for them?

Son: What kinds of problems are they having and why are they happening?

Mom: I'd say that's a pretty good answer. What is the girl thinking about her parents' relationship?

Son: She's probably thinking her parents do not have a good relationship and that they don't like each other that much, so they might get a divorce.

Mom: Does she want them to try and get help?

Son: She probably would want them to get help, because she doesn't want her parents to get a divorce.

Mom: Do you think that kids can really help in this situation?

Son: I don't know. Not really, because if they don't like each other, they don't like each other. The kids can't really do anything.

Mom: That's right. The divorce isn't really about the kids, is it?

Son: No, it's not.

Mom: If you were in a situation like this, how would you feel? What would you do?

Son: I'd be worried, but I'm not sure I'd say anything. I'd just be worried.

Mom: But you wouldn't talk about it?

Son: I wouldn't talk about it.

Mom: What might be the advantage of talking about it with your parents?

Son: You might get some things straight that you thought of that were wrong. It might make you feel better, a little bit.

Mom: All people argue, so maybe the parents were just arguing. Maybe they didn't mean it when they said they wanted a divorce—maybe they were just saying all kinds of mean things to one another. They may not have been serious. If the child doesn't talk about it, she could walk around worrying that they were real serious.

Son: Yeah. So it'd make them feel better.

Mom: Yeah. Also, maybe the parents are so caught up in their problems they don't realize the kids are being affected by this. So it's good for the parents to know that. It can help.

Son: Yeah.

Lessons Learned from This Sample Talk

The mother in this talk got some valuable information about her son: that he would not want to talk about something as serious as divorce. Would he feel threatened by talking about other issues like money or relationships with friends? The mom might address that in later talks. The mom did a great job of explaining that sometimes people just say things that they don't mean, and she stresses how important it could be for a child to simply ask, "What's going on?" This mom let her son know that it's okay to ask even difficult questions, an important skill that could serve the son well later in life.

3

Is That What the Doctor Ordered?

Talking about Over-the-Counter and Prescription Drugs

My doctor prescribed some antidepressants for me and they've been helpful. My daughter asked if she could try some "just for fun." I was taken aback. —Teri, mother of one, New York City

Suddenly you can't turn on the TV without seeing tons of commercials for pills—for everything from curing shyness to sexual problems. Why is that? —Tom, father of two, Tucson, Arizona

My kid asked me if my pills for high blood pressure were "downers."
—Linda, mother of three, Charlotte, North Carolina

The development of drugs to treat depression and anxiety has been a medical miracle for millions affected by those and other emotional problems. But for every person who has used prescription drugs wisely, there are many others who misuse the drugs, taking them when they do not have a diagnosed medical condition. Some people may use a drug longer than its prescribed course; others may take more than the recommended amount. Still other people turn to a variety of methods to obtain prescription drugs that they desire.

Due to looser U.S. government regulations, which now allow drug companies to advertise drugs directly to consumers, the misuse of prescription drugs actually may be worsening. You've probably seen the drug ads yourself; it's not likely you've missed these images of formerly debilitated people prancing in flower-filled fields after taking this or that pill. The Internet, through overseas pharmacies not bound by U.S. law, also has made prescription drugs more easy to obtain than ever.

Family talks need to address the widespread use of prescription drugs, and should address the health benefits as well as the potential for abuse. There are many benefits to that conversation. As your children become adults, they—not just their doctors—will need to be savvy consumers and will have to decide for themselves whether or not to use which drugs, and how.

In this chapter we will discuss how feelings are changed by a variety of legal drugs commonly marketed directly to consumers. We'll also help you clarify your concerns about misusing drugs, and look at whether prescription and over-the-counter medicines should be included in your definition of drugs.

Preparing for the Talk

This talk will give you the chance to discuss prescription drugs with your kids, both their healthy uses and the potential for abuse. It also will help you explain the short- and long-term effects of prescription drug use on our ability to feel our feelings.

In this talk you will help your child understand that

- prescription drugs are a part of our culture.
- there is a difference between prescription drug use and abuse.
- some prescription drugs change our feelings, and it's important to know which feelings are changed and in what way.
- there are family rules about using prescription and over-the-counter drugs.

What You Can Expect from This Talk

After the talk your child will be able to

- define the term "prescription drug."
- define prescription drug use and abuse.
- understand how the entire family suffers when a family member is misusing drugs.
- express the family rules about using prescription and over-the-counter drugs.

How Do You Define "Prescription Drug"?

The term "prescribed" implies that a medical doctor has, after a careful review of your emotional and physical health, recommended that your symptoms be treated with a particular drug. We have no intention of demonizing prescription drugs; they may have saved the life of someone in your family. But we do think it is important that you and your child look at both the positive and negative sides of prescription drug use.

This chapter will help you answer a number of questions including: How does a parent set rules about using prescription and over-the-counter drugs? Does your family consider such drug use harmless, or as dangerous as using street drugs?

"I explained to my daughter that there is a huge difference between being clinically depressed and experiencing a short-term depression due to a specific incident—like a death of a loved one. And there are different drugs that doctors can prescribe to help people cope with both situations." —Tess, mother of one, Buffalo, New York

Influence of the Media

"I remember this moment in the Madonna film in a movie theatre filled with teenage girls. It was 'Desperately Seeking Susan,' where this suburban housewife turns to another character who is feeling incredibly stressed and says, 'For God's sake, take a Valium, like a normal person.'" —Judith, mother of two, Washington, D.C.

"I saw this movie called 'Requiem for a Dream,' where this New York grandma gets addicted to diet pills and ends up having electroshock therapy in a mental ward."

—Ted, father of one, Seattle, Washington

"I remember a film I saw in the 1970s as a kid that showed all kinds of drugs—it was called 'Valley of the Dolls.' I remember a scene where this Hollywood star complains that she's required to 'sparkle, sparkle, sparkle,' and that she just can't without her 'dolls,' which the movie taught me was slang for pills."

—Mara, mother of two, Columbia, South Carolina

Quotes to Consider

"An estimated 4 million people age twelve and older used prescription drugs for nonmedical reasons in 1999; almost half of that number reported using prescription drugs nonmedically for the first time in the previous year."

—National Institute on Drug Abuse, "Prescription Drug
Abuse and Addiction," www.nida.nih.gov

"Data from the National Household Survey on Drug Abuse indicate that the most dramatic increase in new users of prescription drugs for nonmedical purposes is occurring in 12- to 17-year-olds and 18- to 25-year-olds. In addition, 12- to 14-year-olds reported psychotherapeutics, for example, painkillers or stimulants, as two of the primary drugs used."

—National Institute on Drug Abuse, "Prescription Drug
Abuse and Addiction," www.nida.nih.gov

"Overall, men and women have roughly similar rates of nonmedical use of prescription drug use. An exception is found among 12- to 17-year-olds: In this group, young women are more likely than young men to use psychotherapeutic drugs nonmedically."

—National Institute on Drug Abuse, "Prescription Drug
Abuse and Addiction," www.nida.nih.gov

"Ritalin: For millions of children who suffer from attention deficit hyperactivity disorder, or ADHD, drugs like Ritalin have been a godsend. Yet at the same time there is real concern that the use of Ritalin to curb all manner of fidgety behavior has become too casual and that the drug is actually being abused as a performance booster."   —"The Year in Medicine," *Time* magazine, January 15, 2001

"In August 1997, the F.D.A. relaxed its rules governing television advertising; rather than having to run the same fine print required in magazine ads, drug commercials could satisfy F.D.A. rules by giving a toll-free number, mentioning a magazine advertisement and instructing viewers to 'ask your doctor' for more information. In a daring move closely watched by the rest of the industry, Schering-Plough poured $322 million into pitching Claritin to consumers in 1998 and 1999, far more than any brand, according to the National Institute for Health Care Management Foundation, a nonprofit group in Washington."

—*New York Times* magazine, March 11, 2001

"Harried police detectives in dozens of rural areas in Eastern states are combating what they say is a growing wave of drug abuse involving a potent painkiller prescribed for terminal cancer patients and other people with severe pain. Addicts favor the drug because they have learned to circumvent its slow time-released protection and achieve a sudden, powerful, morphine-like high."

—"Can Painkillers Pose New Abuse Threat?" *New York Times*, Feb. 8, 2001

"The overdiagnosis of learning and behavioral disorders in ever-younger children has gone so far that even psychologists joke that Huck Finn and Tom Sawyer, were they alive today, would be on Ritalin and in special education for hyperactivity."

—Kate Zernike, "Ritalin to the Rescue: A Children's Story for Our Time," *New York Times*, Feb. 4, 2001

Different Families: Different Values

Everyone interprets behavior in his or her own way. You'll have your own take on these situations, depending on your background and experiences:

An aunt is visiting her sister and nieces. At bedtime, the nieces watch their favorite aunt get ready for bed and see that she has brought pills in a plastic container. The youngest niece asks, "What are those pills for?"

How do you feel about about an older relative taking medications in front of children? Or about the child's question? Some parents would say that it's perfectly normal for kids to ask questions about pills—let the aunt answer the question any way she likes. Other parents would prefer that the aunt not go into detail about the reasons she is using antidepressants, while other parents would prefer that their kids not see adults taking pills at all. Some parents would explain to their children how people can use antidepressants, prescribed by a doctor, to help them deal with difficult feelings. What would you do?

■

A mom brings her son to the doctor. The boy has been showing signs of clinical depression for several months. The doctor, after talking with the boy and the mother at length, suggests to the mother that her son be prescribed medication.

It's difficult to know what to do in this situation without knowing a lot more about the boy and his emotional life, family life, and physiological makeup. If your child were struggling with depression would you ever consider, with the counsel of a medical doctor, putting your child on an antidepressant? Some parents believe that it's okay for young people to use prescription medication to treat a diagnosed condition, as long as a trusted doctor thinks it's a good idea. Others might be worried that the son is too young to be placed on these medicines and wonder if some other form of treatment might be wiser. Some parents might get a second medical opinion or switch doctors. Some might wonder whether the depression was preventable by other means. What would you do?

◼

A girl is at a dance club when her boyfriend offers her some pills. She asks him where he got them and he says, "I got them from my dentist when I had oral surgery—they make you feel great!" Later that weekend, the girl tells her little sister what happened, and how the pill made her feel. The little sister tells her mom.

Most parents would be unhappy to hear a story like this about their daughter. There might be serious consequences for breaking family rules about misusing drugs. Some parents would want to talk with their daughter about how her boyfriend had not made a healthy choice. Still other parents would want to talk with the boyfriend or call the boyfriend's parents and talk with them about the situation. What would you do?

◼

A mom and her family are watching TV, when a commercial comes on showing the calming effects of a new pill. The commercial suggests that you can ask your doctor "whether it's right for you."

Some parents would ask their kids what they thought of the commercial, using the moment to discuss why people might use prescription drugs to deal with stress. Others would ignore the commercial, hoping their kids didn't get any negative or confusing messages from it. Some parents might write down the phone number or web site address to find out more about the drug. What would you do?

■

A girl is using diet pills to lose weight. She is already thin.

Most parents would be alarmed and urge their daughter to discontinue use of the pills. Some parents would trust their daughter to do whatever feels healthy. Some parents, perhaps those who make staying thin a high priority, might even encourage her use of the pills. What would you do?

Different Perspectives

"I think back on my own upbringing, where we had a very strong sense of tradition and family values, but I could never have imagined my parents talking with me about any of these issues. It just seems so strange for me to attempt to discuss prescription drugs with my child." —Ming, father of one, Seattle, Washington

"I know kids that are downing two bottles of cough medicine to get high." —Jerry, father of two, Phoenix, Arizona

"I wanted my daughter to know that drugs that have been tested and approved of as having helpful medical uses are needed by many people. It is when drugs are taken with disregard to the medical use just for their effect on how you feel, it can be dangerous and unhealthy to use them."

—Judy, mother of two, Orlando, Florida

So, How Are We Feeling Today?

Talks about drug use should not only focus on the dangers and health risks. Those are important topics, but not the only ones to raise. It's vital that parents and kids talk about not only what a particular drug does to one's feelings, but *why* a person would want to change their feelings by using drugs in the first place. Drug use is often the tip of the iceberg, and an indicator of a deeper problem.

These talks often force parents themselves to look inward at their own actions. Parents should go into the talks prepared for unexpected turns in the conversation.

Before you talk with your child, take a moment right now to think about the following questions:

How are you feeling today, right now?
What are your biggest stresses?
How do you think your child is feeling today?
What do you think your child's biggest stresses are?
What does your child say her biggest stresses are?
How can people deal with such stresses in a healthy way?

Last-minute Checkups before the Talk

Before you talk with your child, think back on what, if anything, your parents taught you about prescription drugs when you were growing up.

- Did a parent ever talk to you about the misuse of over-the-counter and prescription drugs?
- Did they model healthy coping skills by not misusing over-the-counter and prescription drugs?
- Did they use prescription drugs in a way that was healthy and helpful?

As a parent, what are you teaching your child about over-the-counter and prescription drugs?

- Do you encourage her to talk about any misuse she might see of over-the-counter and prescription drugs?
- How do you let your child know that you welcome a discussion of any concerns she has about prescription drugs?
- Do you talk to your child about the importance of finding friends who don't misuse over-the-counter or prescription drugs?
- Do you model the ability to deal with stress without misusing over-the-counter or prescription drugs yourself?

Do you have any stories you can share with your child about drug use, or how you confronted someone who was misusing over-the-counter or prescription drugs? For example:

- The time a friend tried to get you to take some pills from her mom's medicine cabinet.
- The time you used prescription drugs, in consultation with a doctor, and how it helped you.
- How you learned to use over-the-counter and prescription drugs responsibly as an adult.
- The time you felt worried by a family member's prescription drug use.

Sharing your stories lets your child know how you feel about over-the-counter and prescription drug use and what effect it had on you when you were growing up.

What Are Your Family Rules?

Do you have family rules about using over-the-counter and prescription drugs, along with clear consequences for breaking them? If not, this is a good time to think about what rules you might want to put in place.

The illustrated scenarios in this chapter are meant to give you a chance to further discuss your definition of drug use. You'll be able to address how prescription drugs can be used carefully, how they can be abused, and how there is sometimes pressure to abuse them. The stories and questions are open-ended, allowing your child to reflect on a range of topics, including the things friends do to protect one another, peer pressure, and other problems or concerns. Depending on your child, the talk could touch on TV commercials promoting drug use and mixed messages about drug use from adult family members. Discussing these situations will give you an opportunity to share your family rules about using over-the-counter and prescription drugs as well as your views on acceptable behavior.

The Talk

Introduce the Talk

To start this talk you could say, "I've got some questions for you about the kinds of drugs that doctors give out."

Your child may respond, "Why do we have to talk about that?" or "You worry too much!" As we will stress throughout this book, this talk is much easier with an elementary-school student than with a middle-school or high-school student already used to a good deal of privacy. Remember, even if you talk for only three minutes, you have accomplished something important. For older children, it is important to address your family rules, the reasons for them, and the consequences for breaking them.

You can add, "Do you know what it means to use a prescription drug?" He might respond with "Yeah, a doctor gives you medicine," or "Nope."

If he is both older and candid he might try to test your reaction with something like, "I know that Aunt Rita gets pills." A favorite conversation stopper used by kids is, "Do you use them?" (And yes, this chapter includes helpful quotes from parents who share how they responded to that question.)

Review These Words

Please review the terms in this section. Discussing all the terms with your child is optional. You know which are appropriate for your child's age and maturity level. It's more than likely that even the youngest children have heard these words on TV.

antidepressant: a drug prescribed to treat clinical depression. There are many different types of antidepressants, and they affect the nervous system in different ways. These drugs are generally not addictive.

depression: a medical illness (beyond a mood) characterized by feelings of persistent low mood, loss of interest and enjoyment in life, reduced energy, and sleep disturbances, all lasting for longer than two weeks. Depressive disorders are estimated to be a major cause of disability worldwide—between 20 percent and 30 percent of people seen by doctors may have depressive symptoms. It is possible to feel depressed without having the illness called depression, a diagnosis made by a doctor or other mental health professional.

opiates: drugs that are used to treat pain. Examples include morphine, codeine, and methadone. These drugs can be highly addictive. These drugs reduce pain and anxiety. When used in excess of prescribed dose, they can be fatal.

over-the-counter drug: a drug available in stores that is dispensed without a prescription from a doctor.

prescription drug: a drug that is dispensed only with the permission of a doctor.

sedative: a drug that often is prescribed to treat anxiety. Sedatives induce sleep, reduce anxiety, promote a feeling of calmness, and can cause slurred speech and lack of muscle coordination. Sedatives are becoming widely available online without a prescription thanks to overseas pharmacies not bound by U.S. law.

self-medicating: using alcohol or other drugs to alter your feelings without the supervision of a medical professional.

stimulants: examples include caffeine, amphetamines, cocaine, and crack. Stimulants increase alertness and reduce the need for sleep in some cases. These drugs have the potential to cause addiction.

Why Is Talking about Over-the-Counter and Prescription Drugs Important?

Ask your child whether she thinks talking about prescription drug use is important. Here are some reasons you might want to offer. Talking about prescription drugs means

- learning the benefits of appropriate over-the-counter and pre-scription drug use.
- clarifying family rules about legal and illegal prescription drug use.
- clarifying the school rules and the law about over-the-counter and prescription drug use.

The Stories

In the next part of the talk, you'll be reading short stories to your child and discussing them together. You don't have to read all of the stories. Pick the ones that you think are appropriate for your child. The stories are very simple. Feel free to embellish them, adding details that you think might make the story more believable to your child.

A Story about the TV Commercial

This story gives you an opportunity to talk about the how prescription drugs are portrayed in the media, how common prescription drugs are, and how they can be used and misused.

"A mom and her daughter are watching TV when a commercial for a drug that calms people and shows them feeling great comes on."

Ask these questions of your child:

- What is the mom thinking?
- What is the daughter thinking?
- What is the mom saying?
- What is the daughter saying?

Now that your child has completed this scenario, ask the following questions:

- What is the TV commercial suggesting about the use of this drug?
- Does the daughter or mom want to take the pills shown in the ad?
- Can a prescription drug like the one in the ad ever be abused? If so, how?
- Does the parent need to talk to the daughter about responsible, adult use of prescription drugs?
- If you were watching the commercial, what would you feel? What would you do?

A Story about a Doctor

This story gives you a chance to talk about how prescription drugs can be used or misused and the important role doctors play in assessing a person's need for a particular drug.

"A mom and her son are at the doctor's office talking about the son's hyperactivity and aggressive behavior at school. The doctor is asking the boy

lots of questions about his feelings and relationships at school and home. The mom asks whether some drug might be helpful."

Ask these questions of your child:

- What is the mom thinking?
- What is the son thinking?
- What is the doctor thinking?
- What is the son saying?

Now that your child has completed this scenario, ask the following questions:

- Does the boy want to take a drug prescribed by the doctor? Why or why not?
- How would the boy feel about taking a prescription drug?
- Can a drug from a doctor be misused? If so, how?
- Does the mom need to talk to the son about responsible, healthy use of prescription drugs?
- What should the doctor know about the son's life before she prescribes any drug?
- If you were the parent in a situation like this, how would you feel? What would you do?
- Should the mom or son ask for a second medical opinion?

A Story about a Boy and His Girlfriend

This story provides an opportunity to talk about how prescription drugs can be abused.

"A boy and his girlfriend are at a party. He offers her some pills and tells her he got them from the dentist. He tells her, 'If we take them, we'll feel great. And we'll feel closer.'"

Ask these questions of your child:

- What is the girl thinking?
- What is the boy thinking?
- What is the girl saying?
- What is the boy saying?

Now that your child has completed this scenario, ask the following questions:

- Does the girl want to take the pill? Why or why not?
- If the girl does not want to take the pills, what can she say?
- Why would the boyfriend want his girlfriend to take the pills?

A Story about an Online Drugstore

This story gives you an opportunity to talk about how drugs are available on the Internet.

"A girl is at the home of an older friend. The friend says that she has just learned how to order diet pills online. They sit down at the computer and look at all the drugs available online."

Ask these questions of your child:

- What is the older girl who's going online thinking?
- What is the older girl who's going online saying?
- What is the younger girl thinking?
- What is the younger girl saying?

Now that your child has completed this scenario, ask the following questions:

- Does the younger girl want to take the diet pills? Why or why not?
- How can a drug purchased from the Internet be harmful?
- What are the consequences of taking any over-the-counter or prescription drugs without a parent's or doctor's advice?

Clarify Your Family's Values

Discuss these questions with your child as a way of sharing your values about prescription drug use. We have included a number of potential responses from children to help you formulate your own responses.

Ask your child: "When someone has a friend who talks about wanting to try prescription drugs for fun, what can a friend do?"

Child response #1: "I don't know."
Parent: Okay. It's hard to know what to do. But maybe talking with the friend about the potential downside of the drug

could help. A talk like that could help someone decide not to misuse a drug.

Child response #2: "Talk with a teacher."

Parent: Finding some help is a good idea. There are all kinds of people who can help, including relatives [name some that you trust], people from our religious community, and people at school.

Child response #3: "Well, one pill couldn't hurt."

Parent: That may be true sometimes. A single pill might not hurt someone. Then again, it might, depending on the person's body chemistry and health status. Prescription drugs are very powerful; they're designed to be given out only by medical doctors.

Child response #4: "My friend uses them, so why can't I?"

Parent: Well, your friend has a medical condition, and is using them under the care of a doctor. And that's a big difference. If you are feeling stressed and want to relax, you can take a long walk, talk on the phone with a friend, write in a journal, play a game, go for a run, or watch TV or a video. If these things don't help, or you find that you don't enjoy doing these things anymore, then you and I should talk more about dealing with stress. I know boredom also leads some people to drugs, so let's also talk about coping with boredom, which is a part of life. Curiosity about drugs is also normal. I'd be surprised if you weren't curious. I hope this is something we can continue to discuss.

The Bare Minimum: A Quick Quiz for Kids

Ask your child the following questions to assess her knowledge and perceptions of prescription drug use.

1. Can you tell me why people need a doctor's prescription to use certain drugs?
   Sample answer:
   • The doctor has an understanding of your unique body chemistry and what medicine is right for you, physically and emotionally.

2. Can you give me an example of why getting drugs without consulting a doctor who knows your medical history might be dangerous?
   Sample answers:
   • The pills you get may harm you.
   • You don't know how much to take.
   • You don't know the possible side effects.

3. What are some appropriate ways people can use prescription drugs?
   Sample answers:
   • With a doctor's approval.
   • With a parent's supervision.
   • Follow all instructions.
   • Don't use other people's prescriptions.

Talk about Your Family Rules

This is an opportunity to review your family rules. Ask your child the following question:

1. What are our family rules about using over-the-counter and prescription drugs?

   Sample answers:

- We discuss, as a family, the use of medical drugs.
- We can use them as long as we are under a doctor's care.
- We don't share prescriptions.
- We always follow the instructions on the bottle.
- No one in this family breaks the law regarding prescription drug use.
- No matter what you see your friends doing or others on TV or in a magazine, only a doctor can help you decide if taking a prescription drug is the best thing to do.
- If you are not feeling good or wonder if you should be prescribed something, you should talk about it with us.

After the Talk

Take a moment to reflect on the talk you just had with your child. How do you feel about it?

- Did anything surprise you about your child's view of over-the-counter and prescription drug use?
- Does she seem susceptible to peer pressure?
- Do you think your child has the ability to deal with the everyday stresses that accompany childhood and adolescence without drugs?
- Does he seem bored and restless—with little to do?
- What lessons did you learn about how to listen to your child?

Warning Signs

The talks can reveal problems that children may be facing. Use your instincts. Review the following warning signs to see if your child might be misusing over-the-counter or prescription drugs:

- Your own supply of prescription drugs seems to have depleted rapidly.
- If over-the-counter or antidepressants are being used by someone in the family, your child is intensely curious about them.
- He doesn't appear to care about school or friends; at home he is listless and unfocused.
- His grades take a dramatic turn downward.
- When you meet your child's friends and their parents, do they appear focused and sober? Above all, trust your instincts on how your child is doing.

Success Stories

You have made it through talk number three. Good job! The talk about prescription drugs may have held a lot of surprises. One mom in New Hampshire found out that her daughter's best friend was on several medications; as a result, her daughter was highly knowledgeable about certain drugs' side effects, and knew which needed to be taken with food and which without. The daughter had a mature understanding of prescription drugs and took their use seriously.

As we've said before, we believe that any talk is a success. Even a short conversation sends a powerful message that you care about your child's well-being enough to sit and listen.

Sample Talks

Between Parents and Children

If you are wondering how a talk based on this chapter might really sound, take a look at the following excerpts from real family talks. These talks are not edited; we've left in the pauses, awkward moments, and childish jokes to show you what real talks can sound like.

Discussing the Story about a TV Commercial

Participants: a mother and her twelve-year-old daughter

Mom: Okay, here's our first story. "A mom and her daughter are watching TV, when on comes a commercial for a drug that calms people down and shows them feeling great!" What is the mom thinking?

Daughter: The mom is thinking that the pill is bad and she doesn't want stuff like this going into her daughter's head, because the daughter might want it and it's harmful.

Mom: What is the daughter thinking?

Daughter: That it is harmful.

Mom: What is the mom saying?

Daughter: She's saying, "Oh, never let these commercials fool you. People never tell the real consequences if they're bad."

Mom: What's the daughter saying?

Daughter: "Don't worry Mom, I'd never take that."

Mom: What is the TV commercial suggesting about the use of this drug?

Daughter: That it will make you feel good—but it doesn't say anything about the negative reactions that it probably will have.

Mom: Does the daughter or mom want to take this pill advertised on TV?

Daughter: No.

Mom: Can a prescription drug like the one on TV ever be abused?

Daughter: I don't get that.

Mom: Abused? Not taken in the correct manner.

Daughter: Yeah.

Mom: How?

Daughter: If you take it more times then it's supposed to be taken.

Mom: Right! Does the parent need to talk to the daughter about responsible use of prescription drugs?

Daughter: Yeah. She should teach that.

Mom: If you were in a situation like this, what would you feel?

Daughter: I wouldn't feel anything. It's just a commercial.

Mom: What would you do?

Daughter: Change the channel.

Mom: Okay.

Lessons Learned from This Sample Talk

This was a very productive talk about a very serious issue. The daughter didn't understand the term "abused" when it came to prescription drugs but she did once her mother explained it in a different way. The daughter said that the commercial didn't make her "feel anything." In future talks, the mom might consider exploring the power of advertising to make viewers feel all kinds of things—like too fat, for example.

Discussing the Story about a Doctor

Participants: a dad and his twelve-year-old son

> *Dad:* "A mom and her son are at the doctor's office talking with the doctor about the son's hyperactivity." Do you know what that is?
>
> *Son:* Yeah.
>
> *Dad:* "Talking about the son's hyperactivity and aggressive behavior at school. The doctor is asking the boy lots of questions about his feelings and relationships at school and home. The mom asks if some drug might be helpful." What is the mom thinking?
>
> *Son:* "I hope he gets better and there's something to cure him."
>
> *Dad:* What would the son be thinking?
>
> *Son:* "Yeah, yeah, yeah."
>
> *Dad:* Do you think the son would really want to take pills?
>
> *Son:* No, he's just all, well, being hyper.
>
> *Dad:* Oh, he's acting hyperactive in the doctor's office. Okay. What is the doctor thinking, when the mom asks if some drug might be helpful?
>
> *Son:* She's probably thinking, "If there is one."
>
> *Dad:* What is the son saying?
>
> *Son:* Nothing.
>
> *Dad:* Does the boy want to take the drug? Why or why not?

Son: I don't know.

Dad: Would he care?

Son: Probably wouldn't. Well, either way it could be bad, because he could take an overdose and get over-depressed.

Dad: Can a drug from a doctor be misused?

Son: Yeah.

Dad: How?

Son: When it says to take two you take fifteen.

Dad: Does the parent need to talk to the son about responsible, adult use of prescription drugs?

Son: If he gets a drug.

Dad: What should the doctor know about the son's life before she prescribes any drug?

Son: If he's allergic to something. I don't know.

Dad: I think that's right. That question needs to be refined. "The son's life" is kind of broad. If you were in a situation like this, that is, if you were in a doctor's office and the doctor said you needed to take some medicine, how would you feel? What would you do?

Son: I'd say, "Okay."

Dad: You would? Would you ask any questions about the side effects of this drug? Or how long do I have to take it?

Son: No, Mom would ask that.

Lessons Learned from This Sample Talk

This father and son had a good talk about doctors, parents, young people, and drugs. The son's comment about taking an overdose could be followed up with other questions about the use and misuse of drugs. The dad could also talk about reasons for people being hyperactive, both emotional and physiological. The boy's comment about his mom's responsibility for asking about any drugs her son might be prescribed could be further explored to probe his ideas about the responsibility of the drug user to be informed personally.

Discussing the Story about a Boy and His Girlfriend

Participants: a dad and his twelve-year-old-son

Dad: "A boy and his girlfriend are at a party. He offers her some pills and tells her he got them from the dentist. He tells her, 'If we take them, we'll feel great. And we'll feel closer.'" What do you think a girl would be thinking if someone told her that?

Son: That they are probably just, like, drugs.

Dad: Are they good drugs?

Son: No, like off-the-street drugs.

Dad: What is the boy thinking?

Son: "Take 'em!"

Dad: Why do you think he's saying that?

Son: Because he's offering it, so he probably wants to take them.

Dad: So what do you think the girl would be saying?

Son: "Noooooo, thank you."

Dad: How about the boy?

Son: "Why not?"

Dad: Does the girl want to take the painkiller? Why or why not?

Son: No. Because she doesn't know what they are.

Dad: You're right. And the story doesn't say they are painkillers. If the girl does not want to take the pills, what can she say?

Son: "No, I don't want to take the pills."

Dad: So be firm, be positive, and just say no?

Son: Yeah!

Dad: Why would the boyfriend want his girlfriend to take the pills?

Son: I don't know.

Dad: Maybe so she would feel so good that he could kiss her?

Son: I don't know.

Dad: To hold her? Get her addicted?

Son: [agitated] I don't know, maybe.

Lesson Learned from This Sample Talk

This talk is a good beginning. The son said that a simple "no" is all one needs to say to decline drugs, and often it is. The dad could follow up by asking why some people want to take drugs, and how the drugs might change a person's feelings and perceptions. The son showed some agitation at the end of the talk, when the topic turned to the boyfriend's motivation. In future talks the dad might want to come back to some of the issues raised, such as manipulation and sexual behavior.

Discussing the Story about an Online Drugstore

Participants: a mother and her fourteen-year-old son

Mom: "A girl is over at her older friend's house. The friend says that she has just learned how to order diet pills online. They sit down at the computer and look at all the drugs available online." What is the older girl, the one who's going online, thinking?

Son: She's thinking these drugs could help her lose some weight, and she'd probably want to order these drugs.

Mom: Hmmm, okay. What do you think the advantage is of being able to order drugs online?

Son: That you wouldn't have to go out to a store to buy them and it'd be more convenient.

Mom: And you don't have to have an ID if you aren't old enough.

Son: Yeah, kids who aren't old enough could get ahold of drugs.

Mom: What is the older girl saying to the younger girl as they look at all these drugs that are available?

Son: That they should order some of these diet pills.

Mom: What is the younger girl thinking?

Son: She might be thinking that's not such a good idea—maybe they shouldn't get the drugs because they are too young.

Mom: What do you think the younger girl is saying to the older girl? Is she saying anything?

Son: She's just thinking.

Lessons Learned from This Sample Talk

This talk was a great start at explaining the pros and cons of ordering drugs online. The son had a hard time imagining how two girls might talk with each other, but he got the major concepts that were presented. In future talks, the mom could ask the son to think about how taking over-the-counter medicines could be harmful, whether they are purchased online or at a pharmacy.

The mom can also assure the son that prescription and over-the-counter drugs can be very beneficial when used properly. The mom might try focusing more on stories and situations with boys to see if her son is better able to imagine conversations between males.

4

Want a Drink?

Talking about Alcohol Use and Misuse

An ice-cold beer on a hot summer day is always okay in my book.
—Jim, father of one, New York City

I grew up in a Greek household, and wine was a part of life. We never had any problems with alcohol.
—Elaine, mother of two, San Francisco

My husband thinks that having our kids watch us drink teaches them about moderation. All I know is that I grew up in a house with an alcoholic parent and I don't like having alcohol in the house at all.
—Patty, mother of two, Gaithersburg, Maryland

My neighbor took in an exchange student—a fifteen-year-old boy from France. She received an E-mail from his mother stating he could have a small glass of wine with the family meal.
—Tami, mother of two, New York City

When we first conceived this book we knew that talking about alcohol would be tricky. First of all, should we call the book *Ten Talks About Drugs* or *Drugs and Alcohol*? We asked parents that very question. Their answers were, in a word, sobering. Most people said alcohol wasn't a drug, and thought the book should focus on street drugs alone. Some parents even warned that we might get ourselves in trouble with the alcohol industry by using the word "drug" to describe their products. And yet nearly every person we interviewed told of someone in their family who had had, at one time or another, serious problems related to drinking alcohol.

Alcohol is the most widely used mood-altering substance in the United States. While millions of people use it wisely and in good health, alcohol abuse plays a role in some of our society's biggest problems. Alcohol causes 100,000 deaths annually in this country, according to the American Medical Association, making it the third leading cause of preventable death. One study estimates that about a quarter of all people admitted to hospitals are there to be treated for the consequences of their drinking alcohol.

Alcohol also plays a large role in violent crime; about 37 percent of all rapes and 27 percent of aggravated assaults involve alcohol use by the offender. The numbers are even higher for homicides; half of all murders involve alcohol use by the offender, victim, or both.

At the same time, alcohol is a constant presence in movies, on TV, and in ads, which link drinking with highly valued traits like popularity and attractiveness, and with desirable outcomes such as sex, adventure, relaxation, and success.

Because alcohol is so readily available and promoted with images that are attractive to young people, the use of alcohol is widespread, even among youth. Family talks need to address responsible ways adults can use alcohol, as well as its risks, health benefits, and potential for abuse.

In Chapter 2 we talked about feelings. In this chapter we will discuss how feelings can be changed by drinking alcohol. This chapter will also help you clarify your concerns about alcohol and whether you include misuse of alcohol in your definition of drug abuse.

"A friend of mine goes to a lot of business-related social functions. She was complaining that all the alcohol was causing her to gain weight. When I asked why she didn't just drink water, she gave me a look that said it all—'That would be an insult to the host—it just isn't done.'"   —Andrea, mother of three, Columbia, South Carolina

"During my senior year, two of the coolest guys in high school were killed in a car accident. Everyone knew they had been drinking. It changed the whole culture after that—unfortunately, it took that to knock some sense into us."

—Lynn, mother of two, Seattle, Washington

"My parents always told us, when we were in high school, if you're going to drink, bring your friends here and do it. That kind of took the excitement out of drinking. We had a few beers with friends a couple of times, but that was about it."

—Bob, father of two, Boston, Massachusetts

Preparing for the Talk

This talk will give you the chance to talk to your children about alcohol, both its legal uses and potential for abuse. It also will help you explain the short- and long-term effects of alcohol use on a person's ability to experience healthy, normal feelings.

In this talk you will help your child understand that

- alcohol use is a part of our culture.
- there is a difference between alcohol use and misuse.

- some amounts of alcohol change our mental abilities, body co-ordination, and feelings, and it's important to know what parts of us are affected and in what way.
- the use of alcohol does not excuse harmful or violent behavior.
- there are family rules and laws about alcohol use.

What You Can Expect from This Talk

After the talk your child will be able to

- define the term "alcohol misuse" and identify some of its different forms.
- understand how the entire family suffers when a family member is misusing alcohol.
- express the family rules about alcohol use.

How Do You Define Alcohol Misuse?

In your eyes, what is a healthy way to use alcohol? And when does alcohol use become misuse? We're not suggesting that that's an easy question, but it's one you might want to consider before you talk with your child. If you use alcohol without negative results, then you can probably see the enjoyable aspects of its use. At the same time, statistics show that half of all people reading this book will have had a family member who has problems with alcohol. If that holds true for you, you are probably able to see the alcohol's downside more easily. Are you ready to help your child see both sides of alcohol use?

This chapter will help you answer a number of questions, including, How does a parent set rules about alcohol use? Does your family consider alcohol use normal or as dangerous as any street drug? Guidelines for conduct become more and more important as children get older and begin to interact with peers who have their own beliefs about alcohol use. Starting early, parents can help their children understand the role of alcohol in everyday life. You can help your kids understand your family's values about alcohol use as well as the emotional and legal consequences of its abuse.

What Is Moderation?

Families from various cultures and backgrounds see moderation in the consumption of alcohol differently. Your family will have its own definition of moderation—one glass of wine, say, or one or two beers. Experts agree, however, that two servings of alcohol per day is the upper limit of moderation. What is a serving? A can of beer, a glass of wine, and a shot glass of liquor all have about the same amount of alcohol, and each is considered one serving. More than two servings a day is considered heavy drinking by some. This is not a hard and fast rule. How drinking affects you also depends on your body size, gender, and brain chemistry, your eating habits, and how your body metabolizes alcohol. Some people can have more than two drinks without ill effect, while others, because of their body chemistry, can hardly tolerate even a single serving.

Influence of the Media

Alcohol is prominently featured in movies, on TV, and in other media. If you read a magazine, you'll see slick ads that tie liquor with money, good taste, and sex appeal. Watch TV and you'll see ads sending the message that one beer gets a man three blonde women in bikinis. Parents can get discouraged by those messages. Fortunately, your kids have you to talk with about reality vs. Hollywood hype.

"I asked my fifth grade son, after we saw a beer commercial with those funny frogs that drink beers, why the beer commercials never show the consequences of drinking, like drunk driving and hangovers and drunken fights." —Rachael, mother of two, New York City

Is Alcohol a Gateway Drug?

A gateway drug is one that is thought to lead to harder drugs. Marijuana is often called a gateway drug. The idea is that people who smoke pot might soon be enticed to try other, more damaging drugs like cocaine, heroin, or LSD. Most anti-drug campaigns still include this message. Do you agree that using some drugs can lead us to try others? Does that ring true in your experience? Does it seem logical to assume that since drinking alcohol changes your feelings and perceptions, that it might lead to a natural curiosity about other drugs that alter perceptions? How would describing alcohol as a "gateway" drug impact its use and regulation by the government?

Quotes to Consider

"Although purchase of alcoholic beverages is illegal for those under 21 years of age, 10.4 million current drinkers were age 12–20 in 1999. Of this group, 6.8 million engaged in binge drinking, including 2.1 million who would also be classified as heavy drinkers."
—Substance Abuse & Mental Health Services Administration (SAMHSA), "National Household Survey Highlights," 1999, www.samhsa.gov

"Although most parents think peer pressure is the main reason teenagers drink, 79% of teens say they drink because it feels good; 67% say drinking helps them forget their problems; 66% say peer pressure is the reason; and 47% say they drink because they have nothing better to do."

> —American Academy of Pediatrics, "Things You Should Know
> about Alcohol and Children," 1998, www.aap.org

"Fifty-six percent of students in grades 5–12 say that alcohol advertising encourages them to drink."

> —Mothers Against Drunk Driving, "Underage Drinking
> Information Parents Need to Know," www.madd.org

"Traffic crashes are the greatest single cause of death for ages 6 to 28. Almost half are alcohol-related."

> —Mothers Against Drunk Driving, "Underage Drinking
> Information Parents Need to Know," www.madd.org

"Alcohol and tobacco together kill more than 50 times the number of people killed by cocaine, heroin, and every other drug combined."

> —Mothers Against Drunk Driving, "Underage Drinking
> Information Parents Need to Know," www.madd.org

"Between 1972 and 1996, the proportion of young adults of both sexes who had some experience with alcohol rose from 82 percent to 90 percent, but heavy drinking seemed to decline."

> —Theodore Caplow, Louis Hicks, and Ben J. Wattenberg, *The First
> Measured Century: An Illustrated Guide to Trends in America, 1900–2000*

About Language

As you discuss alcohol with your child, it might be helpful to be aware of your language. Do you use the same words to describe using alcohol as you do with other drugs? Kids are very sensitive to mixed messages about drug use and will pick up perceived differences between alcohol misuse and drug misuse.

Language can stigmatize or romanticize a behavior, depending on the use of words. Imagine if you said to your party guests, "Let's all do drugs," and then offered them a bottle of wine. Obviously most of us don't use the language of "drug use" to describe alcohol use. How might this affect the way we drink?

> "I gave my twenty-one-year-old son a rule: never more than one drink if he's going to drive. Then he laughed and said, 'Your rule is funny, because one Long Island Iced Tea has about four big shots of booze in it.' Then I had to clarify that one drink meant only one shot, and it would be better if he had no booze and found a designated driver. My son still loves testing me every chance he gets."
>
> —Barbara, mother of one, New York City

Different Families: Different Values

Everyone interprets behavior in his or her own way. Here are some behaviors that may be experienced differently, depending on a person's background and experience:

> *At dinner Dad pulls out a bottle of wine and proceeds to drink constantly through the evening, becoming louder and more agitated. By the end of dinner he is drunk. At bedtime, the youngest daughter asks, "What's wrong with Dad?"*

What would your answer be? Would you encourage the daughter to ask more questions, or discuss how some adults use alcohol to deal with difficult feelings? Some parents would never go into the reasons that an adult family member got drunk, while others might want to discuss it, and talk about healthier and safer ways to deal with stress. What would you do?

■

A family is on vacation and is having dinner at a restaurant, when the waitress brings complimentary cocktails to their table. She gives one to the older son, who is only fifteen but looks much older.

Should the son be allowed to have that drink? Some parents would see nothing to worry about. Others would allow him a few sips and no more. Still others would insist that he abstain from drinking until he was of legal age, and order him a soft drink. What would you do?

■

A group of college kids has been watching football and drinking beer all day. After the game, one of them wants to drive and get food. His girlfriend, seeing that her boyfriend is under the influence of alcohol, asks for the car keys so she can drive, but the young man insists on driving himself.

Have you ever been in a situation like this? Some people would look the other way and hope for the best. Others would try to back the girlfriend up, or at least urge her to stay out of the car. Still others would want to have a talk with the boyfriend once when he sobers up. What would you do?

■

A teenage girl is at a party at a friend's house. There are older guys there who are drinking. She walks into a back bedroom and finds two guys whom she likes drinking on the couch; they offer her a beer. She joins them, and after a while they begin to make inappropriate sexual comments. She leaves feeling shaken. Later that weekend, she tells her mom about the older boys, but not about her own drinking.

What would your response be? Most parents would be unhappy to hear an incident like this, but glad that their daughter felt she could come to them. Some people would talk with their daughter about how alcohol use can lead to unsafe situations. Others would call the boys' parents, or the house where the party was held, and try to talk about the situation. What would you do?

Different Perspectives

"Since alcoholism runs in my family, my mom always told me to stay away from it. She would constantly remind me that four of my paternal uncles died of cirrhosis of the liver resulting from alcohol abuse."   —Kim, health educator and aunt, New York City

"I remember when I was a child I saw my dad getting drunk and nearly choking a relative to death."

—Yolanda, mother of three, Orlando, Florida

"My four-year-old son knows that I pull people over for drunk driving. One day as I was going to work he said, 'Go get the beer drinkers!'"

—Deputy Sheriff James Quattrone, Chautauqua County, New York

Last-minute Checkups before the Talk

Before you talk with your child, try to remember what, if anything, your parents taught you about alcohol when you were growing up.

- Did a parent ever talk to you about alcohol?
- Did they ever talk to you about alcohol misuse?
- Did they tell you how to identify alcohol abuse?
- Did they model healthy coping skills to deal with stress without using alcohol?
- Did they use alcohol in a responsible way that helped you see how it should not be abused?

As a parent, what are you teaching your child about alcohol?

- Do you encourage her to talk about situations that have the potential for alcohol abuse?
- Do you talk about the legal issues for the sale and use of alcohol?
- How do you let your child know that you welcome the discussions of any concerns he has about alcohol?
- Do you talk to your child about finding friends who don't use alcohol?
- Do you model the ability to deal with stress, anger, fear, insecurity, and other emotions without alcohol?

Do you have any stories you can share with your child about alcohol use, or how you confronted someone who was abusing alcohol? For example:

- The time you and a friend got drunk and what the consequences were.

- The time you had a special dinner with good friends and good wine, and how wonderful it was.
- How you learned to use alcohol responsibly and legally as an adult.
- The times you felt worried about a family member's drinking.

Sharing your stories lets your child know how you feel about alcohol use and what impact it had on you when you were growing up.

"I struggle with how to discuss my past with alcohol without glorifying the situations or making them seem like an ordinary rite of passage." —Ned, father of two, New York City

What Are Your Family Rules?

Do you have family rules about alcohol use, along with clear consequences for breaking them? If not, this is a good time to think about what rules you might want to put in place.

The illustrated scenarios in the next section are meant to provide an opportunity to discuss your experiences with alcohol, what you consider healthy drinking, and your definition of drug use. The stories and questions are open-ended, allowing your child to reflect on a range of topics including things family members do to protect one another from harm, peer pressure, and other concerns. Depending on your child, the talk could even include issues of mixed messages that come from you or other family members. Discussing these situations will allow you to share your family rules about using alcohol and give them meaning and credibility.

The Talk

Introduce the Talk

To start this talk you could say, "I want to show you something in this book," or "I'm reading this chapter about alcohol and I want your opinion on it."

Younger children are often happy to offer an opinion, while older ones may respond with, "Do we have to talk about this again?" Remember, even if you can get only a few sentences out of your child, you've had a success—perhaps even a successful beginning to later talks.

You can add, "Do you know what alcohol does to a person?" He might respond with "Yeah, it makes people drunk." If he is both older and candid he might try to press your buttons with, "I know that Grandpa gets drunk every night." A favorite conversation stopper used by kids is, "Did you ever drink when you were a kid?" You might want to think through your response before you begin.

"When my son asked me if I ever got drunk as a kid, I told him the truth. I said that I made a few mistakes that almost cost me my life when I was in college and was binge drinking. I told him that I was trying to fit in with a group of guys who were all getting drunk. I talked to my son a lot about peer pressure as well as a complete description of how sick I was for days. I ended up saying that I hoped he would not make my mistakes."

—Tim, father of four, El Paso, Texas

"My daughter knows about my difficult childhood. One day she told me that she thought drinking was a rite of passage, and that since I had indulged in drinking, why shouldn't she be able to? I said that was an excellent point and she'd eventually make that decision herself. But I told her that I found that in drinking alcohol at an early age, I gave up a lot of my young adulthood and had very few happy memories of being a teenager. Remembering that time means thinking back on a miserable time, involving embarrassment and some shame and that's mostly because I gave in to the peer pressure of friends who did not have my best interests at heart. My daughter was taken aback by my candor, and very thoughtful afterwards."

—Maria, mother of two, New York City

Review These Words

Please review the terms in this section. Discussing all the terms with your child is optional. You know which are appropriate for your child's age and maturity level. More than likely, even the youngest children have heard these words on TV. Keep in mind that many of the terms about drugs found in previous chapters are also appropriate to the talk about alcohol.

alcohol: a depressant that affects a person's feelings by reducing inhibitions, coordination, and ability to focus. For some people, alcohol creates feelings of relaxation and tranquility; for others, it brings up anger and hostility. Alcohol is physically and psychologically addictive; withdrawal from alcohol addiction can be life-threatening.

alcoholic: term for an individual who is addicted to alcohol. Many alcoholics consider themselves alcoholics for life, even after they have stopped drinking.

Alcoholics Anonymous: a twelve-step support program based on faith and personal responsibility for people who are concerned about their relationship to alcohol. It's also an organization offering emotional support to members.

binge drinking: consumption of five or more servings of alcohol in one sitting. Considered high-risk behavior that can be life-threatening.

blackout: a memory lapse, reflecting inability to recall events that occurred during a drinking episode.

drunk: physically and mentally impaired because of alcohol consumption.

drunk driving: operating a vehicle while under the influence of alcohol.

enabler: a friend or family member who unknowingly supports someone's addiction, by making excuses or otherwise helping the drinker avoid facing the consequences of their drinking.

fetal alcohol syndrome: a set of birth defects caused by a pregnant woman's excessive drinking. Consequences to the baby may include serious mental and physical disabilities.

withdrawal syndrome: the effects on the body when a person who is addicted to alcohol suddenly stops using it. These include, but are not limited to, seizures, dangerous heart rhythms, convulsions, and in some cases, death.

zero-tolerance laws: laws that include mandatory penalties for people arrested for drunk driving. For example, some states automatically suspend the drivers licenses of people caught driving while under the influence.

Why Is Talking about Alcohol Important?

Ask your child whether she thinks talking about alcohol use is important. Here are some reasons you might want to offer. Talking about alcohol means

- learning the responsible use of alcohol and the perils of irresponsible use.
- learning to identify potential alcohol abuse in others or oneself.
- clarifying family rules about alcohol use.
- clarifying school rules and the law.

The Stories

In the next part of the talk, you'll be reading short stories to your child and discussing them together. You don't have to read all of the stories. Pick the ones that you think are appropriate. The stories are very simple. Feel free to embellish them, adding details that you think might make the story more believable to your child.

A Story about a Family Dinner

This story gives you a chance to talk about how alcohol can be used responsibly by adults.

"Two teenagers are having dinner with their parents and grandparents. The adults are drinking wine. The teens ask if they can have some."

Ask these questions of your child:

- What is the daughter thinking? What is she saying?
- What is the son thinking? What is he saying?
- What is the mom thinking? What is she saying?
- What is the dad thinking? What is he saying?

Now that your child has completed this scenario, ask the following questions:

- Why do the kids want to have some wine?
- How can wine be misused?
- Do their parents need to talk to the kids about responsible, adult use of alcohol?
- If you were in a situation like this, how would you feel? What would you do?

A Story about a Beer Commercial

This story gives you an opportunity to talk about how common alcohol use is.

"A mom and her son and daughter are watching TV, when a commercial for beer comes on."

Ask these questions of your child:

- What is the mom thinking? What is she saying?
- What is the daughter thinking? What is she saying?
- What is the son thinking? What is he saying?

Now that your child has completed this scenario, ask the following questions:

- Do the mom or kids want to drink the beer advertised on TV?
- Can beer ever be misused? If so, how?
- What does the beer company want the viewer to think? Is the advertisement giving the viewer the whole truth about the product?
- Does the parent need to talk to the kids about responsible, adult ways to drink beer?
- If you were in a situation like this, how would you feel? What did you do?

A Story about an Uncle's Feelings

This story is an opportunity to talk about how alcohol can become addictive, how to recover from addiction to alcohol, and the abuse of alcohol.

"A mom and her brother are talking about why he left a big family dinner early. He talks about his recovery from alcohol addiction and how difficult it is for him to be around the family when they drink alcohol heavily. While they're talking, the mom's young son walks into the room."

Ask these questions of your child:

- What is the mom thinking?
- What is the mom saying?

- What is the uncle thinking?
- What is the son thinking?

Now that your child has completed this scenario, ask the following questions:

- Does the mom feel comfortable talking to her son about the family's drinking or about her brother's recovery? Why or why not?
- Does the uncle feel comfortable discussing his recovery from addiction with his nephew? Why or why not?
- Does the parent need to talk to the child about alcohol misuse, addiction, and recovery from alcohol-related problems?
- If you were the parent in a situation like this, how would you feel? What would you do?

A Story about Taking Risks

This story provides an opportunity to talk about the way alcohol can change a person's feelings, and how some situations where people are drinking can become unsafe.

"A girl is at a party and goes into a back bedroom, where some older boys are drinking beer. She has a crush on one of them, and he offers the girl a beer."

Ask these questions of your child:

- What is the girl thinking?
- What are the boys thinking?
- What is the girl saying?

Now that your child has completed this scenario, ask the following questions:

- Does the girl want to take the beer? Why or why not?
- What might happen if the girl stays in the back room drinking with the boys?
- How might this situation become alcohol misuse?
- Does the parent need to talk to the daughter about responsible, adult use of alcohol and the potential dangers of being around people who are drinking?
- If you were the girl in a situation like this, how would you feel? What would you do?

Clarify Your Family's Values

Discuss these questions with your child as a way of sharing your values about alcohol use. We have included a number of potential responses from children to help you formulate your own responses.

Ask your child: "When a young person has a friend who wants to drink alcohol, or is drinking, what can the young person do?"

Child response #1: "I don't know."

Parent: It's hard to know what to do. Sometimes it might seem okay to sneak a drink of a parent's beer or wine. But alcohol is something for adults only, and even adults have to make sure that they are careful with how much they drink, and what they do when they are drinking.

Child response #2: "Well, one drink couldn't hurt."

Parent: That may be true sometimes, and for some people. But it's not true for everybody in every situation. The point is that one drink can lead to more. And when a person is growing up, it's important that they be clear-headed and able to deal with life's problems with clarity. This builds strength of character and the ability to deal with stress, anger, fear, and other emotions.

The Bare Minimum: A Quick Quiz for Kids

Ask your child the following questions to assess her knowledge and perceptions of alcohol use.

1. How does drinking alcohol effect a person's feelings?
   Sample answers:
   - It makes some feelings stronger and others dulled.
   - It makes it harder to deal with *real* feelings.
   - It makes some people angrier.
   - It makes some people less inhibited.
   - It makes people more willing to take chances, which can sometimes be life-threatening.

2. Can you give me a reason why young people might wait till they are adults to drink alcohol?
Sample answers:
- Alcohol makes you less clear-headed.
- It's dangerous to drink alcohol when your brain is still forming.
- Alcohol takes away stressful feelings, and learning to deal with stress is very important as a teen. It builds character.
- Drinking too much alcohol can make you very sick.
- It's illegal to purchase alcohol when you're still a teenager.

3. What are some healthy and legal ways adults can use alcohol?
Sample answers (yours will vary, depending on your family's values):
- As long as people don't have a history of alcohol abuse, they most likely should be able to drink in moderation with meals.
- Most people can drink moderately, as long as they don't mix alcohol with prescription or over-the-counter drugs, and as long as they don't drive or operate machinery while they're under the influence.

Talk about Your Family Rules

This is an opportunity to review your family rules. Ask your child the following questions:

1. What are our family rules about using alcohol?
Sample answers:
- Adults may use alcohol—but only responsibly and in moderation.
- We do not drink alcohol and drive.
- No one in this family breaks the law regarding alcohol use.

After the Talk

Take a moment to reflect on the talk you just had with your child. How do you feel about it? Think about whether your child has the ability to deal with everyday issues that accompany childhood and adolescence.

- Were you surprised by anything in your child's view of alcohol use?
- Do you think your child might, at some point, abuse alcohol to deal with negative emotions or stress?
- Does she seem susceptible to peer influence?
- What lessons did you learn about how to listen to your child?

Warning Signs

This talk can reveal potential problems children face when dealing with alcohol. Trust your instincts. Did you get the feeling that your child was under stress, or was having trouble navigating the use of alcohol? Check in with your kids often on how they're doing, and how they are handling life's everyday stresses. Review the following warning signs to see if your child might be using alcohol:

- He is defensive about how his friends use alcohol.
- She makes jokes about "drunk driving" or "being blasted."
- He has a sudden change in friends or his grades take a sudden downturn.
- His friends appear drunk or hung over.
- She is very interested in drinking, and unhappy when she's denied alcohol at the dinner table.

Trust your instincts on how your child is doing, and act accordingly.

Finding Help

This talk can reveal serious issues that a child is facing. Your child may have hinted at having problems. Or he may have made up serious problems for the characters in the stories. While presented as fantasy, the situations your child describes may be based on real situations in her life. If needed, support and help is available for your child and other family members. As we said earlier in the chapter, when one family member has a problem with alcohol, the entire family has a problem. Your child's school or public health agency or employee assistance programs may have resources for dealing with alcohol abuse and dependence. Family and friends may also give you helpful insight into how they deal with alcohol use and abuse.

Success Stories

You have made it through the talk about alcohol. This can be one of the toughest talks, since alcohol use, though often problematic, is so widespread and seen as normal. Some parents have broken the silence by opening up about their own problems with alcohol and how they dealt with them. One mom in New York City told her son about her problem drinking when she was younger, and how she felt she had lost years of her life to alcohol. She told her son that she didn't want to burden him with rules, but wanted to help him avoid the pitfalls she faced.

No matter what you discussed, remember that by having this talk, you reinforced the notion that your home is a safe place to deal with everyday challenges. You sent the message that it is healthy and normal to have conversations about problems and ask the family for help and support. And no matter how brief, your talk has laid the foundation for further discussions about illegal drugs.

Sample Talks

Between Parents and Children

If you are wondering how a talk based on his chapter might really sound, take a look at the following excerpts from real family talks.

Discussing the Story about a Family Dinner

Participants: dad and two daughters, ages eleven and nine

Dad: "Two teenagers, a boy and a girl, are having dinner with their parents and grandparents. The adults are drinking wine. The teens ask if they can have some." Do you understand the story?

Daughters: Yes.

Dad: All right. What is the daughter thinking?

Younger daughter: She's thinking, "It's just a sip. We aren't going to get drunk or anything."

Older daughter: "And it's the cool thing to do."

Dad: What is the son thinking?

Younger daughter: "We're old enough to have a sip of wine."

Dad: What are the kids saying?

Older daughter: "It's just a sip. It won't hurt us. It'll be fine."

Younger daughter: But they are probably pleading really badly, because they really want some.

Dad: What about the mom and dad?

Younger daughter: The mom is thinking they are still too young. They can't even drive.

Dad: And the dad?

Younger daughter: He's thinking the same thing.

Dad: Why do the kids want to have some wine?

Younger daughter: It makes them feel more grown up.

Older daughter: Because if they did it, they could brag to their friends about it.

Dad: How can wine be misused?

Younger daughter: Sometimes it makes you drunk or very sleepy.

Older daughter: They could have too much of it and start doing crazy things.

Dad: Do the parents need to talk to the kids about responsible adult use of alcohol?

Daughters: Yes!

Dad: If you were in a situation like this, what would you do? Would you ask for a sip of wine?

Younger daughter: I probably wouldn't, because it could do something to my brain and I wouldn't want that to happen to me.

Older daughter: I don't want to drink alcohol.

Lessons Learned from This Sample Talk

This dad and his daughters had a productive talk about alcohol, which raised issues around the adult "status" that kids see in drinking, the impact of alcohol on the brain ("sleepiness," "doing crazy things"), and their interest in drinking. Future talks can explore some of the "crazy things," like drunk driving and even date rape, that can occur under the influence of alcohol. The dad can also talk about his family rules regarding drinking wine with relatives.

Discussing the Story about a Beer Commercial

Participants: a dad and his two daughters, ages eleven and nine

Dad: "A mom and her kids are watching TV, when a commercial for beer comes on." After the commercial comes to an end, what is the mom thinking?

Younger daughter: "My kids won't do it, they're smart enough not to do it."

Older daughter: "They won't even try."

Younger daughter: She might be thinking, "I better change the channel, just in case."

Dad: What is the mom saying?

Older daughter: "It's not good for you. Don't try it!"

Dad: What are the daughter and son thinking and saying?

Older daughter: "Oh, let's try it. It's a cool thing to do. It's on TV."

Dad: Do the mom or kids want to drink the beer advertised on TV?

Older daughter: I think the kids want to, but the mom doesn't.

Younger daughter: Maybe, maybe not. You can't be sure.

Dad: Can beer ever be misused?

Older daughter: Yes, because they could have an overdose of it. It might kill them.

Dad: Do the parents need to talk to the kids about responsible, adult use of alcohol?

Younger daughter: If the kids didn't have the talk, they could be hurting themselves, and it might cost the parents a lot of money.

Lessons Learned from This Sample Talk

This was a productive talk and raised issues around the power and influence of advertising, misuse of alcohol (what one daughter calls "overdosing"), and the importance of family talks about alcohol and other drugs. Further talks can explore why parents might have to spend "a lot of money" to deal with drinking problems (hospital bills, lawsuits?) and the ways kids can "hurt themselves" (drunk driving, alcohol poisoning?).

Discussing the Story about an Uncle's Feelings

Participants: a mom and her nine-year-old daughter. Note that the mom changed the story's character from "son" to "daughter."

Mom: "A mom and her brother are talking about why he left a family dinner early. He talks about his recovery from alcohol addiction and how it's difficult to be around the family when they drink alcohol heavily. Just then the mom's daughter walks into the room." What is the mom thinking? Like if it were between me and Uncle Joe.

Daughter: She's thinking, "What if she heard our conversation about my brother's drinking?"

Mom: What is the mom saying?

Daughter: Maybe, "Me and your Uncle Joe are having a grown-up conversation that I don't think you should get involved with."

Mom: What is the uncle thinking?

Daughter: "My niece really likes me, but she's a really smart kid who knows a lot about drugs, so if she heard anything in our conversation, she might be a little worried."

Mom: Do you think he's worried about what his niece might think of him?

Daughter: Yes, he might. If he was my favorite uncle he might be scared, like, "Uh-oh, what if my niece won't like me anymore? Because I know she knows a lot, I mean a lot, about drugs."

Mom: And alcohol. This is about alcohol.

Daughter: And also alcohol.

Mom: What is the daughter thinking?

Daughter: If I heard the conversation, I'd be like, "Uh-oh, is Uncle Joe drinking? What should I do? Should I ask my mom why he is? Should I talk to my uncle?"

Mom: Remember, he's talking about his recovery, so he has addressed his problem with drinking. He was an alcoholic, but now he's stopped drinking. But he's saying how it's still difficult to be around other people who drink heavily.

Daughter: Well, since he's still in recovery, I would be worried, because when he's with his friends, they might still go to bars and stuff. His friends might drink wine and beer, the way he used to drink. So he might want to drink again and get addicted again. But maybe he'll say, "No, no, no. I'm not going to drink."

Mom: Does the mom feel comfortable talking to her daughter about her family's drinking or her brother's recovery? Why or why not?

Daughter: I think my mom would feel comfortable talking with me because she knows she can trust me. She also explains to me that people sometimes drink at weddings and parties. And about the uncle, this should be explained to families.

Mom: Does the uncle feel comfortable discussing his recovery with his niece? Why or why not?

Daughter: Probably because he knows I know a lot about it and I am one of the most comfortable people speaking about it.

Mom: Does the parent need to talk to the kids about alcohol misuse, addiction, and recovery from alcohol-related problems?

Daughter: Oh, yeah. Yeah, yeah, yeah!

Mom; Do you think it only happens to certain kinds of people or it can happen to anybody?

Daughter: It can happen to anybody.

Mom: Even in your own family?

Daughter: Yes. Anybody.

Mom: So it's good to discuss this and keep the dialogue open so if this ever happens to someone, even you, you can talk about it. Should the family understand that addiction can happen to anybody and help them through it? Or do you think a family should think that they're a bad person and ask, "Why did you do this to yourself?"

Daughter: That's awful to say to somebody. You should talk calmly to someone and never say any of that bad stuff.

Mom: Because it would . . . ?

Daughter: It would just make him more nervous.

Mom: Should the family continue to drink a lot around him?

Daughter: No. Actually everybody in the family shouldn't drink until he's totally stuck to not drinking any alcohol.

Mom: To show him support?

Daughter: Yes. Also, it's healthier to drink water and other things.

Mom: That's true, it is. Good job. What did you think of this talk?

Daughter: That was a great talk.

Lessons Learned from This Sample Talk

This was a very compassionate discussion. This third grader appears to have a good understanding of the situation and the feelings that the uncle may experience. She also had a very thoughtful idea when she suggested that the family not drink alcohol around a relative in recovery. Future talks could explore how someone develops a problem with alcohol in the first place, as well as how early such problems can develop.

Discussing a Story about Taking Risks

Participants: a mom and her eight-year-old daughter

Mom: "A girl is at a party and goes into a back bedroom, where some older boys are drinking beer. She has a crush on one of the boys. He offers her a beer." What is the girl thinking?

Daughter: That she shouldn't take it.

Mom: What are the boys thinking?

Daughter: That she should take it.

Mom: What is the girl saying?

Daughter: "No, thank you. I don't want it."

Mom: Does the girl want to take the beer?

Daughter: No.

Mom: Why not?

Daughter: Because it's wrong to drink beer.

Mom: What might happen if the girl stays in the back room drinking with the boys?

Daughter: She'll get drunk.

Mom: How might this situation become alcohol misuse?

Daughter: The boys might make her get drunk.

Mom: Does the parent need to talk to the daughter about responsible, adult use of alcohol and the dangers of being around people who are drinking?

Daughter: Yes.

Mom: If you were in a situation like this, how would you feel? What would you do?

Daughter: I would feel guilty and I would go back to the front room.

Lessons Learned from This Sample Talk

The daughter seems to have an awareness of the risks associated with alcohol use—especially around unsupervised boys. The mom could ask how boys could "make" a girl get drunk. The mom could also ask how this situation would be different if it were a girl and her boyfriend. Following talks need to stress the potentially dangerous consequences of drinking alcohol (whether alone, with friends, or with strangers at a party), pressure to drink, and ways to refrain from drinking.

5

Where There's Smoke . . .

Talking about Tobacco

Every day my mom smoked a pack or two of cigarettes. When I was about ten I asked her if I could smoke. She said, "sure," and gave me a lit cigarette to smoke. I inhaled and got sick to my stomach. I was never interested in smoking after that.
—Drew, mother of two, St. Paul, Minnesota

My parents' and grandparents' generations all smoked. But our generation and our kids know better. It amazes me that in spite of all the warnings, people still smoke. This says a ton about how addictive nicotine really is.
—Tess, mother of two, Gaithersburg, Maryland

Every day I see a few kids from the local middle school smoking on their way home. Some of the girls actually look like they are posing—trying to be someone they saw in some movie, I guess. What I want to yell is, "Those cause cancer!"
—Barb, mother of two, Boise, Idaho

I remember that when I was a kid, my parents did stuff that wasn't healthy. Their attitude was, "Do as I say, not as I do." And I resented that. Now here I am, a smoker, trying to tell my kids not to smoke. I didn't set out to become a smoker, and I'd really like to quit—but it's not easy. —Andy, father of three, Syracuse, New York

How many of you can remember working in offices where every desk came with its own ashtray? Or flying in airplanes filled with cigarette smoke? How times have changed. Now workers have to step outside to smoke and airport smokers are confined to glassed-enclosed smoking rooms. Even more important, today's parents, unlike those of previous generations, understand the serious health risks of smoking, and their children are taught in school about the addictive qualities of nicotine and the long-term consequences of using tobacco.

Despite these huge changes, smoking continues to be the number-one preventable cause of death in the United States. Tobacco will kill more than 450,000 Americans this year. More than one in four of us still smokes.

Today's kids grasp these contradictions. And they want to know why cigarettes, proven to be both addictive and deadly, can be legal and acceptable, while other drugs, which kill and injure far fewer people, remain on government lists of controlled substances.

Why has tobacco, with all we know about it, retained such a huge cultural presence? Why do so many young people still see smoking as something relaxing, romantic, and mature?

To talk to your child about smoking, you don't need to have all the answers. All you need is a few minutes of free time, and the patience to listen.

The data is in, and this chapter will help you discuss the serious health consequences of smoking or chewing tobacco, as well as the incredible power of addiction associated with nicotine use. Because tobacco products are so readily available and their use so widespread, these discussions are especially important.

How Tobacco Can Alter Feelings

"My biggest dilemma is trying to explain to my fourth grader why people do something that has no redeeming qualities and is fatal."

—Jan, mother of two, Syracuse, New York

As we have discussed in previous chapters, drugs have the ability to change our feelings—and nicotine does it in an insidious manner. For many people, nicotine addiction takes hold quickly—often within two weeks of starting to smoke—and doesn't let go.

Whenever a smoker is not ingesting nicotine, the brain sends a message that it needs more nicotine, now—and agitation or nervousness sets in. When nicotine is finally delivered, the mind sends a message saying, "relax." This is why smokers often find smoking "relaxing." What's "relaxing" is the temporary relief from the cravings and anxieties *caused by absence* of the drug.

How Nicotine Affects the Body

Tobacco is regarded by many medical authorities as poison, pure and simple. Not only does nicotine permanently damage the heart, blood vessels, and lungs, it is also packaged in a cigarette with hundreds of other dangerous substances. Nicotine is thought to be one of the most addictive substances known to science; some researchers think it more addictive than heroin. There is no documented safe level of tobacco. Even if you don't smoke, you are at risk by being around smokers. The unfiltered, burning end of a cigarette emits twenty times the harmful chemicals as the filtered end. Studies have shown that the bloodstream of someone inhaling secondhand smoke contains deadly substances, contributing to organ damage just as if the person were smoking.

What about Moderate Use?

When your child grows up, will she refrain from smoking, smoke occasionally, or become heavily addicted and find daily use of tobacco necessary? Will your son grow up to be chain-smoker, endangering his life and the life of others in his family who breathe secondhand smoke? Family talks need to address the widespread use of nicotine by children and adults, the health benefits of not starting or quitting, and the potential for life-threatening health problems. Health authorities have been clear in their recommendation—there is no such thing as moderate use of tobacco.

This chapter is designed to help you clarify your concerns about smoking and other tobacco use with your child. You can choose to talk about how nicotine is a drug that some adults are addicted to, and talk about whether the use of nicotine products is included in your definition of drug use.

Preparing for the Talk

This talk will give you the chance to talk to your children about smoking tobacco, both in terms of the addictive qualities of nicotine and the potential for health problems to both smokers and people exposed to secondhand smoke. It will also help you explain the short- and long-term effects of tobacco use on a person's feelings and health.

In this talk you will help your child understand that

- the use of tobacco and nicotine is a part of our culture.
- nicotine is highly addictive.
- the use of nicotine changes our feelings and impacts our health. It's important to know what is changed and in what way.
- there are family rules about tobacco use.

What You Can Expect from This Talk

After the talk your child will be able to:

- define the terms "nicotine" and "addiction."
- understand why people usually start smoking and how people quit.
- understand the risks of secondhand smoke and how the entire family can suffer when a family member is smoking.
- express the family rules about smoking or chewing tobacco.

Would You Define Tobacco Use as Drug Abuse?

"Some people put smoking a pipe or cigar, or chewing tobacco, in a different category from smoking a cigarette. But tobacco doesn't care how it gets into your body. I explained to my eighth grader that it just gets in and does damage the same way."

—Allison, mother of one, Syracuse, New York

How does a parent set rules about tobacco use? Does your family consider tobacco a potentially life-threatening drug? Or do you, like millions of Americans, see tobacco as one of life's simple pleasures?

Is there a difference between tobacco use and misuse? Not according to medical experts, who say that since there is no safe level of use, all smoking is therefore misuse. What do you think?

About 70 percent of all smokers say they'd like to quit. And most say they don't want their kids to start, either. But parents, whether they smoke or not, know that all kids turn eighteen eventually and will be able to make their own choices. Parents should be able to understand and explain the health risks of smoking and talk to kids about the pro-smoking messages found in ads, movies, and other media. Most parents who are smokers would have welcomed this guidance.

Does anyone in your family smoke? If so, be prepared to get some questions about mixed messages. Advice to parents: Be honest about your feelings and your frustrations. If you are trying to quit smoking, let your kids know how tough it is.

Influence of the Media

In 1970, the U.S. government banned tobacco ads from television and required warning labels on cigarette packages and print ads. That's had a positive impact, but the promotion of cigarettes has continued unabated. Slick magazine ads link smoking with sexiness, independence, and style (for women) and rugged individualism (for men). Recent studies have found that kids are more familiar with the cartoon characters from cigarette ads than with Mickey Mouse.

Children know about cigarettes—how to get them and how to smoke them. That's something nearly all kids have in common. Not all kids have parents who are willing to sit down with them and explain the facts and the risks associated with smoking.

Quotes to Consider

"If you're like most parents who are smokers, you do not want your child to start smoking. Here are some things you might say: 'Smoking is easy to start, and hard to stop. I've tried to quit, but I haven't been able to.'"

—National Education Association Health Information Network,
"Kids Act to Control Tobacco Parent Advocacy Guide," 1998

"Youths age 12 to 17 who currently smoke cigarettes were seven times more likely to use illicit drugs than youth who didn't smoke. Young adults age 18 to 25 who smoked were four times more likely to use illicit drugs than their nonsmoking peers."

—Substance Abuse & Mental Health Services Administration (SAMHSA),
"National Household Survey Highlights," 1999, www.samhsa.gov

"Every year, approximately 100,000 Americans die from alcohol-related diseases, and about 400,000 die from tobacco-related causes."

Go Ask Alice, Columbia University Health Education Program, 1998

"The average smoker spends about $900 a year on cigarettes. Look through the *Orlando Sentinel* and circle all the things you could buy that cost $900 or less."

—Supplement, *Orlando Sentinel*, Orange County
Coalition for a Drug Free Community, 2000

"The consumption of cigarettes staggers the imagination. The 48 million smokers in the United States in 1997—about 25% of the adult population—consumed an average of about 27 cigarettes a day."

—Theodore Caplow, Louis Hicks, and Ben J. Wattenberg, *The First
Measured Century: An Illustrated Guide to Trends in America, 1900–2000*

"American cigarette packs already have to make space for a straightforward reminder that cigarette smoking is a health hazard. But to our north, Canadian cigarette makers now have to turn over 50% of each pack to graphic representations of just what those hazards look like. And it's not pretty. The 16 designs include photographs of cancerous lungs, stroke-clotted brains, damaged hearts, and bloody mouths in acute periodontal distress."

—"Salient Facts: Antismoking Campaign,"
New York Times magazine, Feb. 2, 2001

"The Scandinavian countries have banned tobacco advertising and heaped so many taxes on the product that in Norway a pack of cigarettes costs $7.28."

—"Blowing Smoke," *New York Times* magazine, Nov. 5, 2000

Starting Young

Most smokers started when they were teens—and got hooked for years, if not for life. More than 70 percent of American youth who smoke started smoking before age eighteen. In many Latin American countries, more than 65 percent of smoking initiation occurs between the ages of fourteen and seventeen. That means that for kids, even trying cigarettes is potentially dangerous. A third to a half of adolescents who experiment with cigarettes go on to become habitual smokers.

On a positive note, studies show that if young people do not begin to use tobacco before the age of twenty, they are unlikely to start as adults. This highlights the importance of preventing smoking among young people.

Risks associated with smoking tobacco include:

- diminished sense of taste and smell
- gastric ulcers
- chronic bronchitis
- premature and more abundant face wrinkles
- emphysema
- heart disease
- stroke
- cancer of the mouth, larynx, pharynx, lungs, pancreas, cervix, uterus, and bladder

"I had a long talk with my teenage daughter about the health risks of smoking and the difference between understanding risk and changing behavior—and how that connection is often not as direct as people like to think. Many, many people—adults included—understand the health risks of tobacco but continue to ignore the warnings. The issue is much greater than understanding risk, especially for young people. It's about lifestyle and it's very complex."

—Tracy, mother of three, Seattle, Washington

Tobacco and the Law

Different countries, states, and counties have different laws regarding the sale and use of nicotine products. Companies have different policies about where people can smoke and how to keep people safe from secondhand smoke. Every state makes it illegal for people under age eighteen to purchase tobacco; however, health advocates have reported that up to 40 percent of tobacco outlets regularly break that law and sell to minors anyway. It doesn't help that for years, major tobacco companies used cartoon pitchmen to lure kids into smoking. The tobacco industry agreed only recently, as part of a legal settlement, to stop targeting youth in their advertising. But doubts remain over the industry's trustworthiness given past behavior.

> "I was watching a public service announcement about kids not smoking. It showed some cute girl wanting to talk to a cute guy at a restaurant. Then the boy takes a puff off a cigarette and his head morphs into a giant puffing fish head. And the girl thinks he looks like a freak and loses interest immediately. I wondered how effective this commercial would be with young people. It seemed lame. I wondered why it didn't show people in hospitals dying of lung cancer to make the point. Then I saw that the ad was sponsored by the tobacco industry itself!" —Phil, father of two, New York City

About Language

How we describe cigarettes sends messages to our kids and families. Explaining drug use to a teen means taking a critical look at how we perceive *all* drug use—legal and illegal. And this means looking critically at how we talk about nicotine—as a drug.

Language can make a behavior like smoking sound acceptable or sound problematic. Imagine saying to a coworker as you stepped outside, "I'm going out to respond to my addiction to a life-threatening drug." The truth is, we don't use the language of drug use to describe smoking or chewing tobacco.

There are many schools of thought about using such clinical

language, especially with people who smoke. Some say such matter-of-fact talk about tobacco only makes smokers more defensive, guilty, or angry, and does little to encourage them to quit. Others say it is time to call tobacco what it is: the most life threatening and addictive substance that's legally available. As you discuss tobacco with your child, it might be helpful to be aware of your language.

As you begin to talk about other drugs, such as marijuana, in upcoming chapters, see if there is a difference in your wording and emphasis. We know that kids are very sensitive to mixed messages about drug use and will question you about the differences between tobacco use and other drug use.

Different Families: Different Values

Everyone interprets behavior in his or her own way. Here are some behaviors that may be experienced differently, depending on a person's background and experience:

An aunt is visiting her brother and his family. At the dinner table, she lights up a cigarette.

How would you feel about this? Some parents would say that it's perfectly normal for adults to smoke in the house around people, even around kids. Others would ask the aunt to smoke outside. What would you do?

■

A family is sitting in the non-smoking section of a restaurant because the mom does not like the smell of cigarettes when she is eating. A person at the next table lights up a cigarette.

Have you ever been in a situation like this? Some parents would see nothing wrong with asking the food server to ask the smoker to abstain. Others would ask the smoker to put out the cigarette or move to the smoking section, if there was one. Other parents would do their best to ignore the smoke. What would you do?

■

A boy has finished high-school football practice. He and his friends start chewing tobacco while they're talking with their coach.

This scene is more common than you might think. What would you want the coach to do? Some parents think that chewing tobacco is fine for high-school students. Others would want the coach to talk to the students about the health hazards of chewing tobacco. What would you say?

■

A mom is smoking a cigarette in the kitchen, when her sixteen-year-old daughter walks in and lights up her first cigarette at home.

Here's a scene that happens every day. What's your reaction? Some parents assume that a sixteen-year-old is old enough to make her own decisions about smoking. And some parents would rather their kids try their first cigarette under adult supervision than sneak out for an illicit puff. Some parents who smoke say they can't ask a teenager not to smoke—wouldn't they be hypocrites? Of course, other parents would be very clear about house rules regarding smoking. What would you do?

Different Perspectives

"I wish my parents would have talked with me about nicotine. I probably wouldn't have been smoking today if they had."

—Rita, mother of one, Kansas City, Missouri

"My mom told me that if I was going to try cigarettes I should try it first at home. Of course my mom was also an alcoholic, which made life real interesting." —Andy, father of two, Columbia, South Carolina

"One of the hardest questions my son has asked me is: If smoking is so bad for you and could kill you, why do people like Grandpa still do it? I told him that some people started smoking before the dangers were widely known and some know the dangers but don't think about them." —Susan, mother of two, San Francisco, California

Last-minute Checkups before the Talk

Before you talk with your child, try to remember what, if anything, your parents taught you about tobacco when you were growing up.

- Did a parent ever talk to you about smoking tobacco?
- Did they ever talk to you about addiction to nicotine?
- Did they tell you how difficult it is to quit smoking?
- Did they use tobacco in a way that put you at risk for second-hand smoke?

As a parent, what are you teaching your child about nicotine?

- Do you encourage her to talk about smoking and the nicotine addiction that results?

- How do you let your child know that you welcome any concerns she may have about tobacco?
- Do you talk to your child about finding friends who are not addicted to nicotine?
- What behaviors do you model regarding tobacco use?

Do you have any stories that you can share with your child about tobacco use, or how you confronted someone who was abusing tobacco? For example:

- The time you tried your first cigarette
- The time you offered a cigarette to a non-smoker
- The time someone got ill as a result of smoking tobacco
- How you learned, if you smoke tobacco, to keep people free from secondhand smoke
- How you declined an offer to chew tobacco
- The time you felt worried by a family member's tobacco use

Sharing your stories lets your child know how you feel about tobacco use and what effect it had on you when you were growing up.

What Are Your Family Rules?

Do you have family rules about tobacco use, along with clear consequences for breaking them? If not, this may be a good time to think about what rules you could put in place.

The illustrated scenarios in the next section are meant to give you a chance to discuss your experience with tobacco, whether you define smoking as drug use, and how long-term use of tobacco can damage a person's health. The stories and questions are open-ended, allowing your child to reflect on a range of topics, including the things family members do to protect one another from secondhand smoke, peer pressure, and other concerns. Depending on your child, the talk could even include issues of mixed messages that come from the media or from family members.

THE TALK

Introduce the Talk

To start this talk you could say, "I want to show you something about smoking tobacco," or "I'm reading this chapter about addiction to nicotine and want your opinion."

Younger children are often happy to offer an opinion on the topic, especially if they've had classes on tobacco's dangers. Older kids, especially those with friends who smoke, may see this talk as just one more attempt to control their behavior. No matter what your child's age or willingness to talk, it's crucial that you clarify your family rules about tobacco use, the reasons you've put them in place, and the consequences for breaking them.

You could ask, "Why do you think people smoke, anyway?"

Be prepared for anything, from "'Cause it's fun," to "I don't know, it stinks," to "Ask Dad, he smokes!" A favorite conversation stopper used by kids is, "Did you ever smoke when you were a kid?" Or, if you smoke, "Why are you still smoking, since it causes cancer?" No matter what your child says, you can explain that smoking tobacco is a complicated issue and you will be happy to sit down and answer his questions.

"At our son's school, smoking tobacco automatically drops you from any sports team or from going on field trips."

—Pam, mother of two, Gaithersburg, Maryland

Review These Words

Please review the terms in this section. Discussing all the terms with your child is optional. You know which words are appropriate for your child's age and maturity level. More than likely, even the youngest children have heard these words on TV.

addiction: a physiological craving for nicotine, usually in the form of a cigarette or chewing tobacco.

long-term effects of tobacco use: Smoking and chewing tobacco causes lung cancer, heart disease, heart attacks, strokes, and emphysema, a debilitating lung disease. Of adults who smoke, fully 50 percent will die as a result of their tobacco use.

secondhand smoke, also called passive smoke: the smoke that comes off the end of a cigarette and is inhaled by people nearby. Secondhand smoke, because it has not passed through the cigarette's filter, is estimated to have twenty times more carcinogens than the smoke the user inhales. Children exposed to secondhand smoke over the long term may experience infections and lung problems.

Smokeless tobacco: chewing tobacco and snuff are used in the mouth. Health risks include increased likelihood of cancers of the mouth and esophagus, and gum disease.

withdrawal: the physical symptoms associated with abstaining from nicotine after regular use. Withdrawal of nicotine can cause acute cravings.

Why Is Talking about Tobacco and Nicotine Addiction Important?

Ask your child whether talking about tobacco use is important. Here are some reasons you might want to offer. Talking about tobacco use means:

- Learning the benefits of never smoking or chewing tobacco.
- Learning the hazards of addiction to nicotine, and ways people can quit.
- Learning ways a person who smokes can keep people safe from secondhand smoke.
- Clarifying family rules about tobacco use.
- Clarifying the school rules and the law about tobacco use.

The Stories

In the next part of the talk, you'll be reading short stories to your child and discussing them together. You don't have to read all of the stories. Pick the ones that you think are appropriate for your child. The stories are very simple. Feel free to embellish them, adding details that you think might make the story more believable.

A Story about Smoking at the Table

This story is an opportunity to talk about how common tobacco use is, and how different families feel about smoking in the house around others.

"A family is visiting their grandparents. A girl and boy watch their grandparents and dad prepare to smoke after a meal. The adults ask the children to leave the table before they light up."

Ask these questions of your child:

- What is the daughter thinking?
- What is the son thinking?
- What is the dad thinking?
- What are the grandparents thinking?

Now that your child has completed this scenario, ask the following questions:

- Do the kids want to smoke? Why or why not?
- Is the secondhand smoke dangerous for the kids? If so, how?
- Does the parent need to talk to the kids about responsible, adult use of tobacco?
- Does having the children leave the table keep them safe from secondhand smoke?
- How likely is it that parents who smoke will have kids who will eventually smoke?
- If you were the children in a situation like this, how would you feel? What would you do?

A Story about a TV Show

This story gives you a chance to talk about how common tobacco advertising is and how tobacco companies use different strategies to get people to smoke.

"A mom and daughter are watching a TV show. It's an action program and the hero and his girlfriend smoke. They are having a lot of fun."

Ask these questions of your child:

- What is the mom thinking?
- What is the mom saying?
- What is the daughter thinking?
- What is the daughter saying?

Now that your child has completed this scenario, ask the following questions:

- Do the mom or daughter want to smoke the cigarettes because of the TV show?
- Do people even notice tobacco use on TV shows or movies?
- Does smoking look fun or sexy?

A Story about Chewing Tobacco

This story is an opportunity to talk about long-term tobacco use and the serious health consequences that tobacco users can suffer.

"A boy is done with baseball practice, and his older friend offers him some chewing tobacco, saying, 'You should try this.'"

Ask these questions of your child:

- What is the boy thinking?
- What is the boy saying?
- What is the older boy thinking?
- What is the older boy saying?

Now that your child has completed this scenario, ask the following questions:

- Will the younger boy try chewing tobacco for the first time? Why or why not?
- Does the boy's knowledge of risk affect his decision? Why or why not?
- Do parents need to talk with their children about addiction or serious health problems?
- If you were the younger boy in a situation like this, how would you feel? What would you do?

A Story about a Girl and an Offer to Smoke

This story offers a chance to talk about the ways people can decline tobacco.

"A girl is at a party, and a guy she likes offers her a cigarette."

Ask these questions of your child:

- What is the girl thinking?
- What is the boy thinking?
- What is the girl saying?

Now that your child has completed this scenario, ask the following questions:

- Does the girl want to take the cigarette? Why or why not?
- What might happen if the girl smokes the cigarette?
- Do you think the girl feels any peer pressure to smoke?
- Should a parent talk to the girl about the health risks of being around people who are smoking tobacco?
- If you were the girl in a situation like this, how would you feel? What would you do?

Clarify Your Family's Values

Discuss these questions with your child as a way of sharing your values about tobacco use. We have included a number of potential responses from children to help you formulate your own responses.

Ask your child: "When a young person has a friend who wants to smoke or chew tobacco, what can the young person do?"

Child response #1: "I don't know."
Parent: Right. It's hard to know what to do. But tobacco is something for adults only, and most adults who smoke wish they'd never started.

Child response #2: "Well, one cigarette couldn't hurt."
Parent: That may sometimes be true. But the point is that one cigarette can lead to more. Most people do not have only one cigarette. The addictive qualities of nicotine should not be underestimated.

The Bare Minimum: A Quick Quiz for Kids

Ask your child the following questions to assess her knowledge and perceptions of tobacco use.

1. How does smoking or chewing tobacco affect a person's health?
Sample answers:
- Smoking or chewing tobacco causes cancer of the mouth and throat.
- Smoking causes life-threatening conditions such as heart disease.
- Smoking causes lung disease.

2. What are some ways people can quit using tobacco?
Sample answers:
- See a doctor.
- Get support from friends and family.
- Try a nicotine patch or chew nicotine gum designed to lower nicotine levels gradually.

Talk about Your Family Rules

This is an opportunity to review your family rules. Ask your child the following question:

1. What are our family rules about using tobacco products?
Sample answers:
- Adults may legally use tobacco, but at great risk to their health.
- People should never smoke around non-smokers, which would expose them to secondhand smoke.
- No one in this family breaks the law regarding the purchase of tobacco.

After the Talk

Take a moment to reflect on the talk you just had with your child. How do you feel about it?

- What surprised you about your child's view of tobacco use?
- Do you think she might, at some point, use tobacco?
- Does she seem susceptible to peer pressure or media influences?
- What lessons did you learn about how to listen to your child?

Warning Signs

This talk may reveal potential problems that your child is facing. Since teens can be very good at hiding their tobacco use, you will need to use your instinct. Review the following warning signs to see if your child might be using tobacco:

- Her clothes smell of tobacco.
- His fingers or teeth are yellowing.
- His friends smoke and he seems unconcerned.
- If tobacco is being used by someone in the family, is he interested in smoking, and unhappy when reminded to wait until he's an adult?

Success Stories

You have made it through the talk about tobacco. Congratulations! What did you learn about your child's relationship to tobacco? One mom in Maryland was shocked to learn that her daughter had tried smoking with friends—then relieved to hear that she'd felt so sick that she never wanted to try it again. A dad in New Mexico said that he'd suspected that his son was smoking outside the home. The son came clean and said he felt he was already addicted and was afraid to ask for help. His father helped him quit with the aid of a nicotine patch.

Talks about tobacco as a drug may be a strange concept to most families. And it may not be the way you chose to describe smoking or chewing tobacco. But talking about the health risks of drug use, legal or illegal, is a very complex issue. With this discussion, you laid the groundwork for future talks about all kinds of drugs and health issues.

Sample Talks

Between Parents and Children

If you are wondering how a talk based on this chapter might really sound, take a look at the following excerpts from real family talks.

Discussing the Story about Smoking at the Table

Participants: a dad and his fifteen-year-old son

> *Dad:* "A family is visiting the grandparents. A girl and boy watch their grandparents and dad prepare to smoke after a meal. The adults ask the children to leave the table before lighting up." What is the daughter thinking?
> *Son:* "Why?"
> *Dad:* You mean why do they have to leave the table?

Son: Yeah. And, "Why are they smoking anyway? It might mess them up."

Dad: That's what she's thinking? And what is the son thinking?

Son: Depends on how old the son is. If he's old enough, he might want to smoke, too.

Dad: Should he smoke?

Son: I don't know. You're the adult. You make all the rules!

Dad: What do you think about that?

Son: Well, I don't know. Is it okay with you if I smoke?

Dad: Well what if it were a friend of yours, someone who you knew from school who smokes? And they were visiting their grandparents. What would that boy say?

Son: He wouldn't say anything, not if he's smoking himself.

Dad: That's what I'm saying.

Son: Well, that's another situation!

Dad: Let's move on. What is the dad thinking?

Son: "I need a cig."

Dad: Do you think he's thinking about it at all?

Son: No, not really.

Dad: He could be a chain-smoker and not even think about it anymore. He just lights up. I used to smoke. I'm an ex-smoker. Have to admit that.

Son: Yeah, I know.

Dad: And at times, it was a habit, you just picked it up. I'm not sure I was thinking anything. But here, the dad must be thinking, because he asked the children to leave the table.

Son: He probably wants to get rid of it. He doesn't want them to get . . . he may be trying to stop. He doesn't want them to get secondhand smoke. He's more concerned for their well-being.

Dad: What is the mom thinking?

Son: "You're going to kill yourself."

Dad: Okay. Do the kids want to smoke?

Son: Maybe.

Dad: Why?

Son: They want to fit in. They want to be like their dad and their grandparents.

Dad: Are the kids at any health risk from the secondhand smoke?

Son: Yeah.

Dad: How?

Son: Same thing. It still gets in your lungs.

Dad: Does the parent need to talk to the kids about responsible, adult use of tobacco?

Son: I don't know what responsible use of tobacco is. It's legalized. The dad's got an addiction, is what he's got.

Dad: It's the same as a drug.

Son: It is a drug. Nicotine is a drug.

Dad: How likely is it that parents who smoke will have kids who will eventually smoke?

Son: I think it's a luck of the draw.

Dad: Well, it's very likely. It's pretty well proven that kids who come from smoking parents often will smoke.

Son: But you smoked.

Dad: If you were in a situation like this, how would you feel? What would you do?

Son: I'd go downstairs and play Nintendo.

Lessons Learned from This Sample Talk

This dad had an excellent conversation with a son who's some-what rebellious and smart-alecky and also very intuitive and smart when it comes to tobacco addiction. The dad may want to further explore the son's comment, "I don't know what respon-sible use of tobacco is. It's legalized." Does the son think that be-cause a drug is legal there might be less danger than from an illegal drug?

Discussing the Story about a TV Show

Participants: a mom and her twelve-year-old son

Mom: "A mom and son are watching a TV show. It's an action program and the hero and his girlfriend smoke. They are hav-ing a lot of fun." What is the mom thinking?

Son: She's thinking, "Oh man, I was trying to watch a nice movie with my son and look what they're doing. They're putting smoking on. They're showing drugs!"

Mom: And what is the son thinking?

Son: "Hey, I thought this was going to be a cool movie. Look, there's a high-paid star playing James Bond or there's Jackie Chan and look at them, they're smoking. They're getting paid more now just to advertise cigarettes."

Mom: Is that what the son's saying?

Son: He's like, "Hey Mom, change the channel. Let's watch something else. This is really stupid."

Mom: Do the mom or son want to smoke the cigarettes because of the TV show?

Son: I doubt it. It's TV. It's a movie. They may not even be real cigarettes. It won't make a big difference. It's more peer pressure that will do it rather than commercials and stuff.

Mom: Even if the guy's a hero and the girl is beautiful.

Son: They're using sex appeal and the bandwagon effect, because they're saying, "If you smoke, you'll be cool like me." And it shows a nice-looking lady smoking, saying, "I look good and I smoke. Don't you want to look good and smoke, too?"

Mom: Do people even notice tobacco use on TV shows or movies?

Son: I'd say 99 percent of what you watch has someone smoking in it; cigar, cigarette, drugs, whatever.

Mom: Does smoking look fun or sexy when you see it?

Son: It looks fun, but you know it's really not.

Mom: What would you think if you had a girlfriend who you thought was cool and sexy and then she lit up a cigarette?

Son: I'd be like, "Aw man, she smokes."

Mom: It would be a turn off?

Son: Definitely.

Lessons Learned from This Sample Talk

This son seems to have lots of knowledge about tobacco as well as an intuitive understanding of advertising and peer pressure. It was interesting that the son referred to tobacco as a drug. Future talks could further explore his views on the "bandwagon" effect when it comes to being influenced to take illegal drugs.

Discussing the Story about a Girl and an Offer to Smoke

Participants: a dad and his ten-year-old son and twelve-year-old daughter

Dad: "A girl is at a party and a guy she likes offers her a cigarette." What is the girl thinking?

Daughter: Me, personally, I think she's thinking that she may look pretty because a guy is offering her a cigarette. But if that were me, I wouldn't take that cigarette even if I liked the guy. I mean, cigarettes are bad for you and they can kill you, so you shouldn't just do that for a guy.

Dad: What is the boy thinking?

Son: Well, I think the boy is thinking he can get the girl to like him, because cigarettes are cool. Except, personally, I think that's just acting dumb.

Dad: What is the girl saying?

Daughter: She's just saying, "Oh, wow! For me?" You know, normal stuff like that. But she should be saying "Yuck, get that away from me. I don't smoke cigarettes, they're bad!"

Dad: Does the girl want to take the cigarette? Why or why not?

Daughter: In this story I think she would want to take the cigarettes because, first of all, if she were at that party, she wouldn't want to feel left out or not act cool. Or . . . she'd take it just because a guy she likes is giving it to her.

Dad: What might happen if the girl smokes the cigarette?

Daughter: Well, since I took a class on drugs, so I know some stuff about it . . . When she first takes it, she'll probably start coughing because she's not used to it. But then, if she starts taking it more and more, she'll get addicted to it, which can lead to lung cancer or even death.

Dad: How is this a situation of peer influence?

Daughter: Well, this is a good example because peer influence is mainly about when all your friends tell you to do something, like, "Oh, have this cigarette, everybody's trying it." But you shouldn't do it, you should do what you want, not what your friends want you to do.

Dad: If you were in a situation like this, how would you feel? What would you do?

Daughter: I wouldn't be taken in by peer influence. If the guy I liked offered me a cigarette, I'd tell him that I don't want it and walk away. But if my friends were around and they wanted me to do it, I'd tell them that I couldn't do it and I'd give them a good excuse. Even if they call me a chicken, I'm doing what's good for my health, not for their health.

Dad: This asks about why parents need to talk to their kids about the risks of smoking. Parents need to talk to their kids because smoking is not only a habit that makes you smell bad, and makes your fingers smell, and makes your clothes and hair smell, but it's also very bad for your health. From what I remember about the dangers of cigarette smoking, each cigarette takes about five minutes off of your life. Life is short enough without that. So I'd strongly discourage any young person from cigarette smoking. It doesn't make you any cooler, it's just unhealthy.

Lessons Learned from This Sample Talk

This dad seems to have had a good talk, and his daughter seems to understand the concept of peer influence. She sounded pretty confident that she could decline a cigarette offered by friends by making excuses. Future talks could focus on the concept of saving face and fitting in. The younger son did not talk a lot, common when two kids of different ages are put together. To bring out the younger child's perspectives, the dad can have a one-on-one talk with him.

Discussing the Story about Chewing Tobacco

Participants: a dad and his fifteen-year-old son

Dad: "A boy is done with baseball practice, and his older friend offers him some chewing tobacco, saying, 'You should try this.'" What is the boy thinking?

Son: "Sure, let me have some."

Dad: What is the older boy thinking?

Son: I don't know.

Dad: Why do you think he'd offer it to you?

Son: For fun, maybe. Maybe his friends made a bet they could get him to make the little kid chew tobacco. Or maybe he likes it and thinks he can get the little kid to like it, too. Maybe to make him feel more grown up.

Dad: Make him feel like he's one of the big guys. Will the younger boy accept his first chewing tobacco?

Son: I don't know. Maybe. Maybe he thinks it's just like chewing gum.

Dad: He thinks it's like chewing gum?

Son: Yeah, he might trust an older friend and know he won't give him anything bad. Even though he would!

Dad: Does the boy's knowledge of risk affect his decision?

Son: Yeah, if he knows it's something that's going to affect him he won't be as willing to try it. It might take some persuasion to get him to do it.

Dad: Why do parents need to talk with their children about addiction or serious health problems?

Son: So that the kids know what causes it and what not to take. So that kids know they shouldn't take chewing tobacco or smoke cigarettes, even if they're offered. You know the "Just say no" line.

Dad: So why wouldn't he do it?

Son: Cigarettes give you lung cancer, but chewing tobacco can do really bad stuff to you. It can give you cancer of the mouth and you could lose your jaw. We learned about that in health class. There was this guy who lost his entire lower jaw from right where his teeth are—just gone. He had no chin.

Dad: Your grandfather chewed tobacco. He chewed tobacco for quite a long time. He stopped a long time ago but he has no teeth. He lost them all because they rotted out of his mouth. If you were in a situation like this, how would you feel? If you were the younger child.

Son: I wouldn't take it.

Dad: What if you knew it was bad, and your older friend kept pushing you to take it?

Son: I would feel like, "Why are you doing this? I'm not going to take it, so what are you trying to do?"

Lessons Learned from This Sample Talk

This dad and son had a nice dialogue. It was a surprise to the son that his grandfather chewed tobacco and an important part of the conversation. The son seemed knowledgeable and even joked about the "just say no" philosophy. This talk was an excellent foundation for future talks about illegal drugs.

6

Changing Perceptions

Talking about Marijuana

I knew that my parents smoked pot—it was unspoken, but I just could tell that it was something they did once in a while. It seems strange, looking back, that we never once talked about it, since they must have known that I knew what was going on.
—Renee, mother of one, Gaithersburg, Maryland

I never smoked marijuana. I think there may be a whole dozen of us in the U.S. I have always been very clear with my son about other drugs, but I don't think I ever mentioned pot specifically, and surprise! I recently found out that he'd already tried it.
—Marcy, mother of three, Charleston, South Carolina

My parents told us not to drink and drive, but they never mentioned any drugs. When I was eighteen, I was at a party, and a friend gave me some "special" brownies to eat. I got very scared when I started feeling the effects of the pot. It was a strange, intense feeling of being sedated and foggy, and I was totally unprepared for the experience. —Jeff, father of two, Portland, Oregon

We decided to include a chapter that focuses on marijuana because, for many parents and their children, this was (and is) one of the first drugs, after alcohol, to be used experimentally. For many curious young people, marijuana is the first illegal drug that alters their perceptions, something that alcohol and nicotine also do.

Parents are divided on the issue of marijuana. Many parents we spoke to felt strongly that pot shouldn't be lumped in with stronger street drugs. One mom told us that comparing pot to heroin is like "comparing a light rain to a hurricane." Other parents felt quite the opposite, stating, "They are both illegal and unhealthy." The parents we spoke to had no problem calling marijuana a drug, unlike alcohol or tobacco. We feel that it is our job to present a range of values about marijuana use and its consequences. You can decide for yourself how you feel about the drug and how you want to talk to your child about it.

In the "Old Days"

"I remember when I was in high school watching a TV movie—about a daughter who smokes pot at a party. At one point she started hallucinating that the hot dog she was eating had the head of a boy. It was very disturbing."　　　—Jan, mother of one, Syracuse, New York

"I remember a movie in school that showed some guy smoking pot and then jumping off a cliff. That image scared the hell out of me for a while."　　　—John, father of two, Portland, Oregon

"As a kid I remember a black-and-white movie that showed some nice guy smoking pot for the first time, and a few hours later he's in an alley hitting some guy over the head with a board because he needed money for heroin. They taught us very clearly that pot leads directly to really dangerous drugs, and that's what kept me from smoking pot until I was in college."

—Paula, mother of two, Boise, Idaho

The marijuana-scare movies that many parents remember from their youth now seem overdramatic and cartoonish. But as you can see from the quotes above, their effects were real and very unfunny. People who were raised on the warning films uniformly say that the movies' dire consequences did not come close to reality. When those same people, as young adults, tried marijuana for themselves, the vast majority of them did not hallucinate, turn to heroin, or jump off cliffs. (Most of them just felt relaxed and sedated, effects that might have encouraged them to use pot to diminish their difficult feelings, much as people use alcohol or other drugs.) And many began to look skeptically at the anti-drug messages they'd been raised on. How could they ever begin to sort out the fact from the fiction?

Your children may be experiencing the same doubts about anti-drug messages. The best medicine for that is honesty. In this talk, be as honest as you feel comfortable being about your experiences with marijuana and other drugs.

> "My daughter asked me if I ever smoked pot. I said that when I was in college, I tried it. I really wanted to fit in. Looking back, I can see that it didn't really help me fit in or feel better."
>
> —Sue, mother of three, Syracuse, New York

The Reality Today

Talking about marijuana raises many daunting issues, and in the course of writing this book almost every person we interviewed knew of a person in their family who, at one time or another, used marijuana. Marijuana is a large part of some people's lives and a constant presence on many high school and college campuses. For many adults, having an occasional few puffs of marijuana, not unlike having a glass of wine or beer, is an enjoyable and relaxing social ritual. But for other people, marijuana may cause serious problems, both with their health and with the law. People who use marijuana too much are subject to similar emotional health problems as alcohol abusers. Daily pot smokers may be keeping themselves sedated, inhibiting their ability to see their situation clearly and live fully.

> "I have a friend who has been smoking pot every day for years now. She is a talented person but is stuck in a dead-end life and frustrated by her situation. She doesn't seem to be able to motivate herself to make any changes."
>
> —Tom, father of two, New York City

Marijuana is so readily available, and its use so widespread, that it's unlikely that you can shield your children from it forever. Will your kids try pot? Might they use it to escape from difficult issues or tough feelings? Will pot lead to a relaxed attitude toward drugs in general and lead them to experiment with other, more harmful substances? Your family talks need to address the widespread use and availability of marijuana and any concerns you may have about its use and misuse.

In this chapter we will help you discuss with your child how feelings are changed by using marijuana. This chapter is also designed to help you clarify your concerns about the illegality of marijuana, and to help you decide whether to include some kinds of pot-smoking in your definition of drug misuse.

Preparing for the Talk

This talk will give you the chance to talk to your children about marijuana, about why people use it, and its potential for abuse. It also will help you explain its short- and long-term effects on our abilities to experience our feelings.

In this talk you will help your child understand that

- marijuana changes our mental abilities, body coordination, and feelings.
- the use of marijuana does not excuse harmful behavior.
- there are family rules about the use of marijuana.
- there are laws against growing, buying, and smoking marijuana.

What You Can Expect from This Talk

After the talk your child will be able to:

- define "marijuana."
- understand how the entire family can be affected when a family member is using marijuana.
- understand family rules and the law about marijuana use and possession.

How Do You Define Marijuana Abuse?

People's viewpoints on marijuana differ based on their experiences. Some parents have never used marijuana, support the laws against it, and consider its use unwise and unhealthy for people of all ages. Other parents remember their own youthful experimentation with marijuana, see it as a natural phase in life, and are reluctant to call occasional adult use "abuse." We've found that regardless of their past, most parents would prefer that their child not be using marijuana. The fact is that marijuana is illegal and the consequences for possession can be severe.

"I want to be open with my kids and have good conversations about drugs. My older sons have pointed out news stories about marijuana use being debated among doctors, lawyers, and law enforcement officials. But I have to make it clear, even though some drug use is debated, that the law is still the law."
—Tad, father of three, Seattle, Washington

"Even those of us who advocate decriminalizing marijuana use admit that there is the potential for marijuana abuse. I told my kids that its constant use can produce a lack of interest in dealing with problems."
—Phil, father of three, El Paso, Texas

"I'm not sure about how to talk about my college years and my experience with marijuana. I'm just not ready to talk about it with my son."
—Emma, mother of two, Columbia, South Carolina

"I told my daughter that I tried pot once at a party when I was in my twenties and that it was not a good experience. Of course, drinking wasn't so great, either! And I made it clear that my hope was that she would follow the law and not get herself into trouble."
—Sandy, mother of two, Orlando, Florida

This chapter will help you answer a number of questions, including, How does a parent discuss the law and family rules about marijuana use? Does your family consider pot-smoking normal or as dangerous as using any other street drug? Conduct guidelines become more and more important as children get older and begin to interact with peers who have their own beliefs about marijuana use. Starting when children are in elementary school, parents can help children understand their family values about pot, and the emotional, physical, and legal consequences associated with its use.

Influence of the Media

Marijuana has been showing up in the media with increasing frequency. Sitcom characters make winking references to it; one popular show even has its teenage characters sitting in a smoky haze and having the kind of absurd conversation that only marijuana can produce. Movies pitched at young people feature marijuana smoking as something ordinary and uncontroversial. Rock and rap songs mention pot all the time, and many of the musicians openly advocate its legalization. Whatever messages about marijuana you want to pass along to your kids will have to compete with those.

How can you even begin to get another message across? When watching TV with your child, if marijuana is mentioned, use that "teachable moment" to ask questions and to communicate your views and concerns.

> "First, I screened the video rentals and movies for sex, then for violence. Now I have to see what kinds of drugs are promoted. The ratings don't always help when it comes to knowing what drugs are being promoted in a video."   —Amy, mother of one, New York City

Is Marijuana a Gateway Drug?

Anti-drug campaigns often refer to marijuana as a gateway drug, implying that if you smoke pot you're likely to move on to other, more damaging drugs like cocaine, LSD, or heroin. Many parents who smoked pot when they were younger and did not try other drugs now find it hard to take that message seriously. But it's not hard to find people who say that they started their experimentation by drinking alcohol, then using marijuana and went on to use a wide variety of other drugs. It's not frivolous to ask whether marijuana might be a gateway drug for some people.

Think about your experiences and those of your friends. Can you envision your child using marijuana and wondering about other drugs? Does it seem logical to assume that since marijuana alters a person's perceptions it might lead to a natural curiosity about other drugs that do the same?

"My son would agree that marijuana could be a gateway drug—once you try it, like it, and get away with it, you could really be tempted to try other things. He also thinks alcohol and cigarettes can do the same thing."　　　　—Carrie, mother of two, Columbia, South Carolina

Quotes to Consider

"Hanging around users of marijuana often means being exposed not only to other drugs later on, but also to a lifestyle that can include trouble in school, engaging in sexual activity while young, unintended pregnancy, difficulties with the law, and other problems."
—Parents, the Anti-Drug, "Why You Shouldn't Allow Your Children To Smoke Marijuana," www.theantidrug.com

"In 1998, the Monitoring the Future Study reported that 54% of all high school seniors said they had at least tried illicit drugs. Marijuana was by far the most commonly used illicit drug; in 1998, 49% of seniors said they had tried marijuana. About half of those who said they used marijuana, or 25% of seniors, said they had not used any other illicit drug."
—U.S. Department of Justice, "Juvenile Offenders and Victims," 1999

"When polled, the number of parents who thought their children had tried marijuana, about 20%, represented only half the number of parents whose teens had actually tried it."
—"Growing Up Drug-Free: A Parent's Guide to Prevention," 1998

"In 1997 there were 5 million current users of marijuana—by far the most commonly used illegal drug—but 33 million people had used marijuana at some point in their lives."
—Theodore Caplow, Louis Hicks, and Ben J. Wattenberg, *The First Measured Century: An Illustrated Guide to Trends in America, 1900–2000*

Other Views

In terms of health risk, how does marijuana compare to cigarettes? The data is interesting. Evidence shows that marijuana cannot compare to tobacco in terms of health consequences. While 460,000 people die every year from smoking cigarettes, only a tiny handful of deaths are directly attributable to marijuana. Research on marijuana's long-term effects continues.

Smoking marijuana does deliver tar and many other harmful chemicals to the lungs and respiratory system, and regular smoking will undoubtedly harm the smoker's health. Unlike tobacco, however, marijuana lacks nicotine. That means that marijuana is not chemically addictive, and there is no known withdrawal syndrome in people who stop smoking it. Users who report feeling addicted are actually suffering from psychological dependence, the feeling that they need to smoke pot to help regulate their feelings.

Some politicians, doctors, and a variety of citizen's groups are calling for marijuana to be legalized. And researchers have discovered some limited medical uses for the drug, including reducing nausea and stimulating appetite, effects often beneficial for cancer patients and others.

As with all drugs, it's hard to separate marijuana's health risk from its social meanings and legal status. It could be said that the health risk of being arrested and jailed for marijuana use is far greater than that which stems from the drug itself.

"At age ten, my daughter found a small bag of pot in my bedroom and said, 'Mom, what are these leaves? You have drugs!' I was horrified. I wasn't prepared to be caught and had no idea what to say. In the end, I couldn't lie to my child, so I said, 'Yes, that is marijuana. It is bad for young people.' My daughter said, 'But Mom, you could be arrested!'"   —Lisa, mother of one, New York City

"Giving a child mixed messages about any drug is not a good thing. You can't have it both ways. I want my children to deal with their problems and not run away from them by using drugs, so I don't use them, either. My kids look up to me as a role model."
                                        —Tracy, mother of two, Dunkirk, New York

Marijuana and the Law

Different countries, states, and counties have different laws regarding the sale and use of marijuana. In the United States, marijuana is classified as a Schedule I drug (that is, among the most threatening) by the Drug Enforcement Administration. This assignment is made for drugs which have, according to the government

- a high potential for abuse.
- no accepted medical use in the United States.
- no safe use even under medical supervision.

This puts marijuana in the same category as heroin and methamphetamines. Do you agree with this assessment? Some people would knock marijuana down to Schedule 5, along with Tylenol with codeine, because of its low addiction potential and increasing use in medicine. Others see no reason to change the law. No matter what your opinion is, it's important that you tell your kids about the penalties for marijuana possession where you live.

> "When I talk with students about the consequences of using marijuana I discuss the legal consequences for possession, about how the long-term health effects are still not known, and how one's judgment is impaired, leading to potentially dangerous situations."
> —Deputy Sheriff James Quattrone, Chautauqua County, New York

About Language

How we describe marijuana says a lot about its widespread and accepted use in some circles. Some of today's generation of parents refer to smoking marijuana as "getting high" rather than "doing a drug."

Explaining drug use to children means taking a critical look at how we perceive all drug use, legal and illegal. This means looking critically at how we talk about marijuana as a drug. The words we use can stigmatize or glamorize a behavior. As you discuss marijuana use, try to be aware of your language. We know that kids are very sensitive to mixed messages about drug use and will question you about the differences between marijuana use and other illegal drug use.

Different Families: Different Values

Everyone interprets behavior in his or her own way. Here are some behaviors that may be experienced differently, depending on a person's background:

A mom is doing the family laundry. She's making sure all the pockets are empty, when she finds the end of a joint in the pocket of her son's jeans.

Has something like this ever happened to you? Some parents would say that it's perfectly normal for kids to experiment with marijuana, and that it was only a matter of time before they'd have to talk with their kids and let them know the law and family rules. Other parents would see this as a sign that their son was abusing drugs, perhaps including harder drugs, and would look for professional help to deal with the situation. Some parents would advocate severe consequences for their child's having marijuana, while others would not. What would you do?

■

A dad is feeling stress at work and comes home late. He goes into his bedroom to relax, and thinks about having a beer, taking a run, or smoking some marijuana.

Some parents would see nothing wrong with smoking some marijuana to relax, while others would prefer alcohol. Others find physical activity a good way to unwind from a stressful day. Some parents might just need to talk with someone about their stress, rather than use marijuana. What do you think the dad should do?

■

A boy is having a hard time making friends in his new school. He meets a nice girl in art class who invites him to sit with her and her friends at lunch. At lunch the friends all seem like nice people, but the boy can tell that they have been smoking marijuana.

Some parents would hope that if their child found a group of "new friends" who were using marijuana, he would have the good sense to find other people to hang out with. Other parents would think that having new friends, whether they smoke marijuana or not, should be a priority for a son who's just switched schools. Some parents have strict rules about the kinds of friends their children can have, while others do not. What would you say?

■

A teenage girl is at a party with her boyfriend. He asks her if she wants to smoke a joint.

Some parents assume that their kids can refuse marijuana and resist peer influence. Others know that the pressures young people face are intense, and that parties are a place where kids are exposed to a variety of drugs, including marijuana and alcohol. Those families might have rules about which parties their kids can go to. Some parents assume their kids know the family rules, even the unspoken ones. What would you like your son or daughter to do in this situation?

Different Perspectives

"My parents told us not to do drugs, but I knew they were smoking marijuana. They didn't think that I knew what it was."

—Tina, mother of two, Miami, Florida

"When my daughter asked, I tried to be honest and told her I used pot in college, but I also think times have changed and so has the pot. We talked about how pot is part of a whole business that is illegal. I tried to tell her that my greater concern is that when you smoke pot you don't think clearly, and in that kind of situation any kind of danger is possible."   —Peter, father of four, Sels, Arizona

Last-minute Checkups before the Talk

Before you talk with your child, try to remember what, if anything, your parents taught you about marijuana when you were growing up.

- Did a parent ever talk to you about marijuana?
- Did they tell you how to identify marijuana?
- Did they model healthy coping skills to deal with stress without using marijuana?

As a parent, what are you teaching your child about marijuana?

- Do you encourage her to talk about any marijuana use she might see?
- How do you let your child know that you welcome discussions of any concerns she has about marijuana?
- Do you talk to your child about finding friends who don't use marijuana?
- Do you model the ability to deal with stress without using marijuana?

Do you have any stories you can share with your child about marijuana use, or how you confronted someone who was misusing pot? For example:

- The time you had some marijuana and felt paranoid or unsettled
- The time you felt worried by a friend's marijuana use

Sharing your stories lets your child know how you feel about marijuana use and what impact it had on you when you were growing up.

What Are Your Family Rules?

Do you have family rules about marijuana use, along with clear consequences for breaking the rules? If not, this is a good time to think about them.

The illustrated scenarios in the next section are meant to give you a chance to discuss your experience with marijuana, your definition of drug use, and how marijuana can impact people as powerfully as any drug. The stories and questions are open-ended, allowing your child to reflect on a range of topics, including the things people do to relieve stress; what parents do to try to protect loved ones from harm and peer pressure; and any other concerns you or your child may have. Depending on your child, the talk may include issues of mixed messages that come from TV or even from other family members. Discussing these situations will give you an opportunity to share your family rules about using marijuana, as well as your views on the law and acceptable behavior.

The Talk

Introduce the Talk

To start this talk you could say, "I'm on the chapter about marijuana. Can I ask your opinion?" (If you have shown your child this book's cover, which we recommend you do, he knows this question is coming.)

Again, younger children may be more willing to talk, while older children, who may already be witnessing marijuana use among friends, may feel more defensive. Teenagers may be more comfortable talking about the "other kids" who use it, and may criticize this chapter's stories as dumb or unrealistic. This reaction is fine. It gives you the chance to ask, "What situations regarding marijuana use are realistic—and what needs to be talked about?

If your child is willing to talk, you can ask, "Do you know what marijuana does to a person?" He might respond with "Yeah, it makes people act funny," or, "I know that Uncle Lou gets high." A favorite conversation stopper used by kids is, "Did you ever smoke it when you were a kid?" It's a good idea to have thought out your answer to that one in advance.

Review These Words

Please review the terms in this section. Discussing all the terms with your child is optional. You know which are appropriate for your child's age and maturity level. More than likely, even the youngest children have come into contact with these words and ideas through TV and movies.

effects of marijuana use: sedation, euphoria, lack of motivation, impaired judgment and coordination; some users experience occasional anxiety and paranoia.

controlled substance: an illegal drug whose sellers and users are targeted for arrest.

Drug Enforcement Administration (DEA): the U.S. government's drug enforcement arm, part of the Department of Justice.

feelings: internal sensations that regulate our choices and behaviors. Stress, anger, sadness, and fear are some feelings that may be difficult to experience and may serve as catalysts for marijuana use.

hashish (hash): a drug with a concentrated form of the active ingredient in marijuana.

law (regarding marijuana use): marijuana is classified as a Schedule 1 substance by the DEA, which puts it with the most harmful drugs known, including LSD and heroin.

medical marijuana: use of marijuana for medical purposes, including treating of wasting syndrome for those living with

AIDS and cancer, due to the effect of reducing nausea and stimulating appetite.

sedative: a drug that decreases brain activity, making the user feel calm or sleepy. Marijuana has sedative properties.

tetrahydrocannabinol (THC): the active ingredient in marijuana.

How Marijuana Alters a Person's Perceptions

It is hard to describe what using marijuana feels like to people who haven't tried it. As with any drug, the effect is tied to the setting in which it is used. A person smoking marijuana alone may have a different experience from a person smoking marijuana with a group of people. The experience is also affected by a person's state of mind and brain chemistry. For some, marijuana causes shifts in perception that seem mildly hallucinogenic. For others, a feeling of relaxation is the main effect. For others still, a feeling of paranoia sometimes sets in.

So, How Are We Feeling Today?

Talks about drugs can get lost in the abstract. And some talks about drugs tend to focus on danger and health risks—important topics, but not the only issues to raise. It's vital that parents and kids talk not only about what a particular drug does to one's feelings, but *why* a person would want to change their feelings by using the drug in the first place.

Consider the following questions:

- How are you feeling today, right now?
- What are your biggest stresses?

- How is your child feeling today?
- What do you think your child's biggest stresses are?
- What does your child say her biggest stresses are?
- How can people–young and old—deal with stresses like that without turning to drugs?

Why Is Talking about Marijuana Important?

Ask your child whether she thinks talking about marijuana use is important. Here are some reasons you might want to offer. Talking about marijuana means:

- Learning ways to deal with stress without using marijuana.
- Learning to identify potential marijuana abuse in others or oneself.
- Clarifying family rules and beliefs about marijuana use.
- Clarifying the school rules and the law about marijuana use.
- Learning how marijuana use could increase other risks, such as vehicle accidents, bad social judgments, and dangerous situations like date rape.

The Stories

In the next part of the talk, you'll be reading short stories to your child and discussing them together. You don't have to read all of the stories. Pick the ones that you think are appropriate for your child. The stories are very simple. Feel free to embellish them, adding details that you think might make the story more realistic for your child.

A Story about Dealing with Stress

This story is an opportunity to talk about how common stress is, and how people can deal with stress in a variety of ways including running, talking with friends, seeing a counselor, or using marijuana. This talk can highlight our chance to make healthy choices rather than unhealthy ones.

"A boy is feeling overwhelmed with schoolwork and money problems. He can't decide how to deal with his stress: to take a run with one friend or go with his other friends to smoke some marijuana."

Ask these questions of your child:

- What is the boy thinking?

Now that your child has completed this scenario, ask the following questions:

- Does the boy want to have some marijuana? Why or why not?
- Why would the boy think that smoking marijuana will help relieve his stress?
- What can the boy do to deal with stress about schoolwork and money?
- How could a good run help deal with stressful feelings?
- People use marijuana for reasons other than stress. What might they be? Boredom? Curiosity?

- If you were in a situation like this, how would you feel? What would you do?

A Story about a Movie

This story gives you a chance to talk about how marijuana use is shown in movies and on TV.

"A family is watching a movie on TV when a scene shows a bunch of young people smoking marijuana at a fun party."

Ask these questions of your child:

- What is the mom thinking?
- What is the mom saying?
- What is the daughter thinking?
- What is the son thinking?

Now that your child has completed this scenario, ask the following questions:

- Does anyone in the family want to talk about marijuana after seeing people smoke it in the movie? Why or why not?
- How is marijuana use shown in movies and on TV?
- In movies and on TV, why do people smoke marijuana?
- Does the parent need to talk to the kids about marijuana use and the law?

- Does knowing what's healthy mean you will choose the healthier option? Why or why not?
- What things would parents need to say to their children to let them know they care about them and don't want them misusing drugs?
- If you were in a situation like this, how would you feel? What would you do?

A Story about a Dad and His Daughter

This story is an opportunity to talk about how marijuana use can become frequent, how people cope when a family member has a problem, and how to discuss difficult family situations.

"A girl whose parents are divorced spends her weekends with her dad. When she arrives at his house on Friday night, she can smell marijuana smoke, something she now smells every weekend. Her dad seems sedated and less interested in doing anything with her outside the house."

Ask these questions of your child:

- What is the dad thinking?
- What is the dad saying?
- What is the daughter thinking?
- What is the daughter saying?

Now that your child has completed this scenario, ask the following questions:

- How does the daughter feel discussing the dad's marijuana use, and the reasons for it, with her dad?
- Is the dad open to talking about his marijuana use?
- Would the daughter feel comfortable discussing the situation with her mother? Why or why not?
- Could there be any connection between her dad's lack of energy and his drug use?
- Does the mom need to talk to the daughter about marijuana use and the law?
- Who could the girl talk to if she couldn't talk with her mom or dad?
- If you were the daughter in a situation like this, how would you feel? What would you do?

A Story about a Boyfriend

This story is an opportunity to talk about the way marijuana can change a person's feelings, the power of peer influence, and the importance of setting personal boundaries with friends.

"A girl is with her boyfriend, and he offers her some marijuana before they go to a party."

Ask these questions of your child:

- What is the girl thinking?
- What is the boy thinking?
- What is the girl saying?
- What is the boy saying?

Now that your child has completed this scenario, ask the following questions:

- Does the girl want to smoke marijuana? Why or why not?
- If she doesn't smoke the marijuana, how might it affect her relationship?
- Does the girl want to ask her boyfriend not to smoke marijuana?
- What is the girl feeling?
- What is the boy feeling?
- What might happen if the girl says, "No"?
- What might happen if the girl says, "Yes"?
- How is this situation different from being offered alcohol?
- Does the parent need to talk to the daughter about marijuana use, the law, and the consequences of being around people who use marijuana?
- Have you ever been in a situation like this? If so, how did you feel? What did you do?

Clarify Your Family's Values

Discuss these questions with your child as a way of sharing your values about marijuana use. We have included a number of potential responses from children to help you formulate your own responses.

Ask your child: "When a young person has a friend who wants to smoke marijuana, what can the young person do?"

Child response #1: "I don't know."

Parent: Right. It's hard to know what to do. It is not a secret that people smoke marijuana. And people do it for a lot of reasons. One of the biggest reasons is stress. But it could also be boredom or curiosity. And in this family we think it is important to learn how to deal with stress without using drugs, whether it's marijuana, alcohol, or anything else. That's why we have family rules about not smoking marijuana.

Child response #2: "Well, one puff couldn't hurt."

Parent: That may be true sometimes. But the point is that when a person is growing up, they need to be 100 percent clear-headed and able to deal with life's challenges with clarity. It's also illegal. We obey the law because it's designed to keep people safe from harm.

The Bare Minimum: A Quick Quiz for Kids

Ask your child the following questions to assess her knowledge and perceptions of marijuana use.

1. How does smoking marijuana affect a person?
   Sample answers:
   • It might relieve stress for a short period.

- It might make a person feel paranoid or worried.
- It might make a person depressed.
- It might make a person feel less inhibited.
- It might affect someone's ability to drive safely.
- It could make a young person feel more grown up.

2. Can you give me a reason why young people should not smoke marijuana?
   Sample answers:
- It's illegal.
- Marijuana can make you less clearheaded and more vulnerable to making unhealthy or unsafe choices.
- Marijuana, like alcohol, takes away stressful feelings in the short term, but learning to deal with stress is very important as a teen (and an adult).
- The long-term effects are still unknown, so there may be health dangers.

3. How can marijuana be harmful to a person and the person's family?
   Sample answers:
- Marijuana possession is illegal, meaning someone who's using it can go to jail, and that affects the person and the entire family.
- If an adult uses it, they send mixed messages to their kids about not doing drugs.

Talk about Your Family Rules

This is an opportunity to review your family rules. Ask your child the following question:

1. What are our family rules about using marijuana?
   Sample answers:
- No one in this family breaks the law regarding marijuana use.
- Marijuana is never to be used as a substitute for working through unwanted feelings or communicating with other members of the family. This goes for the adults as well as the children.

After the Talk

Take a moment to reflect on the talk you just had with your child. How do you feel about it?

- What surprised you about your child's view of marijuana use?
- Do you think she may, at some point, use marijuana to deal with stress or boredom?
- Does she seem susceptible to peer pressure to smoke pot?
- Do you think your child has the ability to deal with everyday stresses that accompany childhood and adolescence without turning to pot?
- What lessons did you learn about how to listen to your child?

Warning Signs

This talk can reveal problems that your child may be facing. Since teens can be very good at hiding their problems related to stress or marijuana, you will need to check in with them often. Above all, use your instincts about how your child is doing. They're probably right. Review the following warning signs to see if your child might be using marijuana:

- He doesn't appear to care about school or friends or other enjoyable activities; at home he is listless and unfocused.
- He and his friends have red eyes, act silly or paranoid, and smell like smoke.
- His grades take a dramatic turn downward.
- She makes jokes about "getting high."
- She becomes less communicative with members of the family and seems withdrawn.
- He avoids interacting with family members when he comes home.

Success Stories

You have made it through the talk about marijuana. The talk about marijuana can raise very important issues. One mom in South Carolina reported the following:

"As a result of my talk with my teenage son I discovered that he has indeed tried marijuana. He knows how I feel about it, but he saw it as a low-risk drug and just wanted to see what it was like. He had never seen anyone harmed by it and the information he had read indicated that it probably wouldn't hurt him. He says it's everywhere in our town, very easy to get. During our talk we weighed the risks and his perceived benefits. This included being a part of the in crowd and having a pleasant, uninhibited feeling. He said it wasn't all that great and decided it's not worth the risk of jail."

This mom made a huge discovery during her talk. But whatever you found out, you have reinforced the idea that your home is a safe place to talk, even about controversial topics. You've introduced the idea that it's healthy and normal to have conversations about problems and stresses in the family. And your talk set a stronger foundation for further dialogue about street drugs.

Sample Talks

Between Parents and Children

If you are wondering how a real talk based on this chapter might really sound, take a look at the following excerpts from real family talks.

Discussing the Story about Dealing with Stress

Participants: a mother and her fourteen-year-old daughter

Mom: Here's our first story. "A guy is feeling overwhelmed with work and money problems. He can't decide how to deal with his stress. 'Should I take a run or go home to smoke some marijuana?'" What is the guy thinking?

Daughter: "Do I want to smoke some marijuana or take a run?"

Mom: Does the guy want to smoke some marijuana?

Daughter: No. He's stressed out.

Mom: Okay, why?

Daughter: I don't know why.

Mom: Let's see if we aren't given that information. The story mentions "work and money problems." Does smoking marijuana help relieve stress?

Daughter: No. Well, maybe for an hour. It might give him some nice thoughts. I don't know.

Mom: That's interesting, because the next question is, "What about in the short term and long term?" You answered that. Next is, "What can the guy do to deal with his feelings of stress concerning work and money?"

Daughter: He could get a better job that pays more money. He could spend less money. If he's thinking of using marijuana, then he's spent money on marijuana, so if he cut that out of his daily life he'd save money there.

Mom: Wow, good thinking. If you were in a situation like this, how would you feel?

Daughter: Well, I'd be stressed out, because they say he's stressed out. I would feel alone in the world.

Mom: What do you think about this talk?

Daughter: I think this talk is fun.

Mom: Anything to add?

Daughter: I think you should go into detail about how you should deal with stress.

Mom: Ah, interesting. How would you deal with the stress?

Daughter: Well, I'd eat and then I'd feel gross. Then I'd eat some more.

Mom: Would that be a good way of dealing with it?

Daughter: No, not really. Well, I'd probably play the piano or practice yoga. But you know there's stress foods, like when you make a bowl of soup? That's a good stress food because it takes time to make soup. And while you're making the soup you figure out how you're going to deal with everything.

Mom: Interesting.

Daughter: Or like hot chocolate. Those are good stress foods.

Mom: Anything else about this talk you want to add?

217

Daughter: Talk about other drugs. Marijuana may be this guy's drug of choice, but there's other drugs he might use.

Mom: What other drugs?

Daughter: Uh, a mixture.

Mom: Such as?

Daughter: Well, that Pokemon drug, the one with the Pokemon on it. That's a drug. Or crack. Or a lot of kids like ecstasy.

Mom: How do you know they like that?

Daughter: Because I hear them talking about it in the hall.

Mom: How do you feel about that?

Daughter: I really don't care. They're going to do what they do.

Lesson Learned from This Sample Talk

This is a perfect example of what kinds of important information can come from a talk and how it sometimes takes a little patience to gain significant insight. The mom found out that her daughter is around people at school (they may be doing more than "talking in the hall") who are using a "mixture" of drugs—including crack and ecstasy. This came as a big surprise to this mother. She followed it up with more questions about how long the daughter had been hearing "stuff" like that in the halls at school. The good news is that her daughter was willing to talk about it. But until this talk, the daughter had not revealed anything about drugs. For this mom and daughter, this was the beginning of many talks about the availability of drugs and the power of peer pressure.

Discussing the Story about a Movie

Participants: a mother and her fourteen-year-old daughter

Mom: "A family is watching a movie on TV, when a scene shows a bunch of young people smoking marijuana at a fun party." What is the mom thinking?

Daughter: Well, if it's my mom, she'd be crossing her legs and looking embarrassed. She'd say, "I don't think they should show this on public television," and she'd switch the channel to animals or something.

Mom: That might be what I'd say. What is the daughter thinking?

Daughter: That this is a good movie. It's not like I'm ever going to do drugs. It's interesting.

Mom: What is the son thinking?

Daughter: He thinks, "Gee, I hope my skates are still in the garage. I wonder if it's cold? Hmm, why don't we have a skating rink around here?"

Mom: [laughs] So he's not really thinking about the movie? Do you think family members talk about marijuana use after seeing it on the movie?

Daughter: Yes.

Mom: Why?

Daughter: Because it bothers the parents.

Mom: Does it bother the kids?

Daughter: No.

Mom: Why not?

Daughter: Because it's in our everyday life. People at school talk about it all the time. There are kids lined up outside of school smoking.

Mom: Huh! All right. How is marijuana use and its effects in real life different from what is shown in movies and on TV?

Daughter: I wouldn't know, because I've never been involved with marijuana.

Mom: Well, from your experience of hearing people talk about it.

Daughter: It sounds like fun.

Mom: [nervous laugh]

Daughter: I'm joking. I think it's fun for two hours and then it's not fun.

Mom: All right. Back to the question, "How is marijuana use and its effect in real life different than what is shown in movies and on TV?" On TV does it look like fun?

Daughter: Yeah, if it shows them having fun.

Mom: So what is different in real life?

Daughter: I think they are playing up the peer pressure thing too much. I don't think it's really peer pressure. I think it's just kids who want to do it, so they do it. They aren't going around saying, "Do it, do it, do it!" It's just kids who want to do it.

Mom: Why do people smoke marijuana in the movies?

Daughter: I don't know. Maybe they're just trying to make a movie to reach out to some teens, so they'll get a wider range of teens coming to see the movie. They do show the negative effects, too, so kids say, "I don't want that to be me."

Mom: Why does the parent need to talk to the kids about marijuana use and the law?

Daughter: I think they really don't. I think the kids know more than the parents do.

Mom: More about what?

Daughter: More about marijuana use.

Mom: Do you think the kids need to know consequences?

Daughter: That's not going to stop them! At parties they have all the windows open and they have people watching at every corner of the house! If someone's coming, they know.

Mom: And how do you know this?

Daughter: People tell me. Like at lunchtime.

Mom: Hmm. What things would a parent need to say to their child to let them know that they care about them and don't want them to misuse any drugs?

Daughter: They can tell their child, "You are a wonderful child and I love you very much."

Mom: How often?

Daughter: Not too often. So it's not a ploy. And kids should be informed by their parents but it's their decision, not their parents'. If you're a good household, a good family, that does determine whether the kid will try drugs.

Mom: What's a good household?

Daughter: A loving one. Some people that are there for them. Both parents can go to work—but as long as they come home and spend time with their children.

Mom: If you were in a situation like this, how would you feel?

Daughter: First of all, I wouldn't be with a bunch of kids smoking marijuana, because my mother would call the parents of the people having the party to make certain I wouldn't be smoking marijuana. So I wouldn't be there. You don't want to hang around people like that. They are just losers.

Mom: Anything else you want to add to this?

Daughter: You know what? People say that marijuana and drug use is this huge problem in our society today. But I don't think it's that prevalent, unless you really look at the bad kids in school. Most of the kids at school don't do it, or very seldom do it. Only a few, a small percent at my high school do. I don't think we should look at the negative aspects. I think we should look at those kids who excel at academics and are well rounded and focus on the positive.

Mom: Interesting.

Lessons Learned from This Sample Talk

As you might have guessed, this was an eye-opening talk for the mother. Until this talk, she had no idea her daughter was exposed to peers smoking marijuana. The daughter was very forthcoming about her attitudes and values on a range of issues, from peer pressure to parenting. It is significant that the daughter doesn't see drug use as a problem, but mentions many instances at school where kids are involved in drugs. The mother and daughter are able to communicate well, and future talks can check in on the daughter's interest, or lack of it, in drugs. The mother could even initiate a talk, revolving around a hypothetical party where marijuana is being used, about family rules and the law.

Discussing the Story about a Dad and His Daughter

Participants: a mother and her fifteen-year-old daughter

Mom: "A girl whose parents are divorced spends her weekends with her dad. When she arrives on Friday night, she finds her dad has been smoking marijuana. Lately he doesn't seem to want to do anything together." What is the dad thinking?

Daughter: Maybe he just wants to get away from things. I don't know. He's not setting a good example for his children.

Mom: What is the daughter thinking?

Daughter: If I were her I'd be freaked out that my dad was smoking, because you always look up to them as an idol and role model. And everything you've been taught, everything they taught you, has been destroyed because he's doing it himself. I'd probably say something to my dad about it.

Mom: What would you say?

Daughter: "What are you doing? You're ruining your life! You're going to ruin mine." He doesn't even want to spend any more time with her.

Mom: How does the daughter feel, discussing her dad's marijuana use with her dad? Would she feel comfortable talking with him?

Daughter: Probably not too comfortable, but it's necessary if they want to have a relationship. If not, she'd just block him out of her life.

Mom: Do you think there could be any connection between the dad's lack of interest in her and his marijuana use?

Daughter: Yeah. He probably wants to just smoke marijuana because he's addicted. And he doesn't want to spend any time with her.

Mom: If you were in a situation like this how would you feel? What would you do?

Daughter: I would definitely be scared for my father and myself. I'd probably confront him about it, and if he didn't want to talk about it, I'd go to my mom and tell her what happened.

Lessons Learned from This Sample Talk

In this talk, the daughter tells her mom that the example a parent makes is much more powerful than anything the parent might say. The daughter also says she would confront a parent if she thought he was engaging in destructive behavior. This might be a good time to talk more about the reasons why the father has chosen to start smoking marijuana and why he has let his daughter become aware of his smoking. The mother could ask where the daughter heard that marijuana is addictive; addiction to pot is psychological, not chemical. The daughter seems very open to communication. Further talks could focus on the role modeling of parents and the laws regarding marijuana use.

Discussing the Story about a Boyfriend

Participants: a mom and her twelve-year-old son

Mom: Here's our next story. "A girl is with her boyfriend and he offers her some marijuana before going to a party."
Son: Yeah, right. I'm not that guy.
Mom: What is the girl thinking?
Son: "Loser!"
Mom: What is the boy thinking?
Son: "Hey, maybe she likes this stuff! It's good."
Mom: What is the girl saying?
Son: "No, thank you. I think I'm going to go now."
Mom: What is the boy saying?
Son: "No, you really gotta try this stuff. This stuff is cool."
Mom: Does the girl want to smoke marijuana?

Son: No. She probably knows it's bad for you.

Mom: What is the girl feeling?

Son: "Why is he doing this? I thought he was cool, but he really isn't."

Mom: What might happen if the girl says no?

Son: Well it depends on how high the guy is.

Mom: Explain that.

Son: Well, if he wasn't very high he'd be like, "Okay, whatever." If he was really high he might, like, threaten her and force her to try it.

Mom: What might happen if the girl says yes?

Son: They might have sex.

Mom: How is this situation different from being offered alcohol?

Son: In ways it's the same, but it's more powerful. Like if you take a sip of alcohol, it's not going to automatically make you addicted to it. But if you have just a little bit of marijuana, you're going to get addicted to it.

Mom: Okay. Is there any legal difference?

Son: Yeah. Marijuana is completely illegal, and alcohol, you have to be 21.

Mom: What happens when you are around people who use marijuana?

Son: It's dangerous. They could pull a knife on you. There's secondhand smoke. Also, you might want to try it.

Mom: What happens if a cop comes to the party?

Son: Well, if they get busted, then the cops ultimately assume they are all on drugs and they'll all go to jail.

Mom: If you were in a situation like this, how would you feel?

Son: I'd leave.

Mom: What did you think of this talk?

Son: I heard a lot of people talking about stories like this, where someone is asked to try marijuana and you're supposed to say no, but I mean, how often do you actually hear that in real life?

Lessons Learned from This Sample Talk

The son shares some incorrect information about alcohol and marijuana when he says that "if you have just a little bit of marijuana, you're going to get addicted to it." Marijuana is not physically addictive, though regular users can become psychologically addicted. One of the dangers of not correcting this misinformation is that the child may one day try a little bit of marijuana and find that he is not automatically addicted. This may lead him to believe that all the information he's gotten about drug abuse is incorrect, which would be unfortunate. This mother can stress her concerns about using both marijuana and alcohol without resorting to untruths, as there are many reasons why a child should not be using marijuana. Also, the child does not have to worry too much about marijuana making users violent. In reality, it is alcohol that is strongly tied to violent crime and physical abuse. There is no such correlation with marijuana. The parent can stress the illegality of the drug.

"I remember being told in high school that we would become addicted to pot, and that we would crave more drugs. We would become addicted to heroin, too. None of my friends became addicted to pot. So I figured it was all a lie—maybe heroin wasn't addictive, either. But of course, it was. The messages about pot being addictive started my mistrust of all messages about drugs."

—Sheila, mother of two, New York City

7

Different Drugs/ Different Dangers

Talking about Definitions and Decisions

I have a friend who told me that he ordered something online from a drug company overseas, and now he's expecting some very interesting drugs in the mail. I asked him if he was out of his mind, taking pills from some unknown lab. It could be poison for all he knows. —Lee, mother of three, Columbia, South Carolina

To be honest, I did some incredibly stupid things when I was young, things I can't believe that I could ever have done— I'm talking about taking drugs from strangers. I'm not sure I want to tell my kid about any of that history.
—Drew, mother of two, Seattle, Washington

People say "designer drugs" to make an illegal drug sound fancy and upbeat. It's basically a marketing ploy.
—Deputy Sheriff James Quattrone, Chautauqua County, New York

There I was, 20 years old and about to enter Canada for vacation. As we approach the border guard my boyfriend tells me he has some "stuff" in his backpack. All I could envision was us spending the rest of our lives in jail for transporting marijuana. We made it through okay. —Jan, mother of one, Los Angeles, California

As a parent, you ought to know something about current drug trends and become familiar with the drugs' street names as well as their physical and mental effects. This chapter is designed to give you an overview of the most common mood-altering substances being bought, sold, and consumed by young people and adults. In the course of developing this book, we had parents look at our drug list, and most were shocked at the variety of drugs available. In this chapter we also will illustrate how accessible illegal drugs have become in neighborhoods, schools, clubs, and other gathering places. We have included input from both youths and adults on their experiences. Finally, we address the law and the consequences of breaking it.

We want to provide you with some basic information and to begin to create a big picture with regard to the use of illegal drugs. We also want to reinforce your interest in your child's daily activities. We'll offer you some opportunities to start conversations on drugs and choices and, in the process, to learn more about how your child gives meaning to the family values you discuss.

Preparing for the Talk

This talk will give you the chance to discuss with your child the topic of illegal drug use, the availability of drugs, and the dangers associated with them. It will also help you explain the legal consequences of buying and selling illegal drugs.

In this talk you will help your child understand that

- people use illegal drugs for many reasons, all of which can be discussed within the family.
- the desire for drugs creates an economic demand, and therefore a market, to supply them.
- illegal drugs are made without any regulations with regard to quality or safety. So the substance someone thinks he is buying is not always what he gets, which can create serious health risks.
- the selling and buying of drugs have legal consequences, often severe.
- there are family rules, school rules, and societal laws about the possession and use of illegal drugs.
- using any mood-altering drug places you at risk of danger, because you may be physically and mentally unable to make good decisions.

What You Can Expect from This Talk

After the talk your child will be able to:

- explain the physical, emotional, and mental health risks that result from using illegal drugs.
- explain the attraction of illegal drugs and why there is a market for them.
- describe how the legal consequences of buying, selling, and possessing drugs affect individuals and families.
- express the family rules and school rules about using and/or possessing drugs.
- describe how people can find help if they are having problems with drug use.

The Availability of Drugs

As we have discussed in previous chapters, alcohol, tobacco, and prescription drugs are legal for adults and widely available. These products are heavily marketed with slick advertising selling an image, or a feeling, as well as the product.

Illegal drugs have alternative avenues for distribution. A sophisticated network of people who make and sell all kinds of controlled substances serves consumers of all ages, races, and economic brackets. The illegal drug industry is a big business, and life is harsh for the majority of its workers. For example, in some neighborhoods young children are used as drug couriers because the legal consequences for them are less severe than they are for adults. Some young people see drug dealing as a source of income with a quick payoff to purchase possessions, gain status, or help to put food on the table. Some dealers are also themselves addicts, which puts them into a cycle of dependency. The motives to sell are as varied as the motives to use.

Many parents wonder why illegal drugs are so available. The answer is simple: There is a large demand for them. While the government may spend millions to control the supply of illegal drugs, very little is spent on reducing the demand for them. Many people believe that until the reasons for the demand—the reasons that people desire to use drugs—are addressed, we will be ineffective in stemming the supply.

Talking about the Demand

We believe that it is possible to reduce the demand for mind-altering drugs, both legal and illegal, if we look closely at why young people and adults use drugs in the first place. What is it about the state of our feelings that makes us want to alter them with drugs? At one time or another we've all sought relief from the stress of everyday life, and we made choices as to how to do that. For some people, drugs look like a quick, cheap answer. For young people as well as adults, there must be safe and healthy options from which to choose.

In earlier chapters we addressed the importance of understanding feelings, which becomes even more critical when talking about illegal drug use. Chapter 2, which focused on feelings, was developed to promote open dialogue about the kinds of situations that lead to stress, frustration, and painful emotions—all of which can leave one vulnerable to turning to drugs. Some of the activities in this chapter will help you revisit some talks you have had with your child about drugs and the impact they can have on a person's feelings and perceptions.

Why We Have Laws about Drugs

In the course of a program on drug prevention, a third grader asked the teacher, "Why are drugs illegal?" It is a simple question with no easy answer. Trying to explain why some drugs are legal— alcohol for adults, for example—while many others are not is a difficult task, but not an impossible one. When parents embark on this challenge it is important to present the information to your child simply, clearly, and confidently. A parent may say, "Drugs as medicine can help your body heal when you are sick with a cold, a headache, or worse. But if misused, drugs can hurt or kill you. Illegal drugs are not regulated in any way, so you can't trust that they can be used safely."

"With my older son, I have had some candid discussions about what he calls the 'double standard' for drug use. He wants to know why a legal drug like alcohol, which causes car accidents, deaths, violence, and severe health problems, is totally legal, while marijuana, which doesn't cause any of those problems, is illegal. We disagree sometimes, but I think it's good for kids to ask questions, and for parents to think about what the next generation can do to show leadership. You want to legalize marijuana? Get involved in politics and work to change the law. Now there's a challenge for you. The great part is, my son and I are able to discuss all of this without yelling."

—Steve, father of two, Syracuse, New York

A Legal Problem, a Public Health Problem, or Both?

How should people who use illegal drugs be dealt with—as patients who need treatment, or as criminals who need to be locked up? This question is complicated and can't be dealt with in depth in this space. But we do want to acknowledge the ongoing debate between law enforcement and the medical community over the best way to deal with illegal drug users.

Most people in law enforcement consider drug users criminals who should be locked up for knowingly breaking the law. People from the world of public health and medicine generally believe that drug users need to be seen as patients needing treatment of some kind. Others believe there is truth in both approaches. Those who believe in the public health approach would like to see more government dollars spent on drug prevention and recovery programs that would allow every addict who wants help a place in a program.

The approaches taken by other countries vary significantly, with some countries spending large sums on recovery programs and law enforcement. Unfortunately, it often comes down to how a limited amount of resources, private and public, are spent, and which approach offers the best hope for helping people and for keeping schools and neighborhoods safe and healthy.

The "Evil Dealer" or the "Best Friend"

Many of us grew up thinking that drugs came from predatory, strung-out dealers in dark alleys, an image encouraged by educational films and popular culture of the 1950s and 1960s. That stereotype hasn't been completely lost. In the drug-themed movie *Traffic,* a teenage girl from an affluent family is shown enjoying drugs with her friends. Within weeks, she becomes a prostitute in a low-income hotel, dependent on her drug-dealing pimp for a fix.

While there are drug dealers out there taking advantage of young people, the likelihood is greater that your child will be offered drugs by a good friend. Don't assume that drugs are sold only by predatory dealers in someone else's neighborhood. Drug dealers do not discriminate. They go where there is a market. They know no socio-economic, racial, or gender biases. Whether your family lives in a gated community or an urban housing project, drugs are sold nearby. Your best prevention and intervention tools are to be a pro-active parent who asks questions and avoids assumptions about who could or could not be involved with drugs.

The following section provides a basic overview of drug categories. The lists of drug type, trade names, and street names are by no means exhaustive. Our hope is that you begin to become familiar with the language and in turn feel a bit more confident about dealing with a subject that you may feel young people know more about than you do.

"To find out the latest terms for the most popular drugs, I just had to ask my fourteen-year-old daughter and her friends. This is very upsetting."   —Bess, mother of two, Columbia, South Carolina

What Are Narcotics?

The term "narcotic" comes from a Greek word meaning "to numb." We can expect adolescent and adult use of narcotics to increase internationally thanks, in part, to "home" chemists.

Narcotics are depressants with calming and painkilling effects. Narcotics include opium, heroin, morphine, methadone, codeine, and rohypnol (also known as "the date-rape drug"). These drugs are taken in pill form or by injection. Their medical use is pain relief. (An exception is heroin, which is used recreationally. Methadone is synthetic heroin and is used in precise quantities to treat heroin addiction.) All of these drugs are illegal if not received by medical prescription.

What Are Hallucinogens?

A hallucinogen is any substance that causes a sensory experience not based in reality. It is different from simply letting your imagination run wild, because the chemical that is introduced into your body confuses and incapacitates the body's natural ability to respond and maintain a sense of what is real. Hallucinogens cause chemical imbalance in the body, which can cause a user to experience an altered state of consciousness. Various hallucinogens have other effects with serious side effects resulting from their use. Some hallucinogens, such as PCP, have been known to cause violent reactions among users.

Hallucinogens can be eaten, and include LSD ("acid"), psilocybin (found in "magic mushrooms"), PCP (called "angel dust"), ketamine ("Special K"), and peyote, which is derived from a plant. The hallucinogens found in plant life, including types of mushrooms and fungi, have a history of use dating back to ancient civilizations. Some are still used in religious or spiritual ceremonies around the world.

What Are Stimulants?

Stimulants are substances that induce a temporary state of alertness, increased energy, suppressed appetite, a feeling of well-being, and a heightened mood. Stimulants include cocaine, crack cocaine, amphetamines ("speed"), methamphetamine (considered the strongest in the amphetamine category), methylphenidate (legally prescribed to treat attention deficit disorder), ecstasy (MDMA), herbal ecstasy, ephedrine, and—are you ready for this?—caffeine. One of the most popular drugs in the world, caffeine is mainly consumed in tea and coffee, but is also present in cola drinks, cocoa, certain headache pills, and diet pills.

What Are Depressants?

Depressant drugs are known as sedative-hypnotics. Sedative means having a quieting effect; hypnotic means inducing sleep. Depressants are synthetic drugs that may be classified as barbiturates, non-barbiturate hypnotics, or tranquilizers. All depressants significantly reduce the activity of muscles, nerves, the heart, and brain; all are habit-forming. Barbiturates are medically used in the treatment of epilepsy and convulsive disorders.

Trade names of depressants include Luminal, Seconal, and Nembutal. Non-barbiturate hypnotics were developed to duplicate the effects of barbiturates without causing unwanted side effects. Trade names include Doriden, Placidyl, Sopor, and Quaalude. Tranquilizers are used medically to relieve anxiety and tension, aid in inducing sleep, and act as muscle relaxants. Tranquilizers include Haloperidol-Haldol, Thorazine, thioridazine, Librium, Valium, Versed, Ativan, and Ambien.

What Are Inhalants?

Inhalants are solvents or chemical compounds that are sniffed or "huffed" to produce a lightheaded and hot feeling, but can also lead to dizziness, nausea, and in some cases, death. The most commonly used inhalants are lighter fluid, gasoline, model airplane glue, paint thinner, varnish, nail polish remover, and the fumes from cans of whipped cream or hair spray. The chemical fumes can be sniffed directly or expelled into a receptacle, such as a paper bag, and then sniffed. Most of these chemicals are found in household products, making their use widespread. One medical inhalant is nitrous oxide, commonly used as a dental anesthetic.

What Is Marijuana?

Marijuana can be smoked or eaten to produce mild euphoria, relaxation, and intensification of ordinary sensory experience. It stimulates the appetite, reduces nausea, and inhibits concentration and coordination.

Some parents are concerned that marijuana might act as a gateway drug—one that leads to the use of other, harder drugs. Data indicate that among teenagers, those who smoke cigarettes are more likely to drink alcohol, and those who smoke and drink are more likely to use marijuana. Those who use all three are in fact more likely to use other illicit drugs. Slang includes "pot," "grass," "weed," "dope," "joint," and "blunt" (a joint with a mixture of pot and tobacco). Any middle-school student will be able to tell you the slang in popular use at a particular school.

The medical use of marijuana is still controversial, and many doctors disagree on its medical benefits. The active ingredient in marijuana, THC, is also available in pill form and is prescribed for cancer and AIDS patients to stimulate appetite, reduce nausea and vomiting, and induce relaxation.

Marijuana is an illegal drug in the United States. The legal consequences for selling and possession vary from city to city and state to state.

What Are Steroids?

Steroids are naturally occurring, powerful hormones. Small quantities of synthetic steroids have enormous therapeutic value and are used as anti-inflammatory drugs, treatments for auto-immune diseases and allergies, growth-stimulating agents, and oral contraceptives. Steroids also are used to treat arthritis, breast cancer, and the side effects of chemotherapy. Steroids given through inhalers have revolutionized the treatment of asthma and allergies, making it easier for many children and adults to lead healthy lives.

The most commonly abused steroids are the growth-stimulating hormones known as anabolic steroids, which are synthetic derivatives of the male hormone testosterone. When used for medical purposes, steroids are closely monitored because their powerful effects have the potential to cause long-term damage, including bleeding ulcers, impaired body response to stress, and bone loss leading to fractures. Illicit steroids have the potential to cause a host of other damage, including liver cancer, sterility, aggression, depression, acne, and mood swings. Steroids are legal only by medical prescription. People young and old have been drawn to steroid use as a way to pump up their bodies and make them look more muscular. Some young people interested in building muscles (whether for sports or to enhance body image) may be tempted to use them.

Revisiting Alcohol and Tobacco

A previous chapter of this book was devoted to both alcohol and tobacco, but we also include them here, to give them their place among other drugs. Alcohol and tobacco are two distinct substances in terms of how they are used and the effects they produce. Both are widely used and readily available to anyone old enough to buy them. Alcohol requires responsible use; for example, it shouldn't be used before driving or operating equipment. In the case of tobacco, there is no safe exposure level either for smokers or for those exposed to secondhand smoke. It's illegal in all fifty states for anyone under age eighteen to buy tobacco. In the case of alcohol, every state has a minimum legal drinking age, but the exact prohibitions vary widely. For example, some states prohibit underage people from buying alcohol, but allow them to drink it.

Drugs and Pregnancy

Pregnancy is a very special time for parents and their children. The choices that women make during the nine months that a fetus grows can affect a child for a lifetime. Many physicians tell mothers-to-be, "Please don't take any drug other than Tylenol without talking to me first." Any medication during pregnancy is typically reviewed carefully by women and their doctors because of the potential for harm to the fetus.

It is well known that smoking tobacco or drinking alcohol can have profound and serious consequences on the development of a fetus, so physicians strongly discourage the use of either of these substances in any quantity during pregnancy. Less is known about the effects of illicit drugs, such as marijuana or cocaine, on the long-term health of children exposed while inside the uterus. For this reason, many doctors encourage patients to be truthful about their use of drugs of any kind, so that any risks can be evaluated and treatment started if necessary.

Quotes to Consider

"When I think of drugs I remember a Japanese proverb that rings true, 'First the man takes the drink, then the drink takes a drink, then the drink takes the man.'"

—Susan, mother of one, New York City

"Children who learn about the risks of drugs from their parents are less likely to use illegal drugs. However, only 28% of teens 'learn a lot about the risks of drugs' from their parents."

—K.I.D.S. Link, fall, 1998, Vol. 1, Issue 1

"[People are] trying to eliminate personal pain without any of the stigma or struggle associated with something like therapy. The goal is on-demand enlightenment [by using ecstasy]."

—Matthew Klam, "Experiencing Ecstasy,"
New York Times magazine, Jan. 21, 2001

Different People: Different Choices

We are always processing the world around us in terms of our values, beliefs, attitudes, and experiences. These tools help us make sense of our daily activities and interactions. An important role of the parent is to help a child develop his own set of tools to interpret his experiences and to learn along the way how to make safe and healthy choices. Think about two people who share a common experience, yet have two totally different perceptions of what happened. The following examples of how behavior can be interpreted differently will allow you to think about your own reactions and response to the situations. Later, you may want to use one or more of these situations to find out what your own child thinks and what he might do in those situations.

A teenage boy is having an eighteenth birthday party, and his parents have allowed beer to be served. Those driving had to turn their keys in upon arriving, so that they can be checked for sobriety before leaving.

Some parents would say the parents in this situation are breaking the law. Others would say they were helping the young people to learn responsible drinking. Others might say they disagree with the law and will monitor the young people themselves, so no harm is done. Still others may be angry that alcohol is served at all and wouldn't want their child getting a mixed message about youth, alcohol, and the law. Others might have had experiences with alcohol in their family or with their child and might resent the teen's parents enabling alcohol use in this case. What would you say?

■

A group of friends are hanging around after school at a girl's home. Both parents work and aren't around. The girl says she found what she thinks is cocaine in her father's dresser drawer. She says her parents used to tell stories about how they enjoyed a good buzz. The girl wants to know who wants to try the powder with her. She thinks that it can't be dangerous if it belongs to her father.

Some teens would see this as very dangerous and refuse, while others may be curious. Others might say they want to stick with what they know, and suggest raiding the liquor cabinet. How do you think your child would act in a situation like this?

■

A girl has heard from a couple of friends how "awesome" the drug ecstasy can be. However, she saw a special on television that talked about the brain damage it can cause. She is invited to go out with those friends on Friday and suspects they will have some ecstasy. She is thinking that one dose couldn't hurt.

Some teens would see this as a serious health problem to discuss. Some would be curious and want to know more about how the drug makes them feel. Others may want to feel good but fear the loss of control and clearheadedness. Still others would question the truthfulness of the television program if they knew people who had taken ecstasy and seemingly not experienced brain damage. What would you want your child to do?

■

A teenage boy is dating a teenage girl who smokes large quantities of pot. He smokes a bit but doesn't like the way it makes him feel. He's worried that she may eventually try something more potent to get her kicks.

Some people might say the girl's smoking is a real problem, while others would point out that she isn't forcing her boyfriend to smoke. Others might say they both need professional help. What's your opinion?

Different Perspectives

"I read an article in *Time* magazine which disturbed me enough to ask my daughter if she'd heard of anyone who used ecstasy. I told her it's popular at clubs because it gives you a sense of energy, you experience a warm feeling toward yourself and those around you, and it makes you feel euphoric. It is also a stimulant. The downside is, it increases your heart rate and body temperature and doctors are still researching what it does long-term to your brain. And when people buy ecstasy, one of the biggest dangers is that you never know what's really in the pill. And I talked about how judgment can be impaired, so one might do things one normally wouldn't do. After she picked up her jaw off the floor, she asked how I knew all that. I simply told her, 'I read about these things,' and we took it from there."

—Julie, mother of four, Gaithersburg, Maryland

"I remember hearing about my dad's stealing from us. He was a crack user. My mom definitely demonized him for his addiction."

—Tracy, mother of two, New York City

"My brother was a drug dealer in high school. My parents just thought he was very popular because he always had lots of friends dropping over!"   —Carmen, mother of two, Florence, South Carolina

DRUG-FREE SCHOOL ZONE
HIGH PROFILE ENFORCEMENT AREA
VIOLATIONS IN THE AREA WILL BE AGGRESSIVELY PROSECUTED
ATTORNEY GENERAL'S OFFICE
DEPARTMENT OF EDUCATION   —Sign on a school fence

What the Media Is Telling Your Child

Movies and TV portray drug use all the time, and send messages about drugs to viewers. The movie *Altered States* includes one of the most riveting views of hallucinogenics ever captured on film, in a scene where a college professor doing research ingests a special fluid as part of a native ritual. The movie *Trainspotting* shows the underbelly of heroin use in Edinburgh, Scotland, where a group of friends are partying wildly and finally descending into addiction, with dire consequences. On the other end of the continuum, one episode of the TV program "The Simpsons" showed cartoon hero Homer Simpson hallucinating on "magic" chili, with all the signs of a "trip" on hallucinogenic mushrooms or LSD. Homer's world took a surrealistic turn as he wandered the desert and talked with a coyote in search of a spirit guide.

Think about the messages about illegal drugs you got from TV and movies when you were growing up. How did those messages shape your view of drug use? Did the messages frighten or intrigue you? Did you ever talk with your parents about the images you saw?

Last-minute Checkups before the Talk

Before you talk with your child, try to remember what, if anything, your parents taught you about drugs when you were growing up.

- Did a parent ever talk to you about illegal drug use?
- Did they tell you the laws about using illegal drugs?
- Did they model healthy coping skills to deal with stress without using illegal drugs?
- Did they talk about how some illegal drugs have been used at various times by native tribes in rituals, or in laboratory settings in research about consciousness and perception?

As a parent, what are the messages you want your children to get regarding illegal drugs?

- Do you create opportunities for your child to talk about the illegal drug use she sees?
- Do you let your child know that you are willing to talk about any concerns she has about illegal drugs?
- Do you talk to your child about his friends and what they do?
- Do you talk with your child about having fun without using illegal drugs?
- Have you talked to your child about what a person needs to do if someone has a violent reaction to an illegal drug?

Do you have any stories you can share with your child about illegal drug use? We understand that some parents would prefer not to discuss their drug experiences, or if they do, to keep them very vague. Do you have stories about how you confronted someone who was using drugs? For example:

- The time a friend tried to get you to take hallucinogenic mushrooms with him
- The time you had to help a friend who mixed alcohol and illegal drugs
- The time you smoked pot to fit in at a party or club
- The time you called a relative when you were having a bad experience after taking too much of a stimulant
- The time you felt scared by the drug use of a family friend

Sharing your stories lets your child know how you feel about drug use and what impact it had on you when you were growing up.

What Are Your Family Rules?

Do you have spoken or unspoken family rules about drug use, possession, or selling drugs, along with clear consequences for breaking the rules and the law? If your rules are unspoken, this is a good time to think how you might make them clearer by stating them aloud.

The illustrated scenarios in the next section are meant to give you a chance to discuss your concerns about drug use and the common peer pressure to experiment with drugs that children face. The stories focus on making choices and the consequences of those choices. The stories and questions are open-ended, allowing your child to reflect on a range of topics, including the things friends do to protect one another, the power of peer influence, and any other concerns you and your child have. Depending on your child, the talk could even include issues of mixed messages about drug use that come from the media or from family members.

The Talk

Introduce the Talk

To start this talk you could say, "I've got some questions about drugs and I need your perspective." Your child may offer the following: "We've already been through this," or "Are you ever going to stop worrying about this stuff?" Assure your child that a talk about illegal drugs does not imply that he is interested in or is using them. You can let your child know that you want him to have a plan and be prepared before he is in a difficult position. That's why talking about it is important.

Since this talk involves how your child's behavior will affect yours, a five-minute talk about family values and rules, school rules, and the legal consequences for breaking drug laws is required. This chapter, even more than others, may require some help from a relative, such as your teen's favorite aunt, uncle, or family friend if your child is noncommunicative.

Review These Words

Please review the terms in this section. Discussing all the terms with your child is optional. You know which are appropriate for your child's age and maturity level. More than likely, most teens have heard slang terms for many of the drugs listed below. If you like, you can also discuss the drug categories discussed earlier in the chapter.

antidepressant: a drug that is most often prescribed to treat depression. Antidepressants may reduce feelings of hopelessness or sadness, and increase confidence and the ability to engage in enjoyable activities.

drug: any substance, legal or illegal, that is used to change a person's mood, feelings or health. Drugs are thought of by doctors as compounds used to treat disorders and improve health. Drugs are defined by police as illegal substances that subject users to arrest.

sedative: a drug that often is prescribed to treat anxiety or insomnia. Also referred to as a depressant or tranquilizer. Sedatives promote sleep and feelings of relaxation. Also known as "downers."

set and setting: the environment a drug is taken in, which affects how a drug feels to the user. Taking a drug with friends who are all using the same drug feels different, psychologically and physically, from taking the same drug alone.

stimulants (examples include amphetamines and speed): substances that create increased alertness and ability to stay awake, and cause feelings of euphoria. Also known as "uppers."

withdrawal syndrome (also called "Jones-ing"): the body's reaction to not having a drug that it has become habituated to. Almost every drug can result in a withdrawal syndrome if it is taken away abruptly. Examples include caffeine (severe headaches), marijuana or cocaine (anxiety and other psychological symptoms), opiates (severe physical withdrawal including shaking, altered sensations, feelings of dread and fear), and alcohol (violent muscle reactions, mental status changes, and heart damage).

Why Is Talking about Illegal Drugs Important?

Ask your child whether she thinks talking about illegal drug use is important. Here are some reasons you might want to offer. After hearing what she says, you could mention that talking about illegal drugs means

- learning that drug use can be progressive, with one drug leading to another.
- seeing how illegal drug use can change a person's behavior, feelings, and perceptions.
- learning about drugs, legal and illegal, that can change relationships and friendships.
- clarifying family values and rules about illegal and unhealthy drug use.
- clarifying the school rules and legal consequences of drug use.

The Stories

In the next part of the talk, you'll be reading short stories to your child and discussing them together. You don't have to read all of the stories. Choose the ones that you think are appropriate for your child. The stories are designed to be simple, so feel free to embellish them, adding details that you think might make the story more engaging and believable to your child.

A Story about a Police Officer

This story provides an opportunity to talk about the law, keeping safe, and the dangers of mixing alcohol or taking other drugs.

"A police officer stops a teenage boy who was driving a car recklessly. The teen had been drinking some beer and then took a pill given to him by friends at a party. He wanted the pill to give him a lift, because the drinking had seemed to slow him down. He didn't really want to drive home, but he thought it would be okay, since he had taken something to stay alert."

Ask these questions of your child:

- What is the boy thinking?
- What is the boy saying?
- What is the officer thinking?
- What is the officer saying?

Now that your child has completed this scenario, ask the following questions:

- Why would the boy have taken the pill after drinking alcohol?
- What other choices did the boy have besides taking the pill to help keep him awake and get him home?
- What should the officer do?
- If you were in a situation like this, how would you feel if you were the boy? What would you do?

249

- If you were in a situation like this, how would you feel if you were the officer? What would you do?
- If you were in a situation like this, how would you feel if you were the boy's parent? What would you do?

Stories for Older Children

These stories are intended for older children, but some children in late elementary school were able to discuss these anecdotes with their parents.

A Story about "Mushrooms"

This story is about two friends talking about trying some "mushrooms" at a party. These particular mushrooms, when consumed, can produce hallucinations. It's an opportunity to talk about hallucinogens, peer influence, and the serious consequences of thinking that you can use a drug safely. While it may be true that many people can boast of using drugs safely, impaired judgment puts you at risk for many negative consequences as well as in physical danger. The damage you cause your body may be immediate or may not show up until later.

"A girl and her older friend are at a party. The older friend's cousin, who is also at the party, offers both girls some tea made from hallucinogenic mushrooms. He says if they drink some they will have an unforgettable time, and that they shouldn't worry, because he'll keep an eye on them so that nothing bad happens to them."

Ask these questions of your child:

- What is the girl thinking?
- What is her older friend thinking?
- What is the girl saying?
- What is the older friend saying?

Now that your child has completed this scenario, ask the following questions:

- Why would the girls want to take a hallucinogen?
- When someone takes a hallucinogen, how does it change the person's perceptions? (Effects can be anything from a sleepy, dreamlike state to new insight about life to a deeply disturbing emotional experience. There is no way to know in advance.)
- What health risks does drinking mushroom tea pose?
- What would the girl's parents say if she told them about the use of the "magic mushrooms" at the party?
- If you were in a situation like this, how would you feel? What would you do?

A Story about "Partying All Night"

This story gives you a chance to talk about the effects of drugs and peer influence.

"A guy is dancing with his friends at a club. One of the older friends offers him something to sniff to 'party all night long.'"

Ask these questions of your child:

- What is the guy thinking?
- What is the older friend thinking?
- What is the guy saying?
- What is the older friend saying?

Now that your child has completed this scenario, ask the following questions:

- Why would the boy want to sniff some drugs?
- When someone sniffs drugs, how does it change his personality?
- What health risks does taking a drug like cocaine present?
- What would the guy's parents say if he told them about his older friend's use of drugs?
- If you were the younger guy in a situation like this, how would you feel? What would you do?

A Story about a Boyfriend's Secret

This story gives you an opportunity to talk about heroin, the law, and peer influence.

"A girl is out with her boyfriend and notices needle marks on his arms. After a long talk he admits that he has been using heroin, but nothing else. He says it isn't really such a big deal and he'll stop when he gets bored with it."

Ask these questions of your child:

- What is the girl feeling?
- What is the guy feeling?

Now that your child has completed this scenario, ask the following questions:

- Why would the guy do heroin?
- What kind of person do you think the guy is?
- When someone uses heroin, how does it change their personality?
- What health risks does shooting up heroin pose? (Sharing a dirty needle could transmit HIV and hepatitis.)
- What legal risks are there as a consequence of this behavior?
- How does the boyfriend's admission affect their relationship?
- What would the girl's parents say if she told them about her boyfriend's heroin use?

- If you were in a situation like this, how would you feel if your boyfriend or girlfriend admitted to doing heroin? What would you do?

Clarify Your Family's Values

Discuss the following questions with your child as a way of sharing your family values about drug use. We have included a number of potential responses from children to help you formulate your own responses.

Ask your child: "When people feel influenced by their friends to 'try some stuff' or to 'experiment a little' with drugs, what can a person say?"

Child response #1: "I don't know."
Parent: It's tough to know what to do. One answer could be, "No, thanks, I don't need anything to help me have a good time—I can do it on my own." I just want you to be prepared. If there comes a time when you're with some friends, and they're all curious and excited about something, you'll need to keep yourself strong and stay true to yourself.

Child response #2: "Well, trying some 'stuff' won't necessarily kill you. People have been doing drugs forever."
Parent: That may be true sometimes. But what I've found in my life is that it's important for me to think about the decisions I make, since I am the one who has to live with what I choose. Sometimes when I'm in a big group, I don't do

what's best for me, and sometimes I've made decisions I wasn't happy with later. Other times, I have excused myself and talked with a close friend, and arrived at a choice that works better for me. I would like to be that person for you, to provide a safe place for you to ask questions and think about what's best for you.

The Bare Minimum: A Quick Quiz for Kids
Ask your child the following questions to assess her knowledge and perceptions of drug use.

1. Can you give me an example of three illegal drugs?
   Sample answers:
   • heroin
   • ecstasy
   • crack

2. Why do people use drugs so much?
   Sample answers:
   • Young people learn from watching adults take drugs.
   • Some people feel very stressed and want to change the way they feel.
   • They are easy to get and take, and that can seem fun if everyone else is taking them.
   • They make a person feel "adult" and "alternative."

3. What are some health problems that can come with sharing a needle to shoot drugs?

Sample answers:
- HIV infection
- Hepatitis

4. What complications to a pregnancy can occur with drug use?
   Sample answers:
- Low birth weight of the newborn (tobacco)
- Deformities and brain damage to the newborn (alcohol)
- Newborn baby with HIV infection (mother using HIV-infected needle)
- Withdrawal syndrome in a newborn (cocaine)

Talk about Your Family Rules

This is an opportunity to review your family values and rules. Try asking your child this question:

What are our family rules about using drugs?
Sample answers:
- No one in this family breaks the law regarding drug use.
- We talk about healthy drug use and drug misuse openly and honestly.
- By talking, we can learn about how not to start, and if something did happen, we would know it was safe to ask for help.
- Our house is a safe place to ask questions and make decisions with help from each other.

After the Talk

Previous generations of parents did not allow for any discussion, dialogue, or family debate about drug use. It was simply, "Drugs are illegal. Don't do it. Period." We are asking you to do much more—to convey the dangers, the health risks, and the law. We are also asking you to tackle some of the complexities that exist. Teens can engage in discussions about the nation's drug policy, the emotional crutch drugs might offer to vulnerable people, and why some countries do better at reducing the demand for drugs than others.

As we said earlier in this chapter, you may need to ask for support during these talks. If your child refuses to have any kind of talk with you about the topics in the chapter, perhaps an aunt or uncle can be recruited to talk to your child. Many teens report it is much easier to talk with another adult relative because of embarrassment or fear of being judged by a parent. Keeping those kinds of feelings in mind, some pre-talk reassurances about what you will do to help them feel comfortable and safe might lay some important groundwork for good talks.

A Moment to Reflect

Take a moment to reflect on the talk you just had with your child. How do you feel about it?

- What surprised you about your child's view of drug use?
- What were your child's perceptions of who uses drugs?
- Does she seem susceptible to peer influence?
- What did you learn about how to listen and talk to your child?
- Were you able to leave the conversation open-ended, by asking if she had any questions or concerns that weren't talked about?

Warning Signs

The talks may reveal potential problems, or you may observe behaviors that cause you to be concerned. Review the following warning signs to see if your child might be using a controlled substance:

- He doesn't appear to care about school or friends; at home he is at extremes, either listless and unfocused or over-energized and hyperactive.
- She seems isolated or alienated from peers.
- She doesn't see anything wrong with using drugs.
- His grades take a dramatic turn downward.
- She describes values about drug use that are dangerous or illegal.
- He thinks people who go to rehab are weak or "stupid."
- She shares some problems in the course of the talk that sound like they could be serious.
- He is unusually sensitive about privacy.
- Relationships with family members have changed.
- She seems to depend on specific individuals or groups to make important decisions, or appears unwilling or afraid to make decisions that contradict her group of friends.

Most important, trust your instincts on how your child is doing. If you have concerns, approach her honestly and openly. Treat your child with the same respect that you expect from her, but clarify the rules, laws, and consequences for breaking them.

Success Stories

You have made it through what might have been a very difficult talk. Conversations about drug use and the law can be very stressful, especially if you were challenged by your child regarding your past choices, or even your present choices. Some children find the double standard of "Do as I say, not as I do" a very unfair reality.

A dad in California told his son that he had, in fact, smoked pot as a teenager, and had even been arrested once for smoking a joint on the sidewalk with some friends. His eighteen-year-old son surprised him by saying that he had tried marijuana, too. The father and son talked for a long time. In the end, the dad said he was relieved; his son had used marijuana but had little interest in it. He was glad he was able to discuss his concerns. The father initiated talks every few months to check in on how his son was doing, and to see whether any new issues needed to be discussed.

You don't need to find the perfect words or even the perfect reasons for your talks. With any talk, no matter how short, you have modeled for your child that when you care about someone you need to try to understand him. These are the key workings of a meaningful parent-child relationship. Give yourself time to reflect on your child's values and perceptions. Keep doing what seems to work with your child. Don't give up on the parts that don't work; try something new. Even if you hit some rough spots during this talk, you must let your child know that you can talk about these issues. You have also reinforced the belief that with the right resources, people can and should help themselves and their loved ones.

Sample Talks

Between Parents and Children

If you are wondering how a talk based on this chapter might really sound, take a look at the following excerpts from real family talks.

Discussing the Story about a Police Officer

Participants: a mom and her eleven-year-old daughter

> *Mom:* "A police officer stops a teenager driving a car. The teen was driving unsafely. He had been drinking some beer and then had taken a pill given to him by friends at a party to give him a lift because the drinking seemed to slow him down. He didn't really want to drive home, but thought it would be okay since he took something to keep himself alert." What is the boy thinking?
>
> *Daughter:* He's thinking everything's going to be okay. And that he's not going to get hurt driving home, driving drunk.
>
> *Mom:* What is the boy saying?
>
> *Daughter:* The boy is lying to the police officer, saying that he's okay, that he only had one beer. Really he's not okay, and he should be helped.
>
> *Mom:* What is the officer thinking?
>
> *Daughter:* She's thinking the boy is too young to be drinking and driving and he needs to get out of the car and not drink.
>
> *Mom:* What is the officer saying?

Daughter: "Get out of the car." She's also saying, "Where have you been? Have you been drinking? Where are you going? What are you up to?"

Mom: Why would the boy have taken the pill after drinking alcohol?

Daughter: Because his friends told him to.

Mom: What other choices did the boy have besides taking the pill to help keep him awake and to get him home?

Daughter: He could have stayed at his friend's house and called his parents and said he was spending the night at whatever's house and he could have hung out there.

Mom: What should the officer do?

Daughter: Take him to the police station and call his parents and have his parents talk to him.

Mom: If you were in a situation like this, how would you feel if you were the boy?

Daughter: I'd feel nervous that the police officer caught me and I'd feel scared that my friends were going to get in trouble and then I wouldn't have any more friends.

Mom: What would you do?

Daughter: I would get out of the car.

Mom: If you were in a situation like this, how would you feel if you were the officer?

Daughter: If I were the officer, I would feel bad for the boy. Because he can't help what his friends tell him to do. I would be sad.

Mom: If you were in a situation like this, how would you feel if you were the boy's parent? What would you do?

Daughter: If I were the boy's parents, I would be very mad at my son and I'd yell at him because he knows he shouldn't be doing that and he could be killed.

Lessons Learned from This Sample Talk

This daughter has no problem articulating her point of view. The mom could ask in future talks about the daughter's comment about why the boy took the pill: "Because his friends told him." Further talks could explore the concept of peer influences. They could also continue to discuss consequences of use and abuse. "Getting in trouble" with parents may be better than finding yourself in a dangerous situation. The mom can reassure the daughter of her support in this sort of situation.

Discussing the Story about "Mushrooms"

Participants: a mom and her twelve-year-old son

Mom: "A girl and her older friend are at a party. The older friend's cousin, who is also at the party, offers both girls some tea made from hallucinogenic mushrooms. He says if they drink some they will have an unforgettable time, and that they shouldn't worry, because he'll keep an eye on them so that nothing bad happens to them." What is the girl thinking?

Son: "I'm not going to take that stuff."

Mom: What is her best friend thinking?

Son: Same thing.

Mom: That they're not going to take this?

Son: Yeah.

Mom: Why would the girls want to take a hallucinogen?

Son: I don't know. If they feel bad?

Mom: Why does anyone take it?

Son: I don't know. They just do.

Mom: What health risks are there from drinking hallucinogenic mushroom tea?

Son: They would get hallucinogenic.

Mom: Okay. But you know, how would they know what it was? It could be poison mushrooms for all they knew.

Son: Yeah.

Mom: What would the girl's parents say if she told them about the use of the "magic mushrooms" at the party?

Son: I don't know.

Mom: Are you too tired to do this now?

Son: Yeah.

Mom: That's okay, let's quit. Thanks.

Lessons Learned from This Sample Talk

A good talk that raised the issue of the health risks associated with taking substances with unknown ingredients. The mom was also aware that this was not the best time for a long talk and cut it short. Future talks can revisit health risks associated with using mind-altering substances.

Discussing the Story about "Partying All Night"

Participants: a mom and her fourteen-year-old son

Mom: "A guy is dancing with friends at a club. One of the older friends offers him something to sniff to 'party all night long.'" What is the guy thinking?

Son: "This guy wants me to sniff something to go all night long. What is this stuff? Is it good? Will it get me high? Is getting high a good thing?" He may also be thinking the girl on the other side of the room is pretty cute.

Mom: What is the older friend thinking?

Son: "This will help my friend out a little bit. He might have a little more fun. It's good stuff."

Mom: What is the guy saying?

Son: He's either saying, "Yeah, sure, I'll get high tonight, yeah!" or he's saying, "No, I don't feel like it."

Mom: What is the older friend saying?

Son: "Come on man, you'll enjoy it, you'll have a great time."

Mom: Why would the boy want to sniff some drugs?

Son: To get high. Have a good time. Forget about whatever else is going on.

Mom: When someone sniffs drugs, how does it change their personality?

Son: They're kind of not there. They are floating around in a little awkward room and they don't know where they are. They're high and can't tell what's going on.

Mom: What health risks does sniffing a drug present?

Son: Depends what drug it is, anywhere from getting sick and throwing up to dying.

Mom: What would the guy's parents say if he told them about his older friend's use of drugs?

Son: "You should not be doing this. Stay away from these kind of people. Don't go to these parties anymore. Don't do any of this stuff."

Mom: If you were in a situation like this, how would you feel? What would you do?"

Son: I would feel the guy was trying to get me to sniff a drug. What would I do? I'd tell him I could have fun without it.

Lessons Learned from This Sample Talk

This mom and son have a good talk and it seems as though the son's values are in synch with his mom's. The son's comment about being able to have fun without a drug is a notion that can be reinforced. The mom can also talk about the legal consequences of being in possession of certain drugs, and the dangers of ingesting drugs without knowing the ingredients.

Discussing the Story about the Boyfriend's Secret

Participants: a mom and her fifteen-year-old son

Mom: "A girl is out with her boyfriend and notices needle marks on his arms. After a long talk he admits that he has been using heroin, but nothing else. He says it's no big deal and he will stop when he's bored with it." What is the girl feeling?

Son: "My boyfriend's a pothead and I never noticed until now."

Mom: He's not a pothead. Pothead means marijuana.

Son: It can mean drugs too, a druggie.

Mom: Okay, well, what is this guy thinking?

Son: "I shouldn't have done that. That was stupid."

Mom: Do you think he's going to get help now?

Son: He might try.

Mom: What is the girl feeling?

Son: Mad, anger.

Mom: What is the guy feeling?

Son: Mad at himself, I guess.

Mom: Why would the guy shoot heroin?

Son: He's a druggie, he's dumb.

Mom: What kind of person do you think this guy is?

Son: A dummy. I mean, if you are going to do any drugs, why inject yourself?

Mom: An overdose could kill you.

Son: Yeah.

Mom: Also, if you share needles, it's not like going to a doctor. You know when you get a shot from the doctor they never use the same needle twice? People who use drugs often use the same needles over and over again and if you share needles, you could get—well, what disease?

Son: AIDS, HIV.

Mom: Or hepatitis. Very good. How does this affect their relationship?

Son: Lots of tension.

Mom: What would the girl's parents say if she told them about her boyfriend's heroin use?

Son: "Don't hang around with him. Dump him!"

Mom: Would you agree with her parents?

Son: Probably.

Mom: Hmm. All right. If you were in a situation like this, if it was your girlfriend and you found out she was using heroin, how would you feel? What would you say?

Son: I'd talk to her about it. Try to get her to stop. Have a long conversation.

Mom: You would try and get her to stop? Would you threaten to leave her and stop being her friend if she continued doing this?

Son: Probably.

Mom: You would do that for her own good?

Son: Yes.

Lessons Learned from This Sample Talk

The son appears to have some good information about heroin and the risk of sharing needles. His comments about the guy being a "druggie" suggest that the son may have some stereotypes about the kind of person who does heroin. The mom may want to discuss why all kinds of people, from brilliant to stupid and rich to poor, use heroin. The mom could also talk about ways people can get off heroin and the kinds of treatment available.

8

Personal Choices

Talking about Sexuality and Alcohol and Other Drugs

Schools really can't do the job. Only a parent can convey morals and values about sexuality, and talking about alcohol and other drugs is also part of the dialogue.
—Susan Coots, sexuality educator, New York City

My sixteen-year-old son and I went back to ways in which drugs affect your behavior. We talked about how you might be tempted to do something that you wouldn't ordinarily do if you hadn't used a drug. We agreed that decisions about sex are too important to be made under the influence.
—Carrie, mother of two, Columbia, South Carolina

When I was in college, I went to a party with some new friends and there was punch, which I think they called "mushroom juice." I don't know what was in it, but the next morning I woke up in bed with some guy I barely knew—at his house. I had no idea how I got there or what had happened. Neither did he! I felt terrible.
—Sue, mother of two, St. Paul, Minnesota

In high school, my home life was miserable. I was desperate for love. I'd do just about anything if it meant a guy would like me, but sometimes I'd have to drink a lot to convince myself to do it.
—Lisa, mother of three, Portland, Oregon

For many people, sex, alcohol, and other drugs are intimately connected. It's a connection that starts as early as puberty. Puberty, the time when a young person begins to mature sexually, can be one of life's most chaotic phases. It's a physical and emotional roller-coaster ride that has a profound impact on our day-to-day feelings.

As if the internal pressures weren't enough, teens are maturing while being bombarded nonstop with images and messages about sex, physical attractiveness, and the need for acceptance. TV, movies, music, magazines, and the Internet relentlessly tell them that looking a certain way, wearing the right clothes, or buying the right product will enhance their attractiveness and reward them with sex and love. Ads tells us that a beer, glass of wine, or bottle of vodka can be a ticket to sexual adventure. It's no wonder that the use of drugs and the experience of adolescence go hand-in-hand for many people.

In this chapter, we will focus on sexual development and the feelings associated with it. And we will look at the connection between those feelings and drug use. The talks in this chapter touch on physical changes, reproduction, healthy relationships, ethics, character, desire, attraction, love, sexual orientation, and trust. These are sensitive topics, but as parents, we cannot avoid these conversations. What's more, we have to start these conversations early in our children's lives; talks about respecting personal boundaries can begin as early as kindergarten. And while this chapter is not meant to cover all the aspects of drug use and sexuality, it will give you the tools you need to begin talking about how drug use and sexual activity can relate to one another.

Preparing for the Talk

This talk will help you and your children discuss alcohol, tobacco, and other drugs and how they affect our feelings about sex and sexual relationships, as well as our decisions about sexual activity.

In this talk you will help your child understand that

- puberty is a time when a child matures and becomes a fully functioning physical adult, often with biological drives to be sexual.
- sexual desire is a common feeling for someone going through puberty.
- puberty is a time when emotions change, often dramatically.
- alcohol and other drugs alter our feelings, and it's important to know how our feelings are altered.
- the use and abuse of alcohol and other drugs does not excuse harmful or irresponsible behavior.
- there are family rules about alcohol and other drug use, as well as sexual activity.

What You Can Expect from This Talk

After the talk your child will be able to

- define "sex" and "sexual activity."
- understand how drug use and sexual activity are often linked.
- understand that puberty is a time when feelings may be overwhelming.
- understand how we can find healthy outlets for dealing with difficult feelings, especially ones related to sexuality and relationships.

- understand how peer influence to be sexually active can lead to alcohol and drug use.
- know the consequences of using alcohol and drugs in sexual situations.

How Do You Define Sex?

"Sex" means different things to different people. You may be surprised to hear what your child thinks it means! A high-school boy swears he is not having sex if all he is experiencing is oral sex. A middle-school girl sincerely believes that as long as she keeps her underwear on, she is not having sex. Even adults use the word "sex" to mean different things at different times. Can kissing ever be called sex? What about flirting? What's important is how you, the parent, define sex and sexual activity. With a shared definition, you and your child can move on to discussing your family values and family rules about sexual activity—from hugging and kissing to pregnancy and sexually-transmitted disease prevention.

Many parents can't imagine that sexual issues will affect their child's life before high school. Sadly, even kindergartners are exposed to explicit sexual slang by older kids on the bus and the playground. Spend ten minutes at any elementary school and you'll hear jokes and insults riddled with sexual slang being hurled by third graders. (Hearing a third-grade boy explain "where babies come from" to a first-grade girl can be a disturbing experience!) By fourth grade, puberty has begun for many kids. By this time, the parent needs to have provided an overview of puberty to the child.

Don't depend on your child's school to tackle this job. Health class, even a good one, is not a substitute for parents' sharing their values and rules about sexual activity. By middle school, a child is living in a new environment and sharing it with young people who are sexually active, as well as some who are experimenting with drugs. By high school, the sexual feelings of students are intensified.

Most parents, no matter their values, can't keep mature young adults from being sexually aware. What's important is that you keep engaging in talks. We recommend having talks about sexuality and character throughout puberty. The bare minimum is three talks: one when your child enters fourth grade (when many kids begin puberty), another upon entering middle school, and another upon entering high school.

"I have been surprised by what my middle-school daughter has told me about some of her peers. The way she describes it, kids view sexual activity more as a sport than as a way to show intimacy."

—Marcy, mother of two, Columbia, South Carolina

"The things you hear on an elementary school playground would shock most parents. You can hear fourth graders calling one another sluts and worse. And they know the name for every body part you can imagine. These kids show little respect to one another, and somehow they think it's all a joke."

—Lisa, mother of two, Seattle, Washington

Influence of the Media

In movies and on TV, sex and drugs often go together. Alcohol flows in soap operas and on prime-time TV whenever strangers hop into bed with one another. Movies directed at teens show people getting drunk and making out. Drinking is often used to explain (or excuse) sexual activity. Slick ads aimed at men suggest a strong connection between drinking a certain beer or liquor and sexual conquest.

In real life it's possible to make it through young adulthood and even explore romance and sexuality without using alcohol, tobacco, and other drugs. But you wouldn't know this from watching popular media. It's difficult to find videos and films that show healthy relationships that are not somehow dependent on alcohol and other drugs. Many parents have told us that the differences between TV fantasy and their family's reality has been good fodder for ongoing talks.

Quotes to Consider

"Most young people begin having sex in their mid- to late teens, about eight years before they marry; more than half of all seventeen-year-olds have had intercourse."

—Alan Guttmacher Institute, "Teens,
Sex and Pregnancy," 1999, www.agi-usa.org

Percentage of preteens who say they have questions . . .
about puberty: 46%
about knowing when they are ready to have a boyfriend or girlfriend: 45%
about HIV and AIDS: 41%

Proportion of parents who say they have never talked with their preteens . . .
about puberty: 44%

**about knowing when they are ready to have a boyfriend
or girlfriend: 56%**
about HIV and AIDS: 58%

*(Source: "Inside Kids," Nickelodeon and the
Kaiser Family Foundation, 2001)*

Different Families: Different Values

Everyone interprets behavior in his or her own way. Here are some behaviors that may be experienced differently, depending on a person's background and experience:

A mom is watching a TV show with her kids, and the two young adults on the program appear nervous and share a beer. They then climb onto a bed and start kissing.

Some parents would wait for the commercial and ask both kids what they thought of that behavior ("Was it realistic? Why drink beer? What might happen to those two?"). Other parents would not see any reason to comment, figuring their kids see this stuff all the time on TV and hoping it doesn't influence them too much. Other parents might be offended and change the channel. Some parents don't know what to say. What would you do?

■

After taking a shower, a teenage girl is looking in the mirror and wondering if her body is normal. She wonders if smoking will keep her weight down and make her look sexier.

Parents usually can tell if a daughter is troubled by her weight or appearance. Some parents would talk to her about the physical and emotional changes she's going through. Others would leave the job to her school, which probably has programs explaining puberty. Still others might feel conflicted about what to do. What would you do?

■

A teenage boy and girl are at a party and are offered a beer by a friend. The beer makes them feel much happier and less inhibited. They have another beer and end up kissing for a few hours.

Some parents would be happy to hear that their kids have a good social life, but might not be thrilled about the beer use. Others might feel that a few beers and a little kissing is nothing to worry about. Many parents would say that drinking beer and kissing is against their family rules, and that there are consequences for breaking them. What would you do?

■

Two adults are on their first date, having been "fixed up" by friends. They are sharing a bottle of wine over dinner. As the dinner progresses, they find themselves more and more sexually attracted to each other.

Some parents would say that a little wine with dinner is perfectly normal and enjoyable for adults. Others would say that a glass or two of wine over dinner is fine but would draw the line at more, as it loosens inhibitions. Others would be against any alcohol use for adults and young people. What do you think about drinking alcohol on a first date?

■

A young woman has started becoming aware of her emotional and sexual feelings, and she's feeling confused by them. She has been attracted to some guys, but now she is aware of her growing attraction to her female friend at college. She does not know whom to talk to about these feelings and finds herself drinking wine more often to deal with her anxiety.

If the daughter revealed her feelings and wine use to her parents, some parents might say that that there are two important issues to discuss: having confusing feelings of attraction to someone, and using alcohol to mask or deaden such feelings. It's common for young adults to keep feelings about their sexual attractions a secret, but parents in such situations would see that their daughter is withdrawn and get a sense that something was wrong. Some parents would want to help, while others might feel angry or sad or fearful about the situation. How would you feel?

■

A girl is feeling sad because she was dumped by her boyfriend—for her best friend. She is keeping her feelings to herself but feeling very sad and angry. To deaden her feelings, she begins sneaking vodka from her parents' supply. The mom starts noticing a big difference in her daughter's behavior.

Some parents would sense something very serious and spend the time to find out what was wrong, even if it meant bringing in an adult friend, aunt, or professional counselor. Others would sense something was wrong, but think that the daughter was just going through a tough stage—let her "work it out on her own," they might say. Others would be too involved in their own problems to notice or to take action. What would you do?

Different Perspectives

"I've had talks about sex and sexuality with my son and daughter separately. My husband and I agreed we'd talk about sex and drugs with all of us together. We got off to a very weird start, but hung in there. We've turned the talk into a 'what if' debate that deals with the differences between men and women, health concerns, and a lot of other ideas. My kids are thirteen and eleven years old, and I know these talks will change as they age, but at least we've done some great groundwork." —Lauri, mother of two, Syracuse, New York

Last-minute Checkups before the Talk

Before you talk with your child, try to remember what your parents taught you about sexuality, puberty, attraction, and the use of alcohol and other drugs when you were growing up.

- Did a parent ever talk to you about sexuality, puberty, attraction, and the impact of alcohol and other drugs?
- Did they tell you how to identify alcohol and drug abuse in yourself, or in a boyfriend or a girlfriend?
- Did they model healthy coping skills to deal with intense emotions without using alcohol or other drugs?

As a parent, what are you teaching your child about sexual relationships and how drugs impact sexual feelings and behavior?

- Do you encourage her to talk about the feelings she is experiencing?
- Do you let your child know that you welcome any concerns he has about sexuality and how alcohol or other drugs impact sexual feelings?
- Do you talk to your child about finding boyfriends or girlfriends who don't misuse drugs?
- Do you model the ability to deal with the complexities of a relationships without misusing alcohol or other drugs?

Do you have any stories you can share with your child about dating, sexuality, and the role of alcohol or other drug use, or how you confronted someone you were dating who was abusing alcohol or other drugs? For example:

- The time a friend who was sexually attracted to you tried to get you high or drunk
- The time you went to a party and a lot of people were drinking and kissing
- The time you used alcohol to deal with shyness around a person you were attracted to
- The time you were with a boyfriend or girlfriend and felt uncomfortable or scared by the friend's alcohol or drug use

Sharing your stories lets your child know how you feel about drug use and sexual relationships, and what impact it had on you when you were growing up.

What Are Your Family Rules?

Do you have family rules about sexual activity along with clear consequences for breaking them? If not, this is a good time to think about what rules you'd like to put in place. This talk focuses on sexuality, puberty, and attraction, as well as drug use.

The illustrated scenarios in the next section are meant to give you a chance to discuss how puberty can be a very stressful time, when feelings can seem overwhelming. These stories will also help you explain that the use of alcohol and other drugs to temporarily deaden difficult feelings or enhance feelings in sexual situations is tempting, and peer influence to use drugs of all kinds is common.

The stories and questions are open-ended, allowing your child to reflect on a range of topics, including self-esteem, peer pressure, and other problems or concerns. Depending on your child, the talk could even include issues of sexual assault, mixed messages from the media and parents, and the complexities of sexual relationships. Discussing these situations will give you an opportunity to share your family rules about sexual activity coupled with alcohol and other drugs, and your views on acceptable behavior.

The Talk

Introduce the Talk

To start this talk you could say, "I've got some questions for you. I am reading the chapter about sex and drugs."

The most common response to such a line is, "I've already learned that in school!" Older kids may be defensive, wondering,

"Is she thinking that I'm having sex?" Almost any conversation about sexuality can cause eye-rolling, joking, and uncomfortable silences. You will set the tone for the talk. While your child may think she is in for a talk about "body parts," the reality is that this talk is much more about values, ethics, self-esteem, and making healthy choices. Let her know that, if you think it will help.

You can add, "Is there a connection between drugs and sex?" Your child might respond with, "Nope," or "Are you thinking about Viagra?" or "You mean drinking beer at a party and stuff?" You might also hear, "I heard from Uncle Ramón that pot and ecstasy makes people want to have sex." Even if your child has no response, you can say, "I can see that we are going to have an interesting conversation."

Review These Words

Please review the terms in this section. Discussing all the terms with your child is optional. It is a long list, but it illustrates many issues related to sexuality and drugs. You know which terms and concepts are appropriate for your child's age and maturity level. More than likely, even the youngest children have heard many of these words on TV or at school.

abstinence: not having sex.

boundaries: A physical boundary is an imaginary area around us in which we can set rules for how and when we wish to be touched. An emotional boundary sets the rules for how a person wishes to be spoken to and treated.

crush: the feeling of being very physically and/or emotionally attracted to someone. This occurs most often in the early stages of getting to know someone and is often confused with being in love.

love: when used in the context of a romantic relationship, a feeling of deep closeness, mutual respect, and desire for companionship. Love includes a desire for the other person's well-being and a commitment to continuing the relationship.

monogamy: being sexually faithful to a partner. A monogamous relationship is one in which both partners are having sex only with each other.

puberty: the stage of growth when reproductive ability starts to develop, producing characteristics such as body hair, pubic hair, heavier sweat and body odor, menstruation and breast development in girls, and production of sperm in boys. This process starts at very different times for different people and has been known to start as early as age eight or nine and as late as the late teens.

rape: a violent act when a person is forced to have sex against his or her will. Rape is considered a violent exertion of power, rather than a sexual act. An opiate, Rohypnol, is often referred to as the "date rape" drug.

risky sexual behavior: any behavior that could result in a person contracting a disease such as HIV, hepatitis, gonorrhea, syphilis, or in an unexpected outcome, such as pregnancy. Examples include not using a condom during intercourse, or women not using contraception when they do not desire to get pregnant. Risky sexual behavior is increased when people are under the influence of substances, and is equally possible in males and females.

sex: sometimes used to define gender, meaning male or female; sometimes used to mean sexual intercourse; sometimes used to mean some kind of bodily contact. This means that when people say "sex" it might be difficult to know what they have in mind.

sex role: a set of characteristics promoted by a culture as appropriate for females or for males. Sex roles change from culture to culture and evolve over time. For example, traditional sex roles in the United States in the 1950s dictated that females should work in the home and be passive, while males should work outside the home and be assertive. Sex roles are learned behaviors and continue to change.

sexual orientation: someone's sexual preference. Most people are heterosexual, attracted to people of the other sex. A small percentage of people, sometimes estimated at five to ten percent of the population, are homosexual, attracted to people of the same sex. Some people are bisexual, and are attracted, to some degree, to both males and females.

sexuality: a broad term referring to the sum total of someone's sexual desire, behavior, and self-identity.

Why Is Talking about Sexuality and Drugs Important?

Ask your child why she thinks talking about sexuality and drug use is important. Here are some reasons you might want to offer. Talking about sexuality and drugs means

- learning to identify the many stresses associated with puberty, and ways to cope with them without using alcohol and other drugs.
- seeing how drugs can change all relationships, both platonic and romantic.

- clarifying family values and rules about sexual behavior and drug use.
- sharing perspectives.
- learning how drugs could increase your risk of contracting sexually transmitted diseases by decreasing your inhibitions and ability to make wise choices.

The Stories

In the next part of the talk, you'll be reading short stories to your child and discussing them together. You don't have to read all of the stories. Pick the ones that you think are appropriate for your child. The stories are very simple. Feel free to embellish them, adding details that you think might make the story more believable to your child.

A Story about a "Normal" Girl

This story provides an opportunity to talk about the ways that puberty can make people feel insecure about their feelings and body, how people compare themselves to peers and people in the media, and how everyone wonders if they are "normal." This story does not explicitly address drug use. Instead, it focuses on feelings.

"A girl is playing soccer. She looks at all the body types of the other soccer players. She is wondering if she is normal."

Ask this question of your child:

- What is the girl feeling?

Now that your child has completed this scenario, ask the following questions:

- Do girls ever worry about their appearance? Why or why not?
- Do girls ever compare themselves to other girls? Why or why not?
- What does a "normal" body look like?
- Does she wish she looked different? In what ways? And why?
- What does a "good" body look like?
- What kinds of feelings might a girl who is going through puberty have?
- If you were in a situation like this, how would you feel?

A Story about a "Normal" Boy

This story is an opportunity to talk about the ways that puberty can make people feel insecure about their feelings and body, how people compare themselves to peers and people in the media, and how everyone wonders if they are "normal." This story does not explicitly address drug use. Instead, it focuses on feelings.

"A boy is running on the track at school. He looks at all the body types of the other runners and wonders if he is normal."

Ask this question of your child:

- What is the boy feeling?

Now that your child has completed this scenario, ask the following questions:

- Do boys ever worry about their appearance? Why or why not?
- Do boys ever compare themselves to other boys? Why or why not?
- What does a "normal" body look like?
- Does he wish he looked different? In what ways? And why?
- What does a "good" body look like?
- What kinds of feelings might a boy who is going through puberty have?
- If you were in a situation like this, how would you feel?

A Story about Friends and Beers

This story gives you an opportunity to talk about how alcohol affects feelings and decision making, and how friends can find themselves drunk and in sexual situations.

"A high-school senior and a high-school junior have been getting to know each other for almost a month. They have not been physical or sexual in any way. One night at a friend's house they both drink a lot of beer and end up on a couch, touching and kissing."

Ask these questions of your child:

- What is the senior feeling?
- What is the junior feeling?

Now that your child has completed this scenario, ask the following questions:

- Was this a good experience for both of these people? Why or why not?
- How could this sexual activity complicate their relationship?
- Do they respect each other?
- Did alcohol play a role in this situation?
- Do you think that they wanted to get physical with each other but didn't know how to without being drunk?
- Did these people break any family rules or the law?
- How could this situation have been prevented?
- What do people in a situation like this usually do, the next time they see each other?
- If you were in a situation like this, how would you feel? What would you do?

A Story about Peer Pressure

This story provides an opportunity to talk about feelings, inhibitions, being shy, and the impact of certain drugs on inhibitions, desire, and decision making about whether to be sexually active. A talk about this story can cover

the dangers of drug use, keeping commitments to parents, following family rules, and feeling pressure from peers.

"A girl is at a party with some friends. Everyone seems to be having a fun time except her. The girl is offered a pill by one of her friends. 'This will make you feel good,' her friend says."

Ask these questions of your child:

- What is the girl feeling?
- What is the girl saying?
- What is the friend feeling?

Now that your child has completed this scenario, ask the following questions:

- Does the girl want to take the pill? Why or why not?
- Why does her friend want her to take the pill?
- If she doesn't want the pill, how can the girl decline the offer?
- What are the kinds of consequences the girl might experience if she takes the pill? What are the consequences of not taking the pill? How does one weigh the two consequences? How could her decisions about whether or not to be sexually active be affected?
- If she takes the pill and feels less inhibited, might she be tempted to use the pill again? Why or why not?
- Is taking the pill breaking her family's rules and the law?
- If she takes the pill, has the daughter betrayed her parents' trust? What if this is the first time she has found herself in a situation like this?
- If you were offered a drug in a situation like this, how would you feel? What would you do?

Clarify Your Family's Values

Discuss these questions with your child as a way of sharing your values about sexual activity and its relationship to alcohol and other drug use. We have included a number of potential responses from children to help you formulate your own responses.

Ask your child: "When people have feelings of frustration or confusion about sexual feelings that make them uncomfortable, what can they do to feel better, outside of drinking alcohol or taking other drugs?"

Child response #1: "Talk to a friend."
Parent: Right. Sometimes talking about problems with a friend, or even with a new acquaintance, can help someone feel better.

Child response #2: "See a school counselor to help with the problem."
Parent: Finding help is definitely a good idea. There are all kinds of people who can help, including relatives [name some that you trust], people from our religious community, and people at school. And I know that talking with a parent isn't always easy, especially when the subject turns to sex. Would you feel comfortable talking with your aunt or uncle?

Child response #3: "Well, a few beers won't hurt."
Parent: That may be true sometimes. A beer or a glass of wine might not hurt at all. It all depends on the situation and the age and emotional maturity of the person who's drinking. If

an adult uses alcohol moderately, that might be fine. But some people become addicted to alcohol, or sedate themselves in order to mask difficult feelings related to sexuality and relationships. For some people, even one glass of alcohol can be a problem."

Child response #4: "I don't know."

Parent: Well, when you feel really bad what do you do to feel better? You can take a long walk, go for a run, take a long bath, talk on the phone with a friend, write in a journal, play a game, watch TV, or just sleep.

The Bare Minimum: A Quick Quiz for Kids

Ask your child the following questions to assess her knowledge and perceptions about sexuality and the connections between sexual feelings and drug use. These answers will give you information about your child's values and morals. This is also an opportunity for you to share your views on sexuality, relationships, and character.

1. Can you give me one example of what might happen to make a person experiencing sexual feelings or situations want to alter her feelings by using alcohol or other drugs?
   Sample answers:
   - If she is nervous or excited about meeting someone
   - If she feels unattractive
   - If she feels lonely
   - If she's confused by her feelings
   - If she wants to forget her difficult feelings and blend in with others

2. How do alcohol and other drugs alter sexual feelings?
Sample answers:
- Alcohol and other drugs can make people feel uninhibited, impair judgment, or make someone eager to have sex.
- Alcohol and other drugs can make people feel relaxed and very sensitive to being touched. It can alter a person's decision-making process.
- Alcohol and other drugs make people feel happy, eager to be sexual, and comfortable ignoring family rules—or their own personal rules—about sexual activity.
- Alcohol and other drugs can make people feel less concerned about putting themselves in dangerous situations, such as having sex with strangers, or taking other unhealthy sexual risks.
- Some drugs make sexual feelings less enjoyable; alcohol can keep a man from having an erection, and over time, smoking can do the same thing by causing permanent damage to blood vessels.

Talk about Your Family Rules

This is an opportunity to review your family rules. Ask your child the following question:

1. What are our family rules about sexual activity and drug use?
Sample answers:
- In this family, we can talk about any concerns you have regarding sexuality and drug use.
- The term "sex" means different things to different people. In this family we can discuss a common definition.

- Drinking alcohol or using other drugs can impact a person's ability to make healthy and safe decisions. Using drugs and being physical in any way are not allowed.
- No one in this family breaks the law regarding sexual activity.
- In our family, we will arrange for you to see a doctor if you have any questions or concerns about your sex and health. If you are worried that you are ill or find bumps, rashes, or anything on your body that concerns you, we want you to see a doctor.
- In our family we always communicate honestly. Lying, especially about issues related to sex and health, is not helpful.

After the Talk

Take a moment to reflect on the talk you just had with your child. How do you feel about it?

- What surprised you about your child's view of sexuality and drug use?
- Do you think she has the self-esteem to deal with peer influence to be sexual without needing to self-medicate? Does she seem susceptible to peer influence? Think about whether your child has the ability to deal with the intense pressures that go with adolescence, puberty, and relationships.

Warning Signs

This talk can reveal potential problems that your child is facing. Review the following warning signs to see if your child might be involved in unsafe and inappropriate sexual activity and drug use:

- She shares some problems in the course of the talk that sound like they could be serious.
- She doesn't appear to care about school or friends; at home she is listless and unfocused, or agitated and uncommunicative.
- He refuses to talk with you or any adult family member about any sexual issues. This continues after many repeated tries to talk.
- Her grades take a dramatic turn downward.
- He becomes obsessed with someone, whether at school or on the Internet.
- He stops enjoying activities that formerly were enjoyable or becomes withdrawn.
- She reports being harassed or threatened at school by others.

Above all, trust your instincts on how your child is doing. They're probably right on target.

Success Stories

You have made it through a very important talk, perhaps one of the most significant talks you'll have with your child. Talking about sexuality is usually uncomfortable for most families. But the talk should have given you the opportunity to discuss your values and family rules—as well as why these rules are in place to keep your child safe and healthy. Talks about sexual activity and drug use can hold some surprises. One mom in Boise, Idaho, found out during her talk that her sixteen-year-old son had not only started drinking beer, but also had been sexually active with two different girls. This came as a total surprise to the mother and led to a series of talks about her religious values and concerns.

The talks about sexuality are ongoing. We want to restate that talks about sexual behavior and drug use are part of many talks that need to be nurtured. Most bookstores and libraries have many books on the topics of sexuality, relationship building, and character development for people of all ages. It is a very complex issue for many families. The use of alcohol and other drugs has the power to destroy relationships—from budding teen romances to marriages. The good news is that there is more awareness of the problems drugs bring, and there are more resources available for people to find help for themselves and their loved ones.

Sample Talks

Between Parents and Children

If you are wondering how a talk based on this chapter might really sound, take a look at the following excerpts from real family talks.

Discussing the Story about a "Normal" Girl

Participants: a mother and her ten-year-old daughter

Mom: "A girl is playing soccer and she looks at all the body types of the other soccer players. She is wondering if she is normal." What is the girl thinking?

Daughter: She's thinking that she is normal.

Mom: What does "normal" mean?

Daughter: That she isn't weird.

Mom: Do girls ever worry about their appearance?

Daughter: Yeah.

Mom: Why?

Daughter: Because they feel they don't have a lot of friends.

Mom: People judge you on the way you look?

Daughter: No. But sometimes you have to look nice.

Mom: Do girls ever compare themselves to other girls?

Daughter: No, because they don't really care.

Mom: What's a "normal" body look like?

Daughter: I don't know.

Mom: Does it have hair?

Daughter: Yeah.

Mom: Does it matter what the body looks like?

Daughter: No.

Mom: Does she wish she looked different?

Daughter: No.

Mom: What does a "good" body look like?

Daughter: One that's clean.

Mom: Anything else?

Daughter: No.

Mom: What kinds of feelings are normal for a girl going through puberty to have?

Daughter: That she's better than anybody else.

Mom: Really? If you were in a situation like this, like the girl playing soccer, how would you feel?

Daughter: That she's not paying attention and the other team might get a goal because she's not paying attention.

Lessons Learned from This Sample Talk

For a ten-year-old, this was a very good beginning to the talk about puberty. At this point in her development, the daughter did not seem very interested in the body (aside from its being "clean") and was more focused on playing a good game of soccer than considering issues of self-esteem and society's notion of beauty. What is wonderful about this talk is that is sets the foundation for other talks that can get more serious as the daughter goes through puberty. Not all talks have to contain earth-shattering revelations. Sometimes they just show that a parent and child can sit together for even a few minutes and have a talk, a major success in itself.

Discussing a Story about a "Normal" Boy

Participants: a mom and her twelve-year-old son

Mom: "A boy is running on the track at school, and as he looks at all the body types of the other runners he is wondering if he is normal." What is this boy thinking?

Son: You usually depict yourself as bigger than you actually are. So he's probably saying, "Wow, am I fat? Look at him, he's so skinny. Is he normal or am I normal? Do I look right? Is this shirt okay?"

Mom: Do boys ever worry about their appearance?

Son: Yeah. A little bit.

Mom: Why?

Son: I don't know. Sometimes to impress the girls. Maybe there's a girl they like. Something like that.

Mom: Do boys ever compare themselves to other boys?

Son: Yeah. Probably.

Mom: Why or why not?

Son: I don't know. We never think about why.

Mom: At work when I'm teaching, I try all day to get the kids to think about "why."

Son: It doesn't matter why! I like Nike, "Just do it!"

Mom: Why do boys compare themselves with other boys?

Son: Probably so they can fit in.

Mom: Why is it important to fit in?

Son: To be cool and have a lot of friends.

Mom: If you don't fit in, you don't have friends?

Son: You don't have cool friends.

Mom: What's a cool friend?

Son: I don't know. One that's normal.

Mom: [laughs] You're going in circles. Let's try this. What does a "normal" body look like?

Son: It's how people think about it. It's different for every person. There's no such thing as a normal body!

Mom: Okay. What does a "good" body look like?

Son: I don't know. Probably pretty well built. Strong, big, tall, and have wide shoulders.

Mom: Wide shoulders are important if you're a boy?

Son: Yeah. Especially for football.

Mom: Can you play football if you have skinny shoulders?

Son: Yeah.

Mom: Are muscles important?

Son: They can be.

Mom: What defines what a good body looks like? Where do you get your ideas?

Son: From looking at people.

Mom: Other people? Not TV?

Son: [loud and sarcastic] TV only shows the really big, strong people who can pull trucks, okay, you can't compare anything to TV.

Mom: What kinds of feelings are normal for a boy going through puberty to have?

Son: This is like your health class.

Mom: Really! Have you talked about thinking that everyone is staring at you?

Son: Sometimes. But do I care? Not really.

Lessons Learned from This Sample Talk

This mom and son appear to have the ability to communicate candidly and the son revealed attitudes about the mass media's image of attractiveness, having "cool" friends, and what makes a male "normal" and good-looking. Further talks could explore his views on what makes males and females attractive emotionally and intellectually, as well as physically. This talk is a good way to find out what "normal" means, and lets the parent explore the child's values and perceptions. The mom can also ask more about what it means to be "cool" and how one fits in.

Discussing the Story about Friends and Beers

Participants: a mother and her fourteen-year-old daughter

Mom: "A high-school senior and a high-school junior have been getting to know each other for almost a month. They have not been physical or sexual in any way. One night at a friend's house they both drink some beers and end up on a couch, groping and kissing. What is the senior thinking?"

Daughter: It depends if it's the guy or girl. If it's a guy, he's probably going to take advantage of the girl, thinking, "I'm older than her. Let's go ahead and have sex." But if the girl's the senior, she says, "You know what? Let's lay off." Unless they were drunk. But the girl would still have some common sense if she were drunk.

Mom: Boys don't have common sense when they're drunk?

Daughter: They don't have common sense, period. If the girl's a senior and the boy's a junior she's going to be like, "I'm older than you. I have more common sense." And he's going to be all drunk, saying, "Come on, let's have sex." He's not going to think.

Mom: Hmm. Was this a good experience for both of them?

Daughter: Well, they had fun, didn't they? They had fun until they wake up in the morning with their ears ringing.

Mom: Okay. So they wake up and their ears are ringing. What do they think when they think back on it?

Daughter: I think they feel kind of stupid. I think they'll feel kind of disappointed. Let's make a scenario that they were both virgins before this night. I think they'll think back and be kind of disappointed that they had lost their virginity to each other because they were drunk. That they could have decided they really loved each other and were really ready for this particular moment.

Mom: Do you think that they wanted to get physical with one another but didn't know how to without being drunk?

Daughter: Yeah. I think they did like each other but they were, just . . . shy. And they didn't know how to carry it further.

Mom: Did these people break any family rules or the law?

Daughter: They broke the law by drinking alcohol but there'd be no kids left in high school if they were all arrested for drinking. So they broke one law, but having sex isn't against the law. It's not like he raped her. That's a whole different area. They were both drunk and they both wanted to have sex.

Mom: Okay. Did they break any family rules? Would it be breaking any rules at our house?

Daughter: Yeah, well, wait, there's no rule. You'd never come up to me and say, "You can't have sex until you're married." But I know from our family morals that it's not right to have sex until you're married.

Mom: Okay. Interesting. How could this situation have been prevented?

Daughter: They could have drunk cola instead of beer. They could have said no. They could have not gone to the party. They could have stopped at the kissing and groping.

Mom: Here's a question. Suppose you really did like him and he was really neat. Could you talk to him about what's okay and what's not?

Daughter: I think that's stupid. That's like a marriage, it's like, "I'll go out with you but here are the things you have to live by. "First, no doing this or doing that, and then I'll go out with you."

Mom: Suppose you were interested in somebody sexually but you don't want to have a sexual relationship.

Daughter: That's the first time I've ever heard those two words out of your mouth in the same sentence. I think, yeah, when it gets to that point, I think one of them should state how far they should go.

Mom: If you were in a situation like this how would you feel? Let's say you were at a party, not drunk, and with a guy you've really liked for a month.

Daughter: I'd probably kiss him.

Mom: What if he was drunk?

Daughter: Then I probably wouldn't have him as a boyfriend anymore.

Mom: What did you think of this talk?

Daughter: This was interesting.

Lessons Learned from This Sample Talk

The daughter and mother explored new territory here and learned some things from one another. Near the end of the talk the daughter says, "That's the first time I've ever heard those two words out of your mouth in the same sentence," commenting on her mother's use of the phrase "sexual relationship." This was a very productive talk that covered all kinds of important topics, ranging from values and morals to sexual activity between peers, and sex roles. This seems to be the first talk this mother has had with her daughter about sexual conduct, and future talks can only get more interesting.

Discussing the Story about Peer Pressure

Participants: a mom and her ten-year-old daughter

Mom: "A girl is at a party with some friends. Everyone seems to be having a fun time but her. The girl is offered a pill by one of her friends, who says, 'This will make you feel good.' What is the girl thinking?"

Daughter: "What's in that pill? Why does she want to give it to me? What's it for?"

Mom: What do you think the girl is saying?

Daughter: If she's smart, she'd say no. If she isn't very smart, she'll say yes.

Mom: Good. And what is the friend thinking?

Daughter: Why am I offering this to her?

Mom: Do you think she should be offering the pill in the first place?

Daughter: No.

Mom: Does the girl want to take the pill?

Daughter: No.

Mom: Why not?

Daughter: Because she doesn't know anything about it.

Mom: Why does her friend want her to take the pill?

Daughter: To make her happy.

Mom: What are the kinds of consequences the girl might face if she takes the pill?

Daughter: Addiction. She might get sick. She might throw up. She might screw up her life.

Mom: How would she screw up her life?

Daughter: If it were illegal. She might get sent to jail.

Mom: What are the consequences for not taking the pill?

Daughter: Her friend not liking her.

Mom: How does one balance the two? How do you decide?

Daughter: Your life is more important.

Lessons Learned from This Sample Talk

This is a very good talk about peer influence to take drugs. The child seems to share her mother's values about drugs. She understands that drugs are used to moderate difficult feelings, has a good grasp of possible bad outcomes, and says that good health is more important than being liked. Future talks could explore the family rules about what to do when offered drugs.

9

Losing Control/ Taking Control

Talking about Addictions

I remember how my mom, every night at six o'clock, would start drinking her cocktails. It was the same when we visited our grandparents—cocktail hour was at six. I never thought of my mom or relatives as addicted to alcohol.
—Pat, mother of two, Montgomery Village, Maryland

I wanted it to be different for my kids than it was for me. My addiction to cocaine just pushed everything else aside.
—Lisa, mother of two, Portland, Oregon

I found that my son was obsessing about Internet chat rooms. I'm not sure that he's addicted, but he seems to be really hooked—he's on every night for hours, chatting away with God knows who.
—Melissa, mother of one, Syracuse, New York

I didn't understand that my parents were alcoholics until I was thirty years old and my mother nearly died from malnutrition due to excessive drinking. Both my parents had been heavy drinkers throughout my childhood, but most of their friends drank heavily, too, and I grew up thinking that it was completely normal. I would never have thought for a minute that I was living with addicts.
—Carrie, mother of two, Columbia, South Carolina

We never talked about my dad's daily alcohol use in our house—it was never a topic that anyone could broach. By the time we did start talking about it, it was way too late.
—Rita, mother of two, Los Angeles, California

When you hear the word "addiction," what comes to mind? Do you think of illegal drugs, or of alcohol and cigarettes? What does addiction mean to you?

In medical contexts, addiction is sometimes referred to as substance dependence. If someone persists in using a drug despite problems related to its use, a doctor might diagnose substance dependence. Heavy use may result in tolerance to the drug's effects, and in withdrawal symptoms when use is reduced or stopped. If you use a substance every day, that doesn't automatically mean that you are addicted to it, of course; some habits are good.

Talking about addiction has always been controversial. One perspective is that kicking a habit is a matter of self-control and will power; in that point of view, addiction represents a moral weakness. Treatments that come from that viewpoint might look, to some, like punishment. Another view is that addiction is akin to a disease, one that needs to be understood and treated. For many people, any definition of addiction contains a little of each of those perspectives.

Science is just beginning to understand how our genes play into addiction. It appears that some people have a genetic predisposition to addiction; alcoholism, for example, often runs in families and can be found even among relatives who live far from each other. Much more research is needed in this area.

Most families have been touched by addiction in some way. But each family's struggle is different, with unique family values and ways of coping. Some families keep problems closely guarded.

Others are open about the issue and may seek help from family members, friends, or professionals. Still other families may cautiously select what is discussed and what is not. Think about how it was for you growing up in terms of the way your family coped with substance use, misuse, or abuse. How have you carried those values on? What values do you feel good about, and what values might you consider changing?

Preparing for the Talk

This talk will give you the chance to explain to your child what addiction is and why it is important to discuss it. You'll also have a chance to discuss your experiences with addiction, your feelings about it, and any concerns you may have.

In this talk you will help your child understand that

- addiction happens to all kinds of people.
- there is a difference between using a substance and being addicted to it.
- addiction to alcohol, tobacco, and other drugs affects our feelings and emotions as well as our bodies.
- addiction can be a serious condition, and families can discuss ways to support people trying to recover from addiction.
- there are family rules about the use of substances and addictions.

What You Can Expect from This Talk

After the talk your child will be able to

- define the term "addiction."
- describe what happens when people become addicted.

- express family rules and the law about addictive behaviors and substance abuse.
- talk about ways to support family and friends who may be struggling with substance abuse.

The Risks of Addiction

Simply put, addiction is use gone very wrong. Some young people may start using drugs as a way of challenging authority, fighting boredom, or warding off tough feelings, but many soon find it more difficult to stop than they'd imagined. As the addiction progresses, isolation may set in. Who else could understand the overwhelming craving and the fear of facing reality? Feelings of shame may be overwhelming, making it even harder for the person to ask for help.

No one wants to picture a child in this position. That's the very reason that family talks about addiction, and what one can do to ask for help, are essential. Talking about alcohol, tobacco, and other drugs is an important part of keeping your children safe and healthy. Talking to them about health risks and family rules before a crisis occurs is part of the plan.

Defining Our Terms: Use, Misuse, Abuse, and Addiction

A comprehensive talk about drugs and choices needs to provide definitions. Consider the following definitions of "use," "misuse," "abuse," and "addiction."

> **use:** partaking of a substance to fulfill an unmet need in a way that doesn't put you or those around you at risk, or interfere with your daily activities or long-term goals.

misuse: partaking of a substance to fulfill an unmet need as an alternative to more healthy options, or in a manner that puts you or those around you at risk.

abuse: partaking of a substance that puts you or those around you at risk, and impacts your daily living or long-term goals.

addiction: losing control over the use of a substance, such as alcohol, or an activity, such as gambling; also, a habituation to a substance or activity, with development of a withdrawal syndrome when that activity or substance is removed.

As a parent, you'll need to define the terms and compare your definitions with your child's. Do both of you view addiction the same way? If not, how does your view differ from that of your child? You will need to understand how you feel about addictive behavior, both drug- and non-drug-related, so that you can clarify your values and think about how to communicate them.

Quotes to Consider

"The bottom line on addiction is that anyone with a brain can get addicted to drugs. However, most people don't, and there are a plethora of reasons. First and foremost, if a person does not experiment with addictive drugs, then he or she won't get addicted. Second, if a person is mentally healthy, has a stable family and work life, including supportive peers, and no family history of substance abuse, she lacks important risk factors and is less vulnerable. However, she still has a brain, and she is not immune to addiction."

—Kuhn, Swatzwelder, and Wilson, *Buzzed: The Straight Facts about the Most Used and Abused Drugs from Alcohol to Ecstasy,* 1998

"Recovery is a continuing process. Each day is a new challenge for a person overcoming addiction."

—Channing L. Bette Co., *About Addiction*, 1993

"All drugs that are addicting can activate the brain's pleasure circuit. Drug addiction is a biological, pathological process that alters the way in which the pleasure center, as well as other parts of the brain, functions."

—National Institute on Drug Abuse, *Mind over Matter: The Brain's Response to Drugs, A Teacher's Guide*, 1998

Different Families: Different Values

Everyone interprets behavior in his or her own way. Here are some behaviors that may be interpreted differently, depending on a person's experience:

A dad is having his fifth cup of coffee at night to stay up and do work, something he finds himself doing more and more.

Some parents might say that it's no big deal for an adult to use coffee to stay awake while working. Other parents would say he's setting a bad example by using a substance as a crutch. If the dad gets irritated when he is out of coffee, or isn't able to function without it, it could be a sign that he is dependent on coffee in a harmful way. What do you think? If he took caffeine pills, which are widely available, to stay awake instead, would you feel differently?

■

A boy plays computer games for three hours and still wants to play on the computer after his mom says it's time to go to bed. He uses the game every night for hours at a time.

Some parents would see nothing to worry about and see it only as harmless play. Other parents would be concerned about the boy's preoccupation with wanting to be on the computer and worry that it may become an obsession. Still other parents would see this as an opportunity to set clear rules and guidelines for computer use. What do you think?

■

A daughter is using diet pills every day. She thinks about her weight all the time.

Some parents would say that it's okay for young girls to want to look good by focusing on their weight; what girl isn't preoccupied with looking good? Other parents would be concerned with whether the pills were affecting their daughter's feelings or behavior. Others might worry if the daughter shuns activities with friends, such as a day at the beach, out of concern for her weight. What would you say?

■

A college student comes back to his dorm room to find his roommate stoned on marijuana again, now a nightly occurrence.

Many parents would be very upset to hear that their son was living with someone using marijuana at all, and they would want their child assigned another room. Others would say that experimenting with marijuana is a normal part of the college experience. What do you think?

■

A boy is in an Internet chat room trying to find someone to go out with. He is online for several hours a night, seven nights a week.

Some parents might ask their kids whether chatting online has replaced other enjoyable activities, such as spending time with friends, exercising, or listening to music. Others would be happy to have the child quietly entertaining himself. What do you think?

■

A mom's brother is visiting from out of town. The mom knows that her brother used to use heroin, something he claims to have quit. But she notices needle marks that look fresh on her brother's arm.

Some parents would make a point to talk to the brother out of concern for his health. Others would resign themselves to saying nothing, hoping to avoid confrontation. What would you do?

Different Perspectives

"When my sister got out of rehab, she asked if she could explain to my twelve-year-old daughter how she got there. Nervously, I agreed. How my sister came to understand her addiction helped us to understand it as well. Sometimes I see my daughter curiously looking at my sister. I'm thankful that we found a way to talk about it, because although I know my daughter has always loved her, at least she's not afraid of her anymore."   —Joe, father of one, Jamestown, New York

Media Influence

It's no secret that the average child raised on TV and Hollywood movies is well aware of all of the different ways to use substances.

Popular stars smoke cigarettes in their movies while popular singers sing about marijuana use. But popular media often leave out how substance use can become substance abuse. Addicts are usually shown as disheveled, dysfunctional people, not "people like us," with jobs, careers, and loved ones who care about them. In fact, that is the typical addict.

We can't shield our children from the media. Instead, our real challenge is helping them interpret the messages they're getting. You don't have to criticize or judge your child's favorite shows. Just make sure to offer a counterbalance of family values and rules. Point out the differences between the messages on TV and the values that hold true in your home. It's okay if you disagree. The talking itself has power.

Last-minute Checkups before the Talk

Before you talk with your child, try to remember what, if anything, your parents taught you about addiction when you were growing up.

- Did a parent ever talk to you about addiction?
- Did anyone ever explain to you what addiction is?
- Did they tell you how to identify addiction?
- Did they model healthy coping skills to deal with stress or problems without turning to a substance that was potentially addictive?
- How were family members or friends who were struggling with addiction treated while you were growing up?

As a parent, what do you want your child to know about the use of alcohol, tobacco, and other drugs whose use can lead to addiction?

- Do you let your child know that you are open to discussing any concerns that she has about addiction?
- Do you talk to your child about her friends and what they do?
- How have you seen addiction or addicts portrayed in popular culture? Does it match your experience?

Do you have any stories you can share with your child about addiction, or how you once helped someone who was addicted? For example:

- The time a friend started taking a drug all the time until it got out of control, and how scary that was
- The time you made some bad choices about smoking because you wanted to fit in, and how you became addicted to nicotine
- How you helped a friend who was dealing with addiction
- The time you felt scared by a family member's addictive behaviors and didn't know whom to talk to about it

Sharing your stories lets your child know how you feel about addiction. It also shows that you have learned from being in situations that were difficult. You might reflect on the fact that you are currently addicted to something—to coffee, for example, or cigarettes—and feel like skipping this talk out of fear or embarrassment. Remind your child that his parents are human, too, and may struggle with addiction in their own lives. It is not hypocritical to have a talk with your child about addiction in this case. One of the most important gifts you can give your children is to teach them how to make good choices—and how to be honest about times when we fail.

"Children *know* if a parent is holding something back, and it's far better to set the example of communicating that they made a mistake, rather than not communicating. I've learned that I should answer every question truthfully and never lie. Many parents who never admit to making a mistake miss a huge opportunity to help their children understand how everyone struggles and copes."

—Diana, mother of three, Seattle, Washington

"My ex-husband has addictions. The kids know it, but are really uncomfortable talking with me about it because we are divorced and don't get along. So I just let them bring things up about him when and if they need to." —Tracy, mother of two, Columbia, South Carolina

What Are Your Family Rules?

It might sound strange to talk about family rules about addictive behavior. But there may already be unspoken rules about what is acceptable behavior in the family. If you had unspoken rules about addictive behaviors, what would they be? How could you help your family understand that if someone was addicted to a particular drug, you would need to work together to address the situation?

The stories in the next section are meant to give you a chance to discuss the definition of addiction, and how alcohol, tobacco, and other drugs can be addictive. Some of the issues raised in these activities may have been addressed during your talks from earlier chapters. The activities in this chapter focus more on addiction and getting help.

The stories and questions are open-ended, allowing your child to reflect on a range of topics, including the things friends do to protect one another, the power of peer influence, and any concerns you may have. Depending on your child, the talk could even include issues of addiction to eating or sex, and mixed messages about drug use that come from the media or from family members.

The Talk

Introduce the Talk

To start this talk you could say, "Do you know what addiction means?"

Your child may offer the following: "Addiction is when you get hooked on a drug." You can add, "Addiction is the loss of control over the use of a substance or an activity." He might respond, "Then you are addicted to coffee!" or "Does that mean Dad is addicted to beer?" The classic conversation stopper, "Were you ever addicted to anything?" may show up, so be prepared.

Review These Words

Please review the terms in this section. Discussing all the terms with your child is optional. You know which are appropriate for your child's age and maturity level. More than likely, even the youngest children have heard these words on TV or on the bus.

addiction: losing control over use of something, like alcohol or food, or an activity, like gambling; or growing habituated to a substance or activity, such that a withdrawal syndrome starts when that activity or substance is removed.

alcoholism: addiction to alcohol.

drug: any substance, legal or illegal, used to alter a person's consciousness. A doctor's definition might be somewhat different, and include substances used to prevent disease and improve health. Police define drugs as illegal substances that subject users and sellers to arrest.

drug rehabilitation center: a recovery health facility staffed by addiction counselors who provide treatment. There are many organizations that support family members and caretakers of addicted people.

ecstasy (also known as "e" or "x"): ecstasy's chemical structure is related to stimulants and some hallucinogens. It was originally developed as an appetite suppressant in 1914, and was used occasionally in the United States in the 1970s and 1980s by some therapists to enhance communication. Effects described by users include an overwhelming feeling of well-being, increased confidence, and the desire to be in physical contact with other people. It's also known to produce insomnia, depression, and paranoia after the high has worn off.

heroin: a synthetic drug derived from the opium poppy. Heroin is similar to morphine but many times more powerful. It impacts a person's feelings by reducing pain, creating euphoria, reducing stress and inhibition, and preventing withdrawal syndrome.

marijuana (also called pot): a psychoactive plant which is smoked or eaten. Causes mild euphoria, stimulates hunger, and reduces nausea. It is psychologically, though not physically, addictive.

nicotine: the addictive substance in tobacco. Nicotine impacts a person's feelings by stimulating heart function, improving concentration, and for those who are addicted, preventing withdrawal syndrome. Tobacco ultimately acts as a poison to the lungs, heart, and blood vessels. Nicotine is physically and psychologically addictive, and considered by some researchers to be the most addictive substance known to humankind, more addictive than heroin.

opiates: a group of drugs derived from the opium poppy including morphine, heroin, and several medications used by doctors to treat pain. Opiates impact a person's feelings by reducing pain awareness, promoting sleep, and for some, inducing a feeling of complacency or euphoria. Opiates are highly physically addictive.

recovery: the healing and treatment process of becoming sober or ending dependency on drugs. Some addicted people see recovery as a lifelong process.

self-medicating: using alcohol or other drugs to alter one's difficult or painful feelings.

stimulants: a category of drugs, including amphetamines and caffeine, that impact a person's feelings by increasing alertness and causing feelings of euphoria. In general, stimulants are psychologically addictive, but they can be physically addictive as well.

withdrawal syndrome (also called "Jones-ing"): a physical and/or psychological reaction that the body has from not having a drug that it is habituated to. Almost every drug can result in a withdrawal syndrome if it is taken away abruptly. Examples include caffeine (severe headaches, nervousness), marijuana or cocaine (anxiety and other psychological symptoms), and opiates (severe physical withdrawal, including shaking, altered sensations, feelings of dread and fear).

Why Is Talking about Addiction Important?

Ask your child why she thinks talking about addiction is important. Here are some answers you might want to offer. Talking about addiction means

- learning to identify addictive behaviors in your life.
- seeing how addiction to anything can change our relationships.
- clarifying concerns about finding help for relatives and friends with addictions.
- clarifying the connection between addiction and other unhealthy behaviors.

The Stories

In the next part of the talk, you'll be reading short stories to your child and discussing them together. You don't have to read all of the stories; just pick the ones that you think are appropriate for your child. The stories are very simple. Feel free to embellish them, adding details that you think might make the story more believable to your child.

A Story about a Guy and a Chat Room

This story provides an opportunity to talk about addictive behaviors that don't involve drugs.

"A guy is online at night in a chat room talking to people. He does this every night for hours. He finds this activity much more fun than spending time with friends or anything else, and his schoolwork is suffering as a result of his time online. His mom sticks her head into his room before going to bed and wonders whether she should talk with him about his obsession with chat rooms."

Ask these questions of your child:

- What is the boy thinking?
- What is the mom thinking?
- What is the mom saying?
- What is the boy saying?

Now that your child has completed this scenario, ask the following questions:

- Why do you think the boy likes spending time in chat rooms?
- Why is the chat room more fun than spending time with friends?
- What is the boy feeling?
- What should the mom say to the boy about his chat room use?
- How can the boy know if he is addicted to chat rooms?

- If you were in a situation like this, how would you feel? What would you do?

A Story about Alcohol Use Getting out of Control

This story provides an opportunity to talk about alcohol, healthy choices, drunk driving, and what may be the early stages of addiction to alcohol.

"After a party, a teenage girl insists on driving home because she doesn't want to get in the car with her boyfriend, who has been drinking alcohol. Lately, he seems to be drinking all the time and hasn't been able to drink without getting drunk. She drops him off and goes home. The next day the boy calls the girl and invites her to another party."

Ask these questions of your child:

- What is the girl thinking?
- What is the boy thinking?
- What is the girl saying?
- What is the boy saying?

Now that your child has completed this scenario, ask the following questions:

- What do you think the girl wants to do?
- Is the boy being honest about his ability to make safe and healthy decisions?

- What might the girl say to communicate her feelings to her boyfriend? When might she say it?
- What should their parents say to the girl and the boy about drinking and driving?
- How might the boy know if he is addicted to alcohol?
- If you were in a situation like this, how would you feel? What would you do if you were the person drinking too much? What would you do if you were the friend?

A Story about Smoking Pot in Secret

This story provides an opportunity to talk about how family members express concerns about addiction and how people may try, often unsuccessfully, to hide drug use.

"A mother keeps telling her son to clean his room, pull up the shades, and stop burning his incense all the time. She complains that he spends too much time in the dark doing nothing. He says she should be glad he's not running around in the street and to leave him alone. The mom wonders if he's doing drugs all the time, but she's just not sure. They are sitting at dinner and the son is being as quiet as usual."

Ask these questions of your child:

- What is the mom saying?
- What is the mom feeling?

320

- What is the boy saying?
- What is the boy feeling?

Now that your child has completed this scenario, ask the following questions:

- Why would the boy spend so much time alone in his room?
- What might be some of the mom's concerns that she's not talking about?
- How can the mom let the son know that she's really concerned about him?
- What do you think will happen if they both keep avoiding talking about what's going on?
- Let's say the son is smoking pot almost every night. How would he know if he was becoming dependent on marijuana?
- If you were in a situation like this, how would you feel? What would you do?

A Story about Drugs on the Weekend

This story is an opportunity to talk about how people sometimes use drugs on the weekend, a time when it's okay to "let loose."

"A mom picks up her daughter at a friend's house. The girls have been out all night. The mom is concerned because the daughter seems exhausted, and she's beginning to think that maybe the daughter should spend more time at home on weekends. What the mom doesn't know is that the daughter has become fond of using ecstasy at dance clubs. Even though it wears her out, she thinks about it all week and can't wait to do it again next weekend."

Ask these questions of your child:

- What is the mom thinking?
- What is the mom saying?
- What is the daughter thinking?
- What is the daughter saying?

Now that your child has completed this scenario, ask the following questions:

- What might the mom want to say to the daughter, but feels she can't?
- Do you think the daughter has things under control? Why or why not?
- What are some warning signs that the daughter may be headed for some serious problems?
- How might the mom address the concerns she has about her daughter's physical health?
- How would the daughter know if she was becoming dependent on ecstasy?
- How would you feel if you were the daughter in a situation like this? What would you do?

A Story about an Aunt's Recovery

This story gives you a chance to talk about how family or friends can offer support to a relative who's in a program designed to treat addiction.

"A young woman has just moved in with her brother and his two children, one in middle school and the other in high school. The young woman has come to town to join a program for people recovering from using cocaine. She wants to be honest about her recovery program with her niece and nephew because she senses their awkwardness around her. The brother says they don't need to know about addiction or her program, because they're only kids. He tells his sister, 'Let's just keep this to the adults who can handle the situation.'"

Ask these questions of your child:

- What is the sister saying?
- What is the sister feeling?
- What is the brother saying?
- What is the brother feeling?

Now that your child has completed this scenario, ask the following questions:

- Do you think it is helpful to keep the woman's information from the children? Why or why not?

- How do you think the children might react?
- What questions do you think they might have for the woman?
- What might the benefits be of talking about what is going on as a family?
- What do you think the woman needs from her family right now?
- How would you feel if you were the woman in a situation like this? What would you do?

Clarify Your Family's Values

Discuss these questions with your child as a way of sharing your values about addictive behaviors. We have included a number of potential responses from children to help you formulate your own responses. Ask your child the following questions to better understand how she expresses her values and gives them meaning.

Ask your child: "Once you start smoking tobacco, how easy or hard do you think it would be to stop?"

> *Child response #1:* "If you wanted to stop bad enough, you just would."
> *Parent:* That's only part of what it takes. Remember that nicotine causes your body to grow dependent on it, so you also have to be prepared to deal with your body telling you not to stop because it thinks it needs it.

> *Child response #2:* "Just tell the person you don't want them to die, and to stop because you love them."

Parent: That would be an important reason to stop, but a person needs to quit because he makes that choice and wants to make the change. If he does it for someone else, he gets all caught up in not wanting to disappoint someone and then he's not being true to himself. You can still keep telling him you love him, though, and that you don't want him to die and you hope that he quits.

Ask your child: "What kinds of people do you think struggle with addiction?"

Child response #1: "I don't know, people with problems they can't handle."

Parent: Virtually no one sets out to become an addict when he uses drugs for the first time. It can happen to anyone. It's impossible to tell who will become an addict and who will be a recreational user. Some people may think using substances will make their problems go away, but after the high, the problems are still there. Eventually, the addiction can become the major problem—even an addiction to something like cigarettes. All of the other problems then can seem minor in comparison.

Child response #2: "People who are selfish and don't care about the other people they hurt."

Parent: That answer tells me you've given this some real thought. It also sounds like you might have anger or other strong feelings toward a person struggling with addiction. It's a very emotional situation for everyone involved. It might be helpful to look at that person's behavior as tied so tightly to addiction that what they really want is getting lost. What's important is to say what you're feeling, so that we can talk about it honestly and address any problems.

The Bare Minimum: A Quick Quiz for Kids

Ask your child the following questions to assess his knowledge and perceptions of alcohol and drug use.

1. Can you give me examples of three addictive substances?
   Sample answers:
   - Alcohol
   - Tobacco
   - Prescription drugs
   - Heroin
   - Crack

2. What are some addictive behaviors that don't involve drugs?
   Sample answers:
   - Gambling
   - Eating
   - Using the Internet all the time
   - Taking chances with danger
   - Sex

3. Where could you go for answers to questions about addiction?
   Sample answers:
   - Parents or other family members
   - A school counselor
   - Health care provider
   - Our church, synagogue, or religious leader
   - Web sites and hotlines

Talk about Your Family Rules

This is an opportunity to review your family rules. Ask your child the following question:

1. What are our family rules about helping family members and friends with addictive behaviors?
   Sample answers:
   - We try to talk about the problems in a helpful, not blaming, way and not hide them.
   - We know that there are always people who can help.
   - We set boundaries and limits that help us to stay safe and healthy.
   - When rules are broken, we know there are consequences.
   - We talk about the addictive behavior we see at school and in the neighborhood openly and honestly to learn about good ways to deal with it.
   - If we are worried that a friend or family member is addicted, we talk about it rather than keeping it inside.

After the Talk

Take a moment to reflect on the talk you just had with your child. How do you feel about it?

- Were you surprised by your child's view of addiction?
- Does your child seem susceptible to peer pressure when it comes to using alcohol or other drugs?
- What did you learn about how to listen and talk to your child?

Warning Signs

This talk can reveal potential problems kids may be facing. Review the following warning signs to determine if you might need to speak with a school counselor or your doctor:

- Your child shares some problems in the course of the talk that sound like they could be serious.
- Your child doesn't appear to care about school or family.
- Your child seems isolated or alienated from peers.
- She doesn't see anything wrong with kids drinking alcohol or using drugs.
- His grades take a dramatic turn downward.
- She describes values about addictive behavior that are dangerous or illegal.
- He has a hard time concentrating or is unfocused.
- He spends hours every night on the Internet, or does anything to the exclusion of other enjoyable activities.

Some tips follow for being actively involved in your child's daily life. Trust your instincts on how your child is doing. Ask often how your child is doing; try to get beyond their answers of "good" or "fine." Ask your child's opinion on important matters. Be prepared to disagree respectfully, and to tell him you're proud of how he is able to think things through for himself. Make sure to meet your child's friends and their parents, if possible. Set rules and consistently enforce them. Above all, let your kids know you love them no matter what challenges they may face.

Success Stories

You have made it through what may have been a challenging talk. Trying to convey the seriousness of addiction to a child or teen is not easy. The talk about addiction can hold a lot of surprises. One mom reported that her seven-year-old daughter said her friends boasted of being "addicted" to a certain candy. The daughter actually thought that was true, and the mom started a long talk about the difference between craving our favorite candy and behavior that's truly self-destructive and out of control. The mom said she had to think about creative ways to describe addiction in a way her daughter could understand.

Now that we have discussed the seriousness of addiction, we want to end on a positive note about how healthy families cope with alcohol and drug-related problems. Your nine previous talks have laid the foundation for the important tenth one.

Sample Talks
Between Parents and Children

If you are wondering what a real talk about addictions would sound like, take a look at the excepts from actual talks conducted by families.

Discussing the Story about a Guy and a Chat Room

Participants: a dad and his two daughters, ages nine and eleven

Dad: "A guy is online at night in a chat room talking to people. He does this every night for hours. He finds this activity much more fun than spending time with friends or anything else, and his schoolwork is suffering as a result of all his time online. His mom sticks her head into his room before going to bed and wonders if she should talk with him about his obsession with chat rooms." What is the boy thinking?

Older daughter: The boy's probably thinking that it's the cool thing to do.

Dad: What do you think the mom is thinking?

Older daughter: "I should really talk to him about the chat rooms and their dangers."

Younger daughter: "He's doing it too much." She's thinking she should talk to him. If he uses it too much, like an hour a day, then she should give him a punishment.

Dad: What do you think a chat room is for?

Older daughter: Pretty much to talk to your friends or maybe just to get to know someone.

Dad: Why is the chat room more fun than spending time with friends?

Younger daughter: Maybe he doesn't have friends.

Dad: What is the boy feeling?

Younger daughter: Well, I think he's feeling lonely if he's in the chat room instead of talking to his friends. On the computer he can say anything he wants, but to his friends, he can't, because they'll tell everything that he says.

Dad: What should the mom say to the boy about his chat room use?

Older daughter: That it's freedom with limits. You can go into chat rooms but only for an hour. That way, he gets to go in the chat room but it's very limited.

Dad: Do you think that's what the mom should do?

Older daughter: Yes. That way he's not being punished, he's just being limited.

Dad: How does the boy know if he is addicted to chat rooms?

Older daughter: The person on the other side could tell him.

Younger daughter: I think that's very unlikely.

Older daughter: It's *my* answer, not yours!

Dad: Okay, fair enough! How else could he know?

Older daughter: Humph! I told you!

Dad: Okay, let's move on. If you were in a situation like this, how would you feel? What would you do if you were the boy in the chat room?

Older daughter: I've never been in a situation like this.

Dad: But if you were? Spending a lot of time in front of a computer.

Younger daughter: I'd probably stop going to the chat room and start doing games.

Dad: [laughs as girls argue]

Lesson Learned from This Sample Talk

While the girls couldn't relate to the chat room experience very well, they were able to share their thoughts about feeling lonely and left out. The dad might want to discuss these feelings, and healthy ways to cope with them, in future talks.

Discussing the Story about Alcohol Use Getting out of Control

Participants: a mom and her eleven-year-old daughter

Mom: "A teenage girl insists on driving her boyfriend home from a party because he has had too much to drink. Lately, he seems to be drinking all the time and he hasn't been able to drink without getting drunk. The day after the party, the boy calls the girl to invite her to another party." What is the girl thinking?

Daughter: She's thinking he needs to stop drinking, and she doesn't want to go to another party.

Mom: Is the boy being honest about his ability to make safe and healthy decisions?

Daughter: No.

Mom: What might the girl say to communicate her concerns and her feelings to her boyfriend?

Daughter: She might want to talk to him and tell him not to do it, and tell his parents to talk to him.

Mom: What should the parents say to the girl or the boy about drinking and driving?

Daughter: The parents should tell the girl to not get into the car if he's drunk and they should tell the boy not to drink, or drive when he's drunk.

Mom: How might the boy know if he is addicted to alcohol?

Daughter: He'd know if he were drinking all the time and he can't stop.

Mom: If you were in a situation like this, how would you feel? What would you do?

Daughter: I would feel sad that my boyfriend couldn't stop drinking and I'd talk to his parents [about talking to] him and I'd try talking to him.

Mom: What if you were in a situation where you were addicted to alcohol?

Daughter: Then I would try to get help to stop.

Lessons Learned from This Sample Talk

This talk provided an opportunity for both mother and daughter to share their attitudes about drinking. The mother could follow up with more about family rules and alcohol and driving. The daughter seems very open and willing to share her thoughts.

Discussing the Story about Smoking Pot in Secret

Participants: a dad and his two daughters, ages eleven and nine

Dad: "A mother keeps telling her son to clean his room, pull up the shades, and stop burning incense all the time. She complains that he spends too much time in the dark doing nothing. He says she should be glad he's not running around in the street and to leave him alone. The mom wonders if he is doing drugs all the time, but she is not sure. They are sitting at dinner and the son is being as quiet as usual." What is the mom thinking?

Older daughter: She's thinking that he's addicted to drugs. But she just has a suspicion.

Younger daughter: If he starts talking he might blurt it out!

Dad: What is the mom feeling?

Younger daughter: Feels suspicious but she really doesn't know what's happening under her own roof.

Dad: What is the boy thinking?

Older daughter: He's thinking, "She doesn't have a clue and I can keep doing drugs."

Dad: What is the boy feeling?

Older daughter: If he was doing incense, maybe drowsy because some incense makes you sleepy, hungry, and those characteristics.

Younger daughter: He wonders if he's going to die or get sick

Dad: Why would the boy want to spend so much time alone in his room?

Older daughter: So he can keep using drugs, so his mom won't know.

Dad: So the incense is being used to hide the smell of the drugs?

Daughters: Yeah.

Dad: What might be some of the mom's concerns that she's not talking about?

Younger daughter: She's concerned he's using drugs without her permission and he might be lying about it and he could be lying to her about other things, too.

Older daughter: I think she might be concerned about his welfare because she wants him to have a good life without drugs.

Dad: How can the mom let the son know she's really concerned about him?

Older daughter: She could write him a note or tell him straight out or pin it on his wall.

Younger daughter: That she's there to talk and advise and stuff.

Dad: What do you think will happen if they both keep avoiding talking about his use of drugs?

Younger daughter: He could get worse and worse, and by the time it's a crisis, he'll finally tell her.

Older daughter: She took my idea.

Dad: Assuming the son is smoking pot almost every night, how would he know if he was becoming dependent on marijuana?

Older daughter: He would waste all his money. Then he'd start stealing from banks and once he'd realized he'd stolen it, then he'd find out.

Younger daughter: He wouldn't rob from banks, but he'd go bankrupt, and then he'd go to his parents for money, and then other people in the family for money just to get more marijuana for himself.

Dad: If you were in a situation like this, how would you feel? What would you do?

Younger daughter: Lonely.

Older daughter: I would feel kind of bad. You know how some drugs really mess with your brain? If you were a really smart kid and then you started taking it, it would mess up your brain and then it would mess up your grades and then you'd feel bad.

Lessons Learned from This Sample Talk

This talk opened doors for more conversations about addiction. The daughter seemed to understand many of the negative outcomes of drug use. The dad could point out other associated consequences, such as legal problems, loss of motivation, and diminished intellectual development.

Discussing a Story about Drugs on the Weekend

Participants: a dad and his two daughters, ages eleven and nine

Dad: "A mom picks up her daughter at a friend's house. The girls have been out until early in the morning. The mom is concerned because the daughter seems exhausted, and she's beginning to think maybe the daughter should spend more time at home on the weekends. What the mom does not know is that the daughter has become fond of using ecstasy and going to clubs."

Older daughter: What's ecstasy?

Dad: Do either of you know?

Younger daughter: I know what it is, but I forgot.

Dad: Ecstasy is a drug that affects your brain and it can kill you.

Younger daughter: Eventually.

Dad: Eventually. But if you misused it, even one time, it could kill you. Then the story says, "Even though it wears her out, the daughter thinks about it all week and can't wait to do it again." The mom is now picking her up. What is the mom thinking?

Younger daughter: She probably doesn't know about it but she's getting suspicious. Because when people take drugs there's usually some kind of sign, like they get drowsy, they start getting mad or—

Older daughter: Grumpy.

Dad: What is the mom saying?

Older daughter: I don't think she'd say anything. She's just trying to figure stuff out. Like trying to find out what her daughter did there.

Dad: What is the daughter thinking?

Younger daughter: "I shouldn't tell my mom about what I did." She'll make up some lies.

Dad: You think the daughter would tell some lies?

Younger daughter: Yeah, it's not like she'd go up to the mom and say, "Hi Mom, I'm using ecstasy!"

Dad: What is the daughter saying?

Older daughter: I don't think she'd say anything. I think she'd be thinking of ways to go back, and how she can't tell anybody or she'd get in trouble.

Younger daughter: She's probably saying, "I had a good time there and we watched TV and played," stuff like that. That way she would actually say what she did.

Older daughter: She'd just tell her everything else except the club part.

Younger daughter: Yeah.

Dad: What might the mom want to say to the daughter but doesn't know how?

Younger daughter: "Have you been using anything that I don't know about?" "Why are you so sleepy?"

Older daughter: "Why are you suddenly always sleepy and grumpy and stuff?"

Dad: Do you think the daughter has things under control?

Older daughter: No.

Younger daughter: I think she has it under control, but she's getting worse. The first time you do it you think it's horrible, you don't like it. But after a while it's like, "That was kind of good, actually." And then you get addicted.

Dad: What are some warning signs that the daughter may be headed for some serious problems?

Younger daughter: Sleepiness, very exhausted. Lots of stress.

Dad: How might the mom address concerns she has about her daughter's physical health?

Older daughter: She could ask her a lot of questions. Maybe write a letter, a note or something? She could say she's there to talk about anything.

Younger daughter: She could talk to her.

Dad: Those are great ideas. How would the daughter know if she was becoming dependent on ecstasy?

Younger daughter: She can't. If she goes to clubs then people might start giving it to her.

Dad: How would you feel if you were in a situation like this? What would you do?

Younger daughter: I don't know. I'd feel stressed out. I'd probably feel like I needed to talk to somebody.

Lessons Learned from This Sample Talk

The dad might follow up by mentioning whom his daughters might talk to and where they could go for help. He should make sure there is a support structure in place. He could also discuss "getting in trouble" and what that means to his daughter. Children often don't reach out for help because they fear the consequences. Rules are important, but so is knowing that they have a place to turn for help without judgment or shame.

Discussing a Story about the Aunt's Recovery

Participants: a mom and her eleven-year-old daughter. Note how the mother changes the story to make it more real for her daughter.

Mom: "A young woman has just moved back to her hometown from New York City. She is staying with her brother and his two children, one who is in middle school and the other who's in high school. The young woman is in a program recovering from using cocaine. She wants to be honest about her recovery program with her niece and nephew because she senses their awkwardness around her. The brother says they don't need to know about addiction or her program because they're only kids. He tells his sister, 'Let's just keep this between adults who can handle the situation.'" What is the sister thinking?

Daughter: She doesn't know if she should tell the children about her cocaine problem.

Mom: What is the sister feeling?

Daughter: She's feeling like she's not telling the truth. I mean, she's not lying, she's just not telling. She could just tell the brother and then the brother could decide to tell the niece and nephew.

Mom: But how does she feel about her brother not wanting to tell the kids the truth?

Daughter: Well, I think she should. They already went through drug class in school and they know.

Mom: What do you think the brother is thinking?

Daughter: That it's right not to tell his children.

Mom: Do you think he's hiding something from his children? Do you think it is helpful to keep the aunt's information from the children?

Daughter: No.

Mom: Why?

Daughter: Because I think she should tell the nephew.

Mom: Why should they know?

Daughter: I think it's wrong to keep secrets from them. But—well, I don't know.

Mom: The aunt senses the kids are feeling kind of funny around her.

Daughter: That's why I would tell, because they would feel uncomfortable.

Mom: Okay. How do you think the children might react? What if they knew? If she told them, how would they feel?

Daughter: They would be shocked.

Mom: What questions do you think they might have for the aunt? If they did find out?

Daughter: How'd you get started and why?

Mom: What good would it be to talk about what is going on as a family?

Daughter: They might have an idea of how to help, even more, even if she's going through a program.

Mom: What do you think the aunt needs from her family right now?

Daughter: Love. Help.

Mom: That's so true. How would you feel if you were in a situation like this? What would you do if you were the aunt?

Daughter: I would probably tell them.

Mom: But the brother says, "Don't tell them."
Daughter: I would try to convince him to tell them.

Lessons Learned from This Sample Talk

This talk brought out issues of telling the truth and of covering up the negative effects of drugs. The daughter talked about love and support as essential elements for recovery from addiction, points the mother could build on in future talks.

10

How Families Cope

Talking about Family Values, Rules, and Consequences

*I started talking with my son early on about some of his relatives'
problems with drugs and the ways we dealt with—and are still
dealing with—the drug use.* —Maria, mother of two, New York City

*I grew up with a mom who was having all kinds of emotional
problems. She was also mixing prescription drugs with alcohol. It
was never talked about openly, even though the entire extended
family met every Sunday for dinner. My mom never got the help she
needed. Being silent on the subject doesn't help anyone.*
—Don, father of two, Washington, D.C.

*My parents both drank a lot. And my sisters and I used to call it
"dad's problem" or "mom's problem" when they got drunk. We never
called it alcohol abuse, and it wasn't until we were adults that we
got a doctor involved to help them out.*
—Jay, father of three, Newport Beach, California

*I was out with my sister one night, and as usual I was getting high
and drunk. The next morning, hung over, I remember her saying
that she was very worried about me and my drug use. It stuck with
me, and her concern eventually got me into counseling, which
helped a ton.* —Kay, mother of two, Sels, Arizona

By the time most parents reach Chapter 10 they have learned a lot about their child's values—and their own. Some parents say that revisiting their childhood has helped greatly in their assessment of their own parenting. Even if you've done only a few of the talks in this book, you've addressed some of the most important issues that your child will face growing up. We hope that both you and your child have learned from each other about the use of drugs and the significant choices teens and adults have to make. Our hope is that these talks have given you the opportunity to share with your child how you feel, what you believe in, and your views on healthy behaviors and good decisions.

What We Mean by "Coping"

Families cope with alcohol and other drug-related problems in many ways. By coping we mean identifying and addressing the problem, two very different things. For some families, the operative word is denial. The situation is ignored and family members are therefore "denying" that the problem even exists. In other families, problems might have been discussed—even fought over, or cried over—but never addressed with a solution. We advocate coping by communicating about the problems and seeking help, either from family members, professionals, clergy, or other members of your support system.

We hope that in the course of nine talks, you and your child have come a fair distance, but we want you two to go a bit further. We invite you to use this last talk to look at the your values and guiding principles, especially as they relate to how people identify problems within the family and seek help to address them.

Preparing for the Talk

In this talk, be sure that your child has a good grasp of how people identify problems with drug use and—equally important—how family members can help one another. To do this, we will revisit some of the situations addressed in earlier parts of this book. This is a good way to know whether the messages you've sent have come through loud and clearly.

In this talk you will let your child know that

- he can depend on you to talk about problems in the extended family.
- you have expectations about his behavior as well as that of all family members.
- there are family values about helping family members and rules about dealing with drug problems.
- the values and rules are here to keep us safe and healthy.

What You Can Expect from This Talk

After the talk your child will

- be able to talk about any concerns she may have about family members' alcohol and drug use.
- know that while different families have different ways of dealing with drug-related problems, *your* strategies are the ones that set the standard for helping people in your home.
- understand how your beliefs and values about caring for others means knowing where to find help in the community.

Seeing Problems and Solving Problems

There are many people who will have an impact on your child throughout her life. Teachers, coaches, religious leaders, media celebrities, family members, peers, and trusted friends will all affect how your child approaches problems and solutions and makes choices. This book is filled with quotes from parents who grew up in households where alcohol and other drug use was common, and where the impact of alcohol or drug abuse was never discussed. For many families, keeping quiet about alcohol or drug problems is still the norm. But silence didn't help families yesterday, and it doesn't help solve problems today.

Building a Strong Set of Values

Your values are your personal guideposts all through life. Every day we make choices, and our values are our guide. Every choice gives us the chance to be caring or uncaring, helpful or unhelpful, supportive or non-supportive. Every situation tests our values and our beliefs. How a parent lives speaks volumes to a child.

This book asks each parent to look at her or his own values. What models of behavior are you giving your children? How sober and healthy are the relationships your kids see in the house? How do we explain our own struggles to them? Our children study us closely and when our values and our actions don't match up, we owe them an explanation.

Quotes to Consider

"Of nearly 200,000 students surveyed, 33% said that their parents often do not set clear rules. And half said that they are not routinely disciplined when they break the rules."

—Mothers Against Drunk Driving, "Underage Drinking
Information Parents Need to Know," www.madd.org

"The mounting trend to resolve thorny public-safety controversies by slapping another restriction on teens ultimately endangers the public, including children and youths, by diverting attention from the paramount issue of adult misbehavior."

—Mike A. Males, *The Scapegoat Generation,* 1996

"Grownups do not always have realistic expectations of teens; we must take teens where they are, not where we want them to be. Think of the young person as shaking his or her head no, but at the same time as shouting in a quiet voice about his or her needs, hopes, dreams, and desires. Listen for the quiet shouting, too. Pay attention to all the signs."

—Dr. Michael Carrera, *Lessons for Lifeguards,* 1996

"Whether or not their parents had talked with them about these tough issues, children as young as 10 still want more information on how to deal with issues such as how to handle peer pressure to use drugs and alcohol."

—Kaiser Family Foundation and Children Now, "Talking With Kids
About Tough Issues: A National Survey of Parents and Kids," 1999

Different Families: Different Values

Our culture presents many different values and perspectives about alcohol, tobacco, and other drugs. You have your own family values and rules. So do your child's friends, their friends' parents, the older kids down the block, and your child's favorite TV characters. The following scenarios illustrate how a person's values are tested as she receives different messages about alcohol, tobacco, and other drugs. The scenarios are somewhat complex and designed to prepare you for questions from your children. Even though these topics might seem very adult, they are issues that have been brought up by elementary, middle-, and high-school children across the country. Feel free to choose the topics that seem most appropriate for your child.

A mother is talking to her son at the breakfast table. The father appears, looking tired, and says that he is too sick to go to work. The night before, he'd gotten drunk and fallen asleep on the floor watching TV, something he does more and more often.

Many parents would see this as a serious situation that needs to be discussed. Others would be uncomfortable talking about the dad's drinking, and would just hope the problem resolves itself. Some parents would talk with each other about the situation but never in front of the children. What would you do?

■

A mother and daughter are watching TV, when they hear a report about tobacco use and the disease and deaths that long-term use causes. The daughter asks the mom, "Why would people still smoke if we know that it can kill you?"

Some parents would use the opportunity to talk about the power of addiction, from alcohol to Internet use, and how it can consume a person's life and affect everyone in the family. Other parents wouldn't be comfortable talking about tobacco use, perhaps because of smokers in the house. What would you do?

■

A fifth-grade girl asks, "Why is Uncle Tim not around anymore? He used to visit all the time." Tim used marijuana for years and is now in jail for selling marijuana.

Some parents wouldn't want to talk to their kids about a relative going to jail, no matter the reason. They might worry that the news would spread and damage the family's reputation. Other parents would want to discuss this situation as a way of teaching kids about the consequences of using drugs. Still other parents would say that Tim does not deserve to be in jail, and that he belongs in a recovery program instead. What would you do?

■

A mother gets a phone call from her sister telling her that her niece has died of an overdose of heroin. Her fourth-grade daughter asks her how the niece died.

Some parents would want to explain how the niece died, since it provides a cautionary tale. Other parents wouldn't want to talk about it at all, fearing that people outside the family might find out. Still other parents would use this moment to talk about the importance of helping relatives who are using drugs. What would you do?

Different Perspectives

"My parents taught me to pray and to ask God to take the taste for drugs away."   —Marion, mother of two, Charleston, South Carolina

" 'But everyone else's parents let them do this or that!' seems to be the cry of my young kids. I told them that it's hard to play a game if you don't know the rules, and you are sure to lose because you don't know how to win. I know life's not a game, it's way more serious. That's why the adults in our family make sure rules and consequences are followed, and our kids know the values that created them. My job as a parent is to keep my kids' minds, bodies, and spirits healthy, and that comes from keeping us grounded in our family beliefs."   —Joan, mother of five, New York City

Last-minute Checkups before the Talk

Before you start the talk, think about your own upbringing and how family beliefs and values about coping with problems were presented to you.

- Did your parents talk with you about any relatives who were misusing alcohol, tobacco or other drugs?
- Did they have strong beliefs about right and wrong, and communicate those beliefs to you?
- How was asking for help perceived, as a weakness or as a strength?
- Did your parents pass on a set of family beliefs, religious or not, to help guide you in facing problems and making healthy decisions?

How are you communicating your family beliefs to your child?

- Do you talk with your family about your beliefs and values on alcohol and other drugs?
- Do you think your behaviors make it clear how your child should face drug-related problems?
- Do you talk to your child about the difference between right and wrong?

This is a good time to think about your childhood experiences with learning about beliefs and values. Do you have any stories that you could share with your child? For example:

- A story about an adult who talked with you about facing problems with alcohol or other drug use
- A time when an adult explained the difference between right and wrong
- A story about how you developed your values and beliefs, and how those values help you make healthy decisions
- A story about how you specifically developed your beliefs about alcohol and drugs
- A time when you talked with someone about self-destructive behavior
- A story about siblings talking about a family member's behavior

What Are Your Family Rules?

In the previous nine chapters we have offered examples of family rules that were shared with us by parents from around the country. We hope that you have had the opportunity to clarify your values and communicate some standards for conduct in your home. Discussing the family rules, the consequences for breaking them, and the law are vitally important.

In the stories in this upcoming talk, families have meaningful conversations about a variety of situations, all involving potential alcohol or other drug use among family or friends. The stories give you an opportunity to see how your child perceives your values about identifying problems and making healthy decisions.

As you think about the ethical issues in these stories, consider what kinds of family rules need to be in place to offer your child practical guidelines. For example, do you have family rules about whether the children can drink alcohol, and under what conditions? Are there clear guidelines about how to act when friends show up at a party with drugs? Does your child know the consequences for breaking those rules? Have you created a climate in your household in which your child feels free to discuss the rules? Do you feel comfortable enforcing them? And, if you need help of any kind, do you know where you can go to find it?

The Support of Aunts, Uncles, and Grandparents

Clearly, discussing family rules with a ten-year-old is going to be a lot easier than with a high-school junior. What should you do if you encounter resistance? As many parents have found, you can change your parenting style at any time, whether that means having regular family talks or developing new family rules. You can develop new strategies when old ones prove ineffective. Some parents will call family meetings when a problem arises.

Especially with teens, ask for allies within your sphere of trusted relatives. Consider bringing in supportive relatives and friends, adults who have good relationships with you and your kids. Once a child turns thirteen, we hear time and time again that grandparents, aunts, and uncles can really help and provide a needed buffer throughout the teen years.

> "My aunt saved my sanity. She helped me understand why some family members were having problems with drinking. It meant a lot when she said I could call her any time."
>
> —Sara, mother of one, Seattle, Washington

> "I was honored when my sister asked me to help out with her son. My nephew's going through a tough time, and I'm happy to spend time and talk with him about all kinds of stuff."
>
> —Phil, uncle of two, Syracuse, New York

The Talk

Introduce the Talk

Congratulations on making it to talk number ten! After nine chapters and talks, you have had the opportunity to hear how your child responds to a variety of situations and problems, and how he makes choices. This talk will give you a chance to hear how your child thinks family members can help one another if a problem arises. Be prepared for disagreement—it's perfectly normal—and be ready to listen to your kids' perspectives.

Find time for an uninterrupted ten-minute talk. Ask your child, "What is a good way to help someone who might be having a problem with alcohol or other drugs?"

Be prepared to hear "I don't know" or "Tell him to go to a doctor." Your child may also offer some good examples. If so, proceed with the next section.

If he asks you, "What kinds of problems?" you can suggest something like this: "Problems may vary, from drinking too much beer and having a hangover, to experimenting with and becoming addicted to dangerous drugs. Have you ever seen anyone with problems like that?"

Review These Words

Please review the terms in this section. Discussing all the terms with your child is optional. You know what's appropriate for your child's age and maturity level. More than likely, even the youngest children have heard these words in classes on character, or on TV.

choice: the ability people have to use free will to make a decision for themselves. This ability can be affected by the use of alcohol and other drugs.

compassion: the act of being aware, caring about, and understanding the feelings of others and providing support and assistance.

coping: the way we manage our day-to-day activities, including handling stress and emotional concerns.

coping mechanisms: behaviors that we develop for dealing with difficult emotions day to day.

counseling: a process of self-discovery and growth led by a trained professional in which people learn how to better relate to themselves and others.

denial: ignoring or refusing to see what exists.

enabling: providing support for another person's dysfunctional behavior, consciously or unconsciously.
ethics: standards for moral conduct.
morals: how we define what is right or wrong.
principles: a person's basic truths.

Why Is Talking about Coping Important?

For some children, talking about coping seems very strange. Isn't that something adults do? Your child may ask, "Why do we have to talk about this stuff?"

Some responses might be:

- Sometimes a family member may face problems that result in other members having problems, too.
- Talking about coping with alcohol and other drugs helps families set standards for behavior.
- Talking about coping with alcohol or other drugs helps children and parents clarify healthy and unhealthy situations, as well as healthy and unhealthy choices.

Last-minute Checkups before the Talk

Before you talk with your child, try to remember what your parents taught you about coping with alcohol- and drug-related problems when you were young.

- Did a parent ever talk to you about alcohol or other drug problems a relative or friend was having?

- What did they tell you about warning signs for alcohol or other drug problems?
- Did they model their spoken values about addressing problems and getting outside help?

As a parent, what are the messages you want to give your child about dealing with problems?

- Do you encourage her to talk about her concerns related to alcohol, tobacco, or other drug use in the family?
- How do you let your child know that you welcome conversations like that?
- Do you talk to your child about the importance of finding friends who share your values about alcohol, tobacco, and other drug use?
- How do you model your family's values?

Do you have any stories that you can share with your child about talking about tough issues, problems, and difficult feelings? Can you share how your beliefs helped you through difficult situations or how you confronted someone who was misusing alcohol or other drugs? For example:

- The time a relative tried to talk to a family member about a drinking problem
- The time you felt you may have misused prescription drugs but found the strength to deal with the problem
- The time you experienced impaired judgment by a co-worker due to marijuana use

Sharing your stories lets your child know how you feel about having strong values and beliefs about dealing with situations in a healthy way, and what lessons you learned when you were growing up.

What Are Your Family Rules?

In the nine previous chapters we have outlined sample family rules for children. As you think about your values and beliefs, you might wish to review some of the rules illustrated in the book. You'll also want to think about clear consequences of breaking rules and the law.

The Stories

In the next part of the talk, you'll be reading short stories to your child and discussing them together. You don't have to read all of the stories. Pick the ones that raise questions that are appropriate for your child. Feel free to embellish them, adding details that you think might make the story more believable and meaningful to your child.

The following stories show family members talking about a problem related to alcohol or drug use. They illustrate

- a mother talking with a son about his older brother.
- a mother talking with her daughter about her dad.
- a father talking with a daughter about her sister.
- a brother and sister talking.

These stories are a little different from the stories in the previous nine chapters in that the parents in the illustrated scenarios ask specific questions of their children. You may wish to review the sample talks at the end of the chapter to see what areas were explored by other parents and children. Some of the children's responses may surprise you.

A Story about a Mom and Her Son

This talk gives you an opportunity to address your values about drug misuse, trust, and divided loyalties, and how best to help people.

"A mother says to her son, 'Your older brother seems very distracted these days. I am worried that he is using some kind of drug. What do you think?'" The son knows that his brother has been misusing prescription drugs and getting drunk a lot.

Ask these questions of your child:

- What is the son feeling?
- What does the son say?
- What is the mom feeling?
- What does the mom say?

Now that your child has completed this scenario, ask the following questions:

- Does the mom have any special concerns?
- Does the son have any special concerns?
- Does the son understand why this question would be important to talk about?
- Might the little brother feel nervous or afraid his brother will get angry? Why or why not?
- Would the little brother think he is betraying his brother if he talks about his older brother's alcohol use? Why or why not?
- What can the family do to help the older brother?
- If you were the child in a situation like this, how would you react? What would you talk about? How would you feel after the talk?

A Story about a Mom, a Daughter, and a Dad

This talk gives you an opportunity to discuss potential drug misuse, trust, and divided loyalties, and how to help people.

"A mother and father are divorced. The mom says to her daughter, 'I'm worried about your dad. When I go to pick you up or call on the phone at his apartment, your dad sounds like he has been drinking or something. Is there a problem?'" The daughter knows that her dad has been very upset during the past few months. He's been smoking marijuana and drinking alcohol often.

Ask these questions of your child:

- What is the daughter feeling?
- What does the daughter say?
- What is the mom feeling?
- What does the mom say?

Now that your child has completed this scenario, ask the following questions:

- Does the mom have any special concerns?
- Does the daughter have any special concerns?
- Does the daughter understand why this question would be important to talk about?
- Why might the daughter feel conflicted about what to tell her mom? Would she feel that she is betraying her dad? Would she fear her dad's reaction?
- If you were the child in a situation like this, how would you react? What would you talk about? How would you feel after the talk?

A Story about a Dad and His Daughters

This talk gives you an opportunity to address your values about drug misuse, related health risks, laws about drugs, and how to find help for people.

"A dad says to his daughter, 'I'm worried about your sister. When she comes back from college, she always seems tired and distracted. She is very skinny and doesn't look healthy. Do you know what's going on with her?' The daughter knows that her sister has tried heroin."

Ask these questions of your child:

- What is the daughter feeling?
- What does the daughter say?
- What is the dad feeling?
- What does the dad say?

Now that your child has completed this scenario, ask the following questions:

- Why does the dad have special concerns?
- Does the daughter have any special concerns?
- Is the daughter worried about betraying her sister's confidence?
- Is she afraid what might happen if she tells?
- Does the daughter understand why this question would be important to talk about?
- What can the family do to help the older sister?
- If you were the child in a situation like this, how would you react? What would you talk about? How would you feel after the talk? Who could you talk with—a parent, grandparent, aunt, or uncle?

A Story about a Brother and Sister

This talk is an opportunity to address your values about finding help for a family member.

"A brother and sister are driving to school. The sister says that she is very upset and worried about her mom's drinking. The mom has been drinking vodka at lunch and throughout the rest of the day and night. This has become a daily routine."

Ask these questions of your child:

- What is the brother feeling?
- What does the brother say?
- What is the sister feeling?
- What does the sister say?

Now that your child has completed this scenario, ask the following questions:

- Why does the sister have any special concerns?
- Does the brother have any special concerns?
- Is the daughter worried about betraying or angering her mother?
- Is she afraid what might happen if she tells an aunt or other relative about the situation?
- Does the brother understand why this issue would be important to talk about?
- What can the brother and sister do to help the mother?
- What can happen to the mother if no family member intervenes?

- If you were the teenager in a situation like this, how would you react? What would you talk about? How would you feel after the talk? Whom could you talk with—a teacher, grandparent, aunt, or uncle?

A Story about a Mom and Her Sons

This talk gives you an opportunity to address your values about discussing treatment for a family member, respecting the privacy of others, and expressing concerns.

"A mom is having dinner with her two sons. The older son is eighteen and has just returned from a few months in a treatment program to address his addiction to cocaine and alcohol. The younger son is thirteen years old and really looks up to his brother. The mom is worried that her younger son will get into drugs. This is their first dinner together in three months."

Ask these questions of your child:

- What is the older brother feeling?
- What does the older brother say?
- What is the younger brother feeling?
- What does the younger brother say?
- What is the mother feeling?
- What does the mother say?

Now that your child has completed this scenario, ask the following questions:

- Why does the mother have special concerns?
- Does the older brother have any special concerns?
- Why would the mother worry about her younger son trying drugs?
- What can the younger brother and mother do to help the older brother?
- What can the older brother do to help keep his younger brother off drugs?
- If you were the older brother in a situation like this, how would you react? What would you talk about? How would you feel after the talk? Who could you talk with, in addition to the mom, to feel supported—a grandparent, aunt, or uncle?

Clarify Your Family's Values

Discuss these questions with your child as a way of sharing your feelings about family members' misuse of alcohol and drugs. We have included a number of potential responses from children to help you formulate your own responses.

Ask your child: "What happens when a teenager starts using drugs?"

Child response #1: "I don't know."
Parent: It depends on the person and the drug. But illegal drugs can get people into big problems with the police. And people don't know who makes the drugs. Someone might experi-

ment with some drug at the urging of a good friend, and find out that they have taken something that causes severe health problems.

Child response #2: "He gets hooked on it."
Parent: That can definitely happen. Some people do become addicted to all kinds of substances. It is very complex, and it depends on the person and the drug.

Ask your child: "What are the benefits of family members talking openly about problems associated with sex and drugs?"

Child response: "How should I know?"
Parent: We can talk about a situation *before* it becomes a serious problem.

Ask your child: "Are there times when family members might not talk about drug or alcohol use? When? And why?"

Child response #1: "It's embarrassing."
Parent: Yes, it can be sometimes.

Child response #2: "If I talk about stuff, you'll think I'm doing it."
Parent: Actually, I won't. I know you get tons of messages from your friends and TV about sex and drugs. Talking about it doesn't mean anyone is actually doing something.

The Bare Minimum: A Quick Quiz for Kids

Ask your child the following questions to assess her knowledge of her own values.

1. How might a friend or family member react if you said you were concerned about his alcohol or other drug use?
   Sample answers:
   - The person might be mad.
   - The person might say it's none of your business.
   - You might lose the friendship for a short time or forever.
   - You might have a long talk about the situation and find out that your friend wants help.
   - You might save your friend's life.
   - You might be threatened.

2. How does someone find help for alcohol or other drug-related problems?
   Sample answers:
   - By contacting the school's psychologist, counselor, or nurse.
   - By calling a help line.
   - By talking to people at your religious or community center.
   - By talking to other family members or trusted friends.
   - By talking with a doctor.
   - By reading about places to go for help at a bookstore, library, or on the Internet.

3. How does a person know when a family member might need help?

Sample answers:
- The family member is losing control.
- The family member becomes violent or threatens violence to others or self.
- He denies having a serious problem when it's clear a problem exists.
- She is unable to concentrate or perform basic tasks.
- The family member asks for help directly or talks about being very sad and upset.
- She shows signs of severe depression.

Talk about Your Family Rules

As you know, *Ten Talks* is filled with sample family rules in every chapter. Take some time to think about what family rules you need to create, reintroduce, change, omit, add, or emphasize. You also may want to think about the consequences of breaking family rules or the law and review those consequences with your child.

After the Talk

Take a moment to reflect on the talk you just had with your child. How do you feel about it?

- What surprised you about your child's answers?
- Are you comfortable with her sense of right and wrong?
- How do you think your child felt about the talk?
- What follow-up talk would you like to have?

Warning Signs

Potential problems that your child is facing may be revealed by the talks or recent behaviors. There may be cause for concern if you hear from the school, or from other parents or child-care providers, that your child

- is extraordinarily hyperactive, agitated, or unusually aggressive.
- is sullen, depressed, or lacks energy.
- has severe mood swings.
- shows little or no empathy or compassion for others.

Always use your instinct as a parent when it comes to looking for warning signs. In any of these situations, you need to find out what is happening by talking with your child. If after your discussion you feel that your child needs more help than you alone can offer, contact the school counselor or look further into one of the many resources available in your community.

Finding Help

Support and help for your child—and you—is available, if needed. Most teachers, school counselors, principals, religious leaders, and employee assistance programs can refer parents to caring professionals with expertise in working with young people and family members. You may need to interview a few professionals before you find one you and your child are comfortable with.

Success Stories

You have made it through *Ten Talks*. Great work! You now have more insight into how your child views drugs and makes healthy choices. You have opened up the lines of communication—which means you can now talk about pretty much anything.

A mom in Maryland said, after doing all ten talks, "Well, I sure know a lot more about my son than I did before I started. I have learned that he knows a heck of a lot more about drugs in high school than I knew in college. He also knows more about me and my past, and even about his grandparents' struggles with alcohol."

Around the country, we are hearing that the *Ten Talks* approach can serve as a catalyst for productive family conversations, helping parents and their children build stronger relationships and open up new lines of communication. As a parent, you have the most important job on earth. The work you are doing with your child affects everyone. Always remember that you are supported by other caring people in your community—we're all in this together. Other families share your struggles. *Ten Talks* salutes your hard work and wishes you the best for your ongoing talks with your child. Know that your work helps strengthen not only your family but the entire community as well.

Sample Talks
Between Parents and Children

If you are wondering how a talk based on this chapter might really sound, take a look at the following excerpts from real family talks.

Discussing the Story about a Mom and Her Son

Participants: a dad and his twelve-year-old son. Note that the dad has changed the gender of the parent in the scenario from a "mom" to a "father."

Dad: A father says to his son, "Your older brother seems very distracted these days. I am worried that he is using some kind of drug. You know your brother has been using some drugs and getting drunk a lot." What is the son feeling?

Son: He's thinking he is sad, but the older brother is cool because he's older than him, so he wants to protect him. He looks up to him and stuff like that.

Dad: Would you feel like you are hiding something?

Son: When the dad would ask me, I'd deny it, I'd stick up for my older brother.

Dad: Is that the right thing to do?

Son: It's not the right thing but, one, I'd want to protect him from my dad and, two—

Dad: You'd protect him even though you know it's bad for him?

Son: Uh, yeah, because—

Dad: Yeah?

Son: Because he'd protect me in situations like that, too.

Dad: Well, let's move on here. What does the son say?

Son: I'd try to gradually tell my dad and see what I could do with my brother to help him stop it.

Dad: What do you think the dad is feeling?

Son: He thinks his son is doing it but he doesn't know for sure. He feels a little worried because his son could be doing drugs and hurting his body as he grows older.

Dad: What does the dad say?

Son: He's asking his sons if they're doing drugs or not. And he's saying, "If you are, just come up and say it and we'll get you some help, we'll help you stop. I'd rather have you tell me than put your body in danger."

Dad: Does the son understand why this question would be important to talk about?

Son: Yes, because he would want to help his brother.

Dad: Might the little brother feel nervous—fearing his brother's wrath?

Son: Yes!

Dad: Why?

Son: Because his brother may have threatened him, saying, "Don't tell dad or I'll beat you up!" He'd feel pressured and threatened.

Dad: Really? Would the little brother think he is betraying his brother if he talks about his alcohol use?

Son: Yeah. Because then he'd think, "My brother told me not to tell and I did, so I guess I'm not being a good brother."

Dad: What can the family do to help the older brother?

Son: Get him help or talk to him.

Dad: If you were the child in a situation like this, how would you react?

Son: I'd really try to help my brother out, really talk to him. But I wouldn't suddenly go to my dad and say, "He's using drugs." I'd do it gradually.

Dad: How would you feel about that? Knowing that it's bad for him but, yet, you're protecting him? Doesn't that make you stop now and think about it being the wrong thing to do?

Son: Umm, yeah.

Dad: Yeah? So you'd be willing to deal with any consequences that came for you and your brother?

Son: Now that I'm thinking about it. If it's actually you . . .

Lessons Learned from This Sample Talk

In this talk the father was surprised by his son's apparent code of silence over an older brother's misdeeds. Don't be surprised if something like this comes up in your conversations with your child. It is important to listen without judgment, even though what you hear may disappoint you. You are learning about your child's attitudes. You are also providing an opportunity for him to hear about yours.

Discussing the Story about a Mom, a Daughter, and a Dad

Participants: a mom and her eleven-year-old daughter

Mom: "A mother and father are divorced. The mom says to her daughter, 'I'm worried about your dad. When I go to pick you up or call him at his apartment, your dad sounds like he has been drinking or something. Is there a problem?' Now, the daughter knows that her dad has been very upset the past few months. He's been smoking marijuana and drinking alcohol a lot." So the mom's asking this question, "I'm worried about your dad." What is the daughter feeling?

Daughter: "Uh-oh, I don't know what to do, because my dad might get mad if I tell my mom." So she doesn't know what she should do.

Mom: What do you think she might say?

Daughter: "Ask him yourself."

Mom: What is her mom most worried about?

Daughter: That her daughter might get hooked on it and the husband might do something to the daughter.

Mom: Because he's doing the drugs?

Daughter: Uh-huh.

Mom: Does the daughter understand why this question would be important to talk about?

Daughter: Depends on how old the daughter is. If she were fifth grade or older, yeah.

Mom: If you were in that situation, what would you do? Parents are divorced and your dad's doing pot and drinking, and now your mom's asking about it?

Daughter: I'd tell my mom.

Mom: How would you feel about that?

Daughter: I would feel bad. I'd try and help my dad to stop.

Lessons Learned from This Sample Talk

In future talks about drugs the mom might want to stress how even adults can get into trouble with drugs. It would be interesting to explore what the daughter thought the dad in the story might do to the daughter. Children are often afraid of adults and feel powerless to intervene or even protect themselves when it is called for.

Discussing the Story about a Dad and His Daughters

Participants: a mom and her eleven-year-old daughter

Mom: "A dad says to his daughter, 'I'm worried about your sister. When she comes back from college she always seems tired and distracted. She is very skinny and doesn't look good or healthy. Do you know what's going on with her?' Now, the daughter knows that her sister is on heroin." Heroin is a very strong drug. How do you think the daughter feels?

Daughter: "I don't know what to do!"

Mom: "Oh, my God!" [both laugh]

Mom: What do you think she might say?

Daughter: "I'll keep a good eye on my sister."

Mom: You think she'll tell the dad?

Daughter: No.

Mom: Do you think the dad has some reason to be concerned about the daughter being skinny and unhealthy looking? You think he should be worried?

Daughter: Yeah. Feed her a lot.

Mom: Is the daughter worried about telling on her sister?

Daughter: Yep.

Mom: Would you tell?

Daughter: Yeah.

Mom: Even if you were afraid?

Daughter: Depends on how old I was. If I was in high school, no.

Mom: You wouldn't be afraid?

Daughter: No.

Mom: Okay. Thanks.

Lessons Learned in This Sample Talk

This talk focused on whether the daughter in the story would tell her dad about her sister's behavior. The mother could explore why the daughter might be afraid to talk to her dad. When is it appropriate to betray someone's confidence? Could the daughter talk to her sister?

Discussing the Story about a Brother and Sister

Participants: a mom and her eleven-year-old son

Mom: "A brother and sister are driving to school. The sister says that she is very upset and worried about her mom's drinking. The mom has been drinking vodka drinks at lunch and throughout the rest of the day and night. This has become a daily routine." What is the brother feeling?

Son: He's worried because his mom is drinking vodka, and that's harmful. He's worried about his sister because she's worried, too.

Mom: What does the brother say?

Son: That they should help their mother.

Mom: What is the sister feeling?

Son: She's feeling worried that her mother is drinking vodka every day and it has alcohol and it could be bad for your health.

Mom: What does the sister say?

Son: "We should help our mother."

Mom: Is the daughter worried about betraying or angering her mother? Is she afraid what might happen if she tells an aunt or other relative about the situation?

Son: Yes.

Mom: Why?

Son: Because then the mom would get mad at them.

Mom: What can the brother and sister do to help the mother?

Son: Help her overcome her drinking. They could get other family members or a counselor to help their mother.

Mom: What can happen to the mother if no family member intervenes?

Son: She can start drinking more and more and more, until she gets real sick.

Mom: If you were the teenager in a situation like this, how would you react?

Son: I'd tell another family member that I'm worried about my mom.

Mom: How would you feel after the talk?

Son: I'd feel good, because then I'd know what we were going to do, and my mom would get better.

Mom: Who could you talk with?

Son: I could talk to an aunt or uncle or even my dad—somebody, a grandparent, or even my teacher.

Mom: Okay. Thank you very much.

Lessons Learned in This Sample Talk

This talk gave the mom an opportunity to discuss resources with the son. The mom might want to probe more about whom the son might talk to and whom he would feel comfortable sharing problems with. This would give the son a chance to problem-solve and identify a support group before problems come up.

Discussing the Story about a Mom and Her Sons

Participants: a dad and his two daughters, ages eleven and nine

Dad: "A mom is having dinner with her two sons. The older son is eighteen and has just returned from a few months in a treatment program to address his addiction to cocaine and alcohol. The younger son is thirteen years old and really looks up to his brother. The mom is worried that her younger son will get into drugs. This is their first dinner together in three months." What is the older brother feeling?

Younger daughter: He might feel proud because he might feel better than he did when he was on drugs.

Older daughter: I think he'd feel sad because he was on drugs and he probably cost his mom a lot of money to pay for his recovery.

Dad: What does the older brother say?

Younger daughter: Maybe he says, "Thank you."

Older daughter: Maybe he says, "Sorry for doing that." And then, maybe he says, "You shouldn't do it."

Dad: What is the younger brother feeling?

Younger daughter: He's probably feeling sorry that his brother went through that.

Older daughter: He's feeling awkward because he doesn't know if his brother still has the addiction and he could be afraid to ask it.

Dad: What does the younger brother say?

Older daughter: "Is the addiction gone or is it still there?"

Younger daughter: She took my idea!

Dad: Okay, then what is the mother feeling?

Older daughter: Probably sad and happy at the same time.

Dad: Why sad and happy?

Older daughter: Sad because he had to go through that and happy because it's over.

Dad: Do we think it's over? What is the mother saying? Either of you know?

Younger daughter: I know, she's probably saying, "Are you feeling any better? Because, if you're not we can take you back."

Dad: Does the mother have any special concerns?

Younger daughter: Yes, because the younger son looks up to the older one, so if the older one does something the younger one might do it.

Dad: Why would the mother worry about her younger son following her older son's example and trying drugs?

Older daughter: She might worry because then she'd have to pay twice as much money for the same thing over again.

Dad: If you were the older brother in a situation like this, how would you react?

Older daughter: I'd be on my best behavior. I mean, after three months you're coming home to somewhere you really want to come home to.

Dad: Who could you talk with about the whole situation?

Older daughter: At my age? There's a counselor at school you can talk to about your problems.

Younger daughter: You could talk to a psychiatrist, your mom, or dad and family.

Dad: Very good!

Lessons Learned in This Sample Talk

Addiction is often difficult to grasp for those who have never experienced it, especially children. This talk might lead to a future discussion of how people who are addicted never recover fully from their addiction. They must always work at maintaining their sobriety and other healthy behaviors.

Afterword

We're All In
This Together

*We need to rebuild the parents movement, to get concerned parents
involved again and give them the information needed—the most up-
to-date information about what drugs do to people.*
—National Institute on Drug Abuse, *Preventing Drug Use Among
Children and Adolescents: A Research-Based Guide*

The topic of drugs raises many complex issues. Certainly there
are no easy answers when it comes to keeping every child free
from drug abuse but there are some things that can be done to
make your child's world a safer and healthier place. Change happens on many levels. *Ten Talks* has focused on the changes you
would like to nurture in your family. This is a healing process
you're already part of if you are holding this book. Change also
happens at the school level, the neighborhood level, and at the city,
state, and national levels as well. No matter where you put your
energies, you are part of the solution.

And you are not alone in this vital health promotion endeavor.
There are people in your community who want to help and support
the vital work you are doing as you educate your child about drugs
and choices. Across the nation, many schools, religious organizations, community groups, and employers are setting up workshops
for parents and their families to help address a broad range of safety
and health issues. Consider getting involved with (or even setting

up) such educational events. Your compassion, energy, and insight are needed, because there is a lot of work to be done.

We encourage you to let us hear how you are doing with your talks, as well as the kinds of support you are finding in your community. Future books in the Ten Talks series will share dialogues from families all over the world (Ten Talks books have been translated into Spanish, Chinese, and Japanese). We will also report on community events, parent workshops, and support from local and state governments for parent-friendly programs. We all have a lot to share and to learn from one another.

We would like to end this book with a wish that you and your family enjoy good health—and great conversations! We salute the meaningful work you are doing in the challenging and important job of parenting.

We would enjoy hearing how your talks are going. Let us know about your successes, challenges, and creative approaches by visiting us on the web at www.tentalks.com.

OPEN THIS BOOK TO ADDRESS BULLYING, TEASING, AND SCHOOL SAFETY

This resourceful book provides parents with the tools they will need to talk openly and honestly with their children about violence, bullying, and keeping safe. With a series of ten easy-to-manage and engaging talks, *Ten Talks Parents Must Have With Their Children About Violence* includes real-life scenarios to which every child can relate.

"Cappello's strategies for getting families talking are simple and effective." —*Jerry Painter, Washington Education Association*

"A book every parent needs." —*Dennis Worsham, "Washington, Can We Talk?"*

"*Ten Talks* gets kids talking."
—*Mike Newton-Ward, Public Health Program Consultant, North Carolina Dept. of Health and Human Services*

"*Ten Talks* is inspiring and empowers parents."
—*Fr. Tom Merkel, S.J., Superintendent, Red Cloud Indian School, Pine Ridge, South Dakota*

0-7868-8549-1 • $12.95 • (paperback)
www.tentalks.com

OPEN THIS BOOK AND CLOSE THE COMMUNICATION GAP

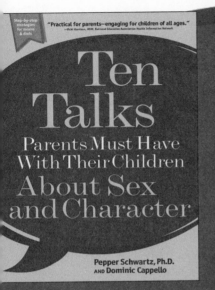

These days it's more important than ever for parents and their children to communicate openly about sexual issues. *Ten Talks Parents Must Have With Their Children About Sex and Character* offers parents advice on what to say to their children—not just about sex, but about safety, character, peer pressure, ethics, meeting people on the Internet, and mixed messages from TV.

"Easy-to-use strategies that get young people talking."
—*Frieda Takamura, Washington Education Association*

"*Ten Talks* is a 21st-century approach to providing much needed sexuality and character education."
—*Dennis Worham, "Washington, Can We Talk?"*

"Now, more than ever, parents need to talk with their children about character, relationships, and yes...sex! Not so easy, you say? Then *Ten Talks* is the book for you."
—*Lynn F. Delevan, Founder, Center for Social and Emotional Learning*

0-7868-8548-3 • $12.95 • (paperback)
www.tentalks.com